FOUNDATIONS FOR THE WORK OF MINISTRY

DAG HEWARD-MILLS

Parchment House

25. How Your Value Is Determined ... 163
26. How to Enjoy Your Work ... 174
27. How to Find Your Life's Work ... 180
28. Why Some People Do Not Prosper at Work ... 184
29. How to Have Favour with Your Boss ... 187
30. How to Choose between Part-Time and Full-Time Ministry ... 193
31. Accept The Season of Full-Time Ministry ... 198
32. Seven Wrong Perceptions About Full-Time Ministry ... 202
33. Why You Must Choose Full-Time Ministry ... 207
34. How God Called Me to "Give Myself Wholly" ... 213
35. The Mysterious Purposes of Full-Time Ministry ... 221
36. The Principles behind Full-Time Ministry ... 229
37. Wrong Reasons for Full-Time Ministry ... 236
38. Right Reasons for Full-Time Ministry ... 239
39. How to Assess Your Readiness for Full-Time Ministry ... 246
40. What it Means to Choose Full-Time Ministry ... 252
41. The Privileges of Full-Time Ministers ... 258
42. Why Some People Leave the Work of Ministry ... 262

SECTION 3 : LAIKOS

43. LAIKOS: The Layman ... 271
44. What Happens When There Are No Laymen and Volunteers ... 275
45. Seven Reasons Why God Operates through Lay People ... 280
46. Seven Things You Must Know about the Lay Ministry ... 283
47. Why You Must Become a Lay Pastor ... 287
48. How I Operated as a Lay Pastor ... 295
49. How to Share the Burden with Lay People ... 301
50. The Ideal Lay Pastor ... 308
51. What Is the Proper Attitude of a Lay Pastor? ... 310
52. Double-Minded Lay Pastors ... 313

53. Understanding How Lay Ministry Is a Measure of Ministry 316
54. Understanding How Lay Ministry Is a Type of Helps Ministry 319
55. Understanding the Deficiencies of Lay Ministry 322
56. Understanding Why God Allows Lay Ministry to Exist 327
57. Develop the Four Essential Skills of a Lay Pastor 330
58. The Struggles of Lay Pastors 333
59. The Example-Setting Ministry of Volunteers 342
60. Why We Must Fight to Protect the Lay Ministry 345
Bibliography 351

Chapter

1

The Four Spiritual Appointments

CHAPTER SUMMARY

Our four appointments are losing, sacrificing, suffering and dying. Are these appointments scriptural? Yes, the Scriptures show us how we are destined to lose, to suffer, to sacrifice and to die because of our faith, our calling and our spiritual destinities.

> **If any *man* come to me, and hate not his father, and mother, and wife, and children, and brethren, and sisters, yea, and his own life also, he cannot be my disciple.**
>
> **Luke 14:26**

To follow Jesus is not easy. Living for Jesus isn't easy. Do not believe anyone who presents a false version of Christianity to you. Christianity is all about following Jesus Christ and becoming Christ-like!

From the things Jesus said about becoming His disciple, it almost seemed as though He did not want anyone to follow Him. He warned different people who attempted to follow Him of the dangers of coming to Him.

Jesus Warns Us

He said, "If you come to me you must hate your parents, your family and yourself" (Luke 14:26).

He said to a rich man who wanted to follow Him: "You must sell whatever you have if you want to follow me" (Matthew 19:21).

He also said, "If you follow me you will not have anywhere to stay because I don't even have the home that foxes and birds have" (Luke 9:58).

He said, "You cannot say goodbye to your family if you really want to follow me" (Luke 9:61).

He said to someone whose parents had died, "You cannot be involved in the burial of your father if you really want to be my disciple" (Luke 9:59).

Jesus Does Not Lower the Standards for Anyone

Obviously, Jesus did not intend to make things easy for anyone. He did not lower the bar for anyone. He did not give anyone special treatment. He knew He was inviting us to the greatest privilege ever given to mankind. The privilege of being saved by the blood of Jesus, the privilege of knowing God and the privilege of going to Heaven!

These warnings by Jesus Christ have not deterred the millions who simply respond to His awesome love. Millions love Jesus Christ in spite of the difficult conditions that He has set for following Him.

Somehow, knowing the living God and His Son Jesus Christ is more than enough compensation for any difficulties we must experience.

Don't listen to anyone who claims that following Jesus is all about getting blessed, rich and successful. That is not Christianity. Christianity is about losing, sacrificing, suffering and dying.

The hardships and difficulties to be encountered by all Christians can be categorised into four main groups: losing, sacrificing, suffering and dying.

These are four spiritual appointments that all Christians must expect in one form or another. No one who truly follows Jesus Christ will escape these four appointments.

Don't take any notice of anyone who tells you otherwise! He is just scratching your itching ears. In one shape, form or another, perhaps with a different name, you will experience the cross of Jesus Christ if you are really His disciple.

This book is intended to show how real these appointments are. It is not as bad as you may think and it will turn out to be a blessing in the end. Notice how the Scriptures below clearly outline these appointments for all of us.

1. Your appointment with "loss and losing"

> **For whosoever will save his life shall LOSE it: and whosoever will lose his life for my sake shall find it.**
>
> **Matthew 16:25**
>
> **But what things were gain to me, those I counted LOSS for Christ. Yea doubtless, and I count all things *but* LOSS for the excellency of the knowledge of Christ Jesus my Lord: for whom I have suffered the LOSS of all things, and do count them but dung, that I may win Christ,**
>
> **Philippians 3:7-8**

Because of Christ you will experience the appointment with "loss and losing". This means a lot to anyone who cares to think about it.

a. Loss means you will come to be without certain things. There may be little or no prospect of recovering the things you will lose.

b. Loss means you will suffer the deprivation of certain things.

c. Loss means you will be unable to keep or maintain certain things in your life.

d. Loss means you will give up and forfeit the possession of certain things.

2. Your appointment with suffering

Because of Christ you will experience an appointment with "suffering". This means a lot to anyone who cares to find out what suffering actually means. Don't take any notice of people who do not include the concept of suffering in their walk of faith. All the great men of faith suffered because they believed in God.

a. Suffering means you will be subject to pain, distress, loss, injury or something unpleasant.

b. Suffering means you will experience adversity, affliction, hardship and misery in your life.

Chapter

2

How to Suffer Loss for Christ

CHAPTER SUMMARY

You must accept to lose everything for Jesus Christ just as Paul did. Paul suffered by losing many things. When you do not lose you will not gain. The twelve disciples of Jesus had lost everything because they followed Jesus. They had left all! They had lost their professions, their families and their friends to follow Jesus. This was a great personal loss to them. You cannot follow Jesus unless you are ready to lose something.

> **Yea doubtless, and I count all things but LOSS for the excellency of the knowledge of Christ Jesus my Lord: for whom I have suffered the LOSS of all things, and do count them but dung, that I may win Christ,**
>
> **Philippians 3:8**

> **Then Peter began to say unto him, Lo, WE HAVE LEFT ALL, and have followed thee.**
>
> **Mark 10:28**

Your ministry is limited by what you keep. If you carry certain things while you run, you will not run fast enough. God is expecting us to leave things behind and follow Him. We may have to leave our sleep, our friendships, our televisions, our careers and our jobs to follow Jesus.

You Must Lose Your Money

Going into the ministry involves losing some money. You will lose financially when you step into the ministry. Many pastors do not realise that they will also have to give their money to the ministry. Every minister must invest personally into the ministry. Of course, you cannot do that if your money is not distinct from the church's money.

It is important that your personal possessions are distinct from the property of the church. If this distinction is not clear, you lose the blessing of giving. You have nothing to give because all you have is church property. And how can you give the church what belongs to it?

You Must Lose Your Comforts and Well-Being

Without sacrificing your leisure time to be with the Lord, there will be no real fruit. Many ministers have time for everything else but the Lord. There is time for TV, useless socializing, computers, business and sports but there is no time for personal fellowship with the Lord. *Your ministry is a reflection of your personal time with the Lord.*

There are many things in the ministry, which may take away your comforts. If you are not prepared to sacrifice the little things of life, you may never amount to much in the ministry.

Insisting on certain comforts on this earth can easily be the reason for your inability to move forward in ministry. You should *"set your affection on things above, not on things on the earth"* (Colossians 3:2). When your heart is set on things above, you will not be so fussy about things on this earth.

> *One night, I was standing by the Pacific Ocean in a foreign country. In front of me were several large expensive yachts belonging to millionaires. I turned to the Christians who were walking with me and said, "I would like to have my yacht in Heaven." One of them laughed at me and said, "Oh no, I want to have mine here." This little conversation reflects two schools of thought in Christendom today. Most Christians want to have their comforts here, while a few want them in Heaven.*

I do not drive the car that I would really like to drive. In fact, I have never driven the car I would really like to drive. I do know which cars are the nicest and the best but I do what I do for the sake of the ministry.

> **But I have used none of these things: neither have I written these things, that it should be so done unto me: for it were better for me to die, than that any man should make my glorying void.**
>
> **1 Corinthians 9:15**

I do not live in the best house or in the best area of my city. I do know where these "best areas" and "best houses" are. I do know that there are many better places than where I live. I am also aware that my church can afford to provide these things for me.

But I am content with what the Lord has given me. In fact, I think I am super blessed. I do not intend to join the struggle to impress people about what I have and where I live. I hope to have the best mansions in Heaven.

You Must Lose Your Family

Your family will make many sacrifices because of the ministry. You will have to give up time and pleasure with your family so that you can do the work of God. In Luke 14, the young man refused to attend the dinner because he had "married a wife".

> **And another said, I have married a wife, and therefore I cannot come.**
>
> **Luke 14:20**

Many people do not fulfil God's will because they try to please their wives. The Bible teaches us to love our wives. But the Bible teaches us to love God first.

> **If any man come to me, and hate not his father, and mother, and wife, and children, and brethren, and sisters, yea, and his own life also, he cannot be my disciple.**
>
> **Luke 14:26**

Jesus talks about hating your mother, your father, your wife, your children, your brethren, your sisters and even your own life in order to be a disciple. If you have to do that to qualify as a *disciple*, how much more would you have to do that as a *Christian leader?*

You Must Lose Your Safety and Security

Jesus sacrificed the safety of Heaven to dwell amongst a group of perverted, depraved and wicked people. We must follow His example if we are to bear fruit.

Walking with the Lord will lead you into many dangers, toils and snares. Every journey you make will put you at risk. If your self-preservation is more important than obeying God, you are not likely to sacrifice your safety and security.

Being in full-time ministry means you must sacrifice your security. It is much more secure to work for Barclays Bank than it is to work for a Pentecostal church led by a twenty-eight-year-old pastor.

I was once invited to Colombia to minister. I was uncertain as to whether I should go or not. I called a pastor in America to ask whether he knew if Colombia was a safe place to go to. He told me he would find out and call me back.

He called me a couple of days later and said, "Brother, it is a very dangerous place. I don't think you should venture there."

He continued, "I talked to a Catholic nun who told me to advise you not to step in Colombia. She told me of a Catholic bishop who had been shot in cold blood while serving mass."

"Are you serious!" I exclaimed.

"Yes," he replied. "It is very dangerous."

Then, I had some further information. I was told about another pastor who had been shot while getting into his car after church. It became clear to me that pastors were being targeted in Colombia. I also remembered a renowned pastor who had almost died in a drive-by shooting incident in Bogotá.

Of course, I decided I would not set foot in Colombia.

However, as I flew down to another country in South America, I had a dream in which the Lord spoke to me. He rebuked me sharply and told me that He was ashamed of me because I was trying to preserve myself. He reminded me that if He removed His protection from me for just five minutes, I would perish instantly. When I woke up, I was frightened and decided to go to Colombia. I needed no further coaxing to take me to Colombia.

Dear friend, I cannot begin to describe the extent of the power of God that was present in those meetings in Colombia. I saw the greatest miracles in my life, including the raising of the dead.

If you are not prepared to lose your security, you will never gain the security of God.

I invited a man of God who lived in one of the richest countries in the world to preach in Ghana, West Africa. His first question was, "Is it safe?" "I would be able to come only if it is safe and there are guarantees for my health, safety ad security".

"Wow," I thought to myself. "How difficult it is to work with people who love themselves and their lives on this earth more than anything else?" But this is typical of Christians who have grown used to the comforts of the modern safety-conscious version of Christianity! That was not Jesus' version of Christianity.

Chapter

3

The Art of Losing

CHAPTER SUMMARY

Anyone who takes up the cross will lose something. The phrase, "if any man" defines those who must take up the cross. Self-denial is one of the basic truths of the Gospel. I do not know of any stronger statement that our Lord made. In this Scripture, He defines those who *cannot* be His disciples. This act of taking up your cross clearly draws a line between those who qualify and those who do not. Those who therefore cannot be Christians are those who are not prepared to deny themselves and lose something.

> **... whosoever will lose his life for my sake shall find it.**
>
> **Matthew 16:25**

Where are crosses usually taken?

Are crosses taken to shopping malls, restaurants, parties, or weddings? No sir! Crosses are carried to the place of execution and suffering. This Scripture has only one meaning: it means that we must follow the example of Jesus Christ and lay down our lives in obedience to Him. Are you obeying the Lord?

I got to know the Lord at about the age of fifteen. I have constantly had to take up my cross, deny myself and follow the Lord. Without doing this, my Christianity would always have been a phantom of what true Christianity is supposed to be. Dear friend, Christianity then and now is not easy.

Losing the Music

During my early years as a Christian, I learned to say "no" to things that ordinary people said "yes" to. One of the first things I had to deny myself of was **non-Christian music**. I used to love music by Lionel Richie, Michael Jackson, the Bee Gees and ABBA. The key verse that guided me in those days was 1 Corinthians 10:23: "All things are lawful but not all things are helpful."

> **All things are lawful for me, but all things are not expedient: all things are lawful for me, but all things edify not.**
>
> **1 Corinthians 10:23**

I really loved and still do love music, but there was no way I was going to continue my walk with Christ and listen to that kind of music. Although nice to the ear, it is not spiritually helpful. There are many Christians who don't do well because they are not prepared to lose certain worldly things.

Losing the Places You Would Usually Visit

There were places I used to go to that I had to stop going to if I was to continue with the Lord. Dear friend, you cannot go to the same old places. Except you deny yourself, you cannot be a Christian. I used to go gambling at the racecourse every Saturday. I was an avid horse lover and a regular patron of the racecourse. When I got saved, I had to lose the pleasure (and foolishness) of gambling.

Losing Your Friends

If you are not prepared to lose certain friends, you will never gain the friends and family God has for you. Even as I write this book, I realize how essential it is for Christians to lose certain friends in order to gain access to a whole new world of friends.

Indeed, if you do not lose the old group you may lose your salvation.

I had a set of friends before I got saved. When I got saved, I realized that these unbelieving friends would not be helpful to my Christian life. One by one, I lost all of them until the old stock was gone. I've basically lost all the friends I used to have.

Losing Your Job

There are times you have to give up certain jobs in order to serve the Lord.

I remember a brother whom I led to the Lord. I saw him saying the sinner's prayer. A few days later, I prayed for him to receive the Holy Spirit baptism. I personally laid hands on him, watched him receive the Holy Ghost baptism and saw him speak in tongues. I also counselled him about his lifestyle.

I told him, "You have to change your lifestyle. You have to say 'no' to the old things, the old people and the old places of your life." One day, I noticed that this brother had stopped coming to church regularly.

I asked him, "What is happening?"

He told me, "I have a new job at such and such hotel."

He continued, "We work in the night and at weekends."

Then I probed further, "What exactly do you do at this hotel?"

He mumbled some feeble answer, and I could tell immediately that it was not a decent job. Night after night, he worked amongst smoking, drinking and rollicking with men and women of sin, as they danced their lives away to Hell.

This was no atmosphere for a good Christian. It was only a matter of time, before my friend completely backslid. The next time I saw him, he was deep in the world and high on drugs. If you are not prepared to lose certain jobs, you will never gain the treasures of Christ.

Losing Your Business

Christians today are not prepared to lose anything. Some ladies are not prepared to give up their unbeliever boyfriends for anything. They say, "You can take away my house, you can take away my job, you can take away my car, but I am not prepared to lose my boy!"

You see, except you deny yourself, you cannot be a disciple of Christ.

I remember a born-again, tongues talking church member, who inherited a thriving nightclub business from his father. I wondered to myself, "What in the world is a Christian going to do with such a nightclub?"

But instead of closing down the nightclub and getting rid of that house of sin, he actually expanded the business.

Because he was not prepared to lose anything, he continued to run the nightclub. How much lower can we go because we are not prepared to lose anything for Christ sake?

One day a church member rented a space to run his restaurant. Somehow, the lease he signed included a dancing room in the building. I asked him "What are you going to do with this dance room?"

He said, "Oh, we will just play music in the evenings." This "music in the evenings" degenerated into a nightclub environment with half-dressed girls singing and dancing every night.

I thought to myself, "How long will this Christian brother be able to stay in the faith?" Not for long! Indeed, the last time I heard of him, he was out of the church and deeply embroiled in the world.

He had fallen into every kind of dark sin that you can think of. I also heard that he had become a mental patient.

There are times you will have to lose your business so that you can follow Christ. Not all jobs are from the Lord. The blessing of the Lord makes rich and adds no sorrow.

Losing Your Films

The films I used to watch, I could watch them no more. That was not easy for me because I really enjoyed watching films. It is not everything we watch that pleases the Lord. I would go to different cinema houses in my city and have a good time watching all kinds of films.

One day, whilst watching a Chinese film at Orion Cinema hall in Ghana, the hero of the film suddenly developed a fever. As he lay shivering under his blanket, it was decided that the only thing that could cure his fever and keep him warm was a group of naked girls.

This film suddenly changed in its character. That was a turning point for me. I knew I had to lose my film-watching hobby!

These things may seem trivial to you, but it is the failure to deny yourself these very things that prevents us from walking with God.

As I have walked with the Lord, I have had to lose many things. Christianity is all about losing.

I also learnt how to deny myself of food so that I could fast.

Little by little, and step by step, you take up your cross, deny yourself and lose your life so that you can follow Jesus.

Chapter

4

The Two Ways of Losing

CHAPTER SUMMARY

There are two ways to lose the things God wants you to give up. You can either give them up voluntarily or they can be taken away from you.

> **Therefore doth my Father love me, because I lay down my life, that I might take it again. NO MAN TAKETH IT FROM ME, but I lay it down of myself. I have power to lay it down, and I have power to take it again. This commandment have I received of my Father.**
>
> **John 10:17-18**

I promise you that giving something is very different from having it taken from you. One is a sacrifice and the other is not. Both end with a loss to you.

Jesus was clever; He knew it was a matter of time before the Pharisees would kill Him. He knew that it was just a matter of time before He would be eliminated. The build up of hatred was obvious to all. *Instead of waiting for this to happen, He gave Himself up to be crucified.*

The Big Difference

There is a big difference between giving up something and having it taken from you. In both cases, you end up losing. I have watched as people tried to preserve themselves and their families but ended up losing them. Many have also tried to prevent financial loss as they avoided going into full-time ministry. Many times, they lost what they were trying to keep.

I remember one lady who was trying to prevent the loss of her husband by keeping him away from the church. Anytime church members came to see her husband for some help, she would shoo them away.

Her nasty and unwelcoming behaviour was a clear indication to the visitors that they were not wanted. Gradually, she warded off the church members until her vision of securing her husband to herself was accomplished.

However, after sometime, her husband began to backslide. He no longer attended prayer meetings and became uninterested in church. As he became less spiritual, he also began to lose interest in his wife. Soon, his eyes were twinkling and his mouth was watering. He considered other girls!

This lady realized that she was about to lose what she was protecting. Then she ran to church and asked the pastor to pray for her marriage. She knew the very thing she was preserving was slipping out of her hands.

Dear friend, be it known unto you that he who keeps his life will lose it and he who loses his life for Christ's sake will find it. These are the irrevocable words of our Saviour.

> **He that findeth his life shall lose it: and he that loseth his life for my sake shall find it.**
>
> **Matthew 10:39**

There are people who think they are preserving their family lives by not getting too involved in church activities. They give themselves to secular pursuits thinking that they are safeguarding the future of their homes. Many of these people have ended up losing their children and their spouses as they followed money on a wild goose chase.

■ Give It before It Is Taken

> **A prudent man foreseeth the evil, and hideth himself: but the simple pass on, and are punished.**
>
> **Proverbs 22:3**

It takes wisdom to see ahead and to know that you are going to lose something. Foolishness often keeps us blinded from this reality.

I once ran a car rental business. At one point, I had a very good customer who was paying me good money. At times, he would rent my car for long periods and promise to pay later. This suited me fine until the payments stopped coming. After one or two months of waiting, I decided to go fetch my car. I eventually got the car but my customer would not pay up and kept telling me stories.

I made several trips to a suburb of Accra trying to get this man to pay me what he owed. One night, the Lord told me that I was never going to get my money. He asked me to give the money to the man as a gift. (The Lord was introducing me to an eternal principle).

I was going to lose something anyway so I might as well give it away first. But I thought I was wiser than the Lord. The man had been so insolent and I didn't feel like giving him anything. I decided to pursue this man until I got my money. My debtor was a smooth-talking liar, who could come up with a different story every day.

I never forgave this man and never obeyed the Lord to give away the money. Can you believe I never got my money back? Up until today, I have not received a dime. I have even forgotten how much I was owed. But God knew I would lose my money anyway. He wanted to bless me, so he asked me to take that step of giving it away but I failed to do so.

I lost my money but I could have given it away freely and reaped a harvest.

Give up your life today and God will use it. Lose your life for His sake, and you will find it. Perhaps the very things you are afraid of losing are about to be taken away from you anyway.

Chapter

5

Why God Wants You to Experience Suffering

CHAPTER SUMMARY

No amount of faith, healing and prosperity teachings can remove the truths about Christians suffering. The Bible is littered with Scriptures that point us clearly to the existence of a divine plan that includes suffering for Christians.

■ Appointed Unto Suffering

For unto you it is given in the behalf of Christ, NOT ONLY TO BELIEVE ON HIM, BUT ALSO TO SUFFER FOR HIS SAKE

Philippians 1:29

That no man should be moved by these afflictions: for yourselves know that WE ARE APPOINTED thereunto.

1 Thessalonians 3:3

Christianity is a religion that does not only involve believing but also suffering. I once attended the funeral of a pastor of a large church. His ministry had similar foundations to mine and the dead pastor had had strong beliefs in the doctrine of faith, prosperity and healing.

However, the unexpected and slow death of this pastor over a number of years had brought untold suffering to the family.

Different people gave speeches at the funeral, paying tribute to this great hero who had passed on. Finally, his wife spoke to the emotional crowd of thousands that were in attendance.

She said, "The death of my husband was not a defeat. It is easy for Christians to think that we were defeated because he did not get healed."

She went on and made a profound statement that encapsulates a missing truth in our teachings.

She said, *"I believe our theology must include suffering."*

When she said this, I recognized the voice of the Holy Spirit speaking through all the pain and difficulty we had been through. God was saying: *Our concept of Christianity must include the concept of suffering!*

We may not like it and we may wish it were not so, but there is so much of it everywhere in the Bible that we cannot escape!

Paul said, "We must through much tribulation enter into the kingdom of God." (Acts 14:22)

The apostle Paul spoke of many sufferings in his letters. He said he was troubled on every side. He went on to say that he was persecuted, perplexed and cast down on many occasions. What do you think these things mean? Are they some kind of enjoyment?

Paul described his life as being always delivered to death for Jesus' sake. What does it mean to be always delivered to death? Do you think it means he is receiving prosperity and healing? Honestly, I don't think so! Indeed it sounds terrifying for anyone to be always delivered to death!

The ministry of Jesus involved two very different aspects. Preaching, teaching and healing formed one clear phase of His ministry. The second phase of His ministry was to basically experience different kinds of suffering. He suffered rejection by the Israeli community, betrayal by Judas, desertion by His disciples, false accusations by the pastors, misrepresentation by the Pharisees, pain from the Roman soldiers, the psychological torment of impending death and the pains and horrors of crucifixion.

But why does following God include all these different kinds of suffering?

Why does someone who obeys God ever have to experience suffering?

Is it not the case that the obedient ones deserve to be exempted from some of these hard and difficult experiences?

Many times, bad people seem to have it easy but the good ones seem to suffer. Indeed, we have tried to eliminate the concept of suffering from our theology because it is a most uncomfortable and difficult-to-explain reality.

But it is time to bring back the concept of suffering into our theology. The teachings on faith, healing, prosperity and long life are the mainstay of a large part of the church. But it's time to include suffering in these faith teachings. If we fail to add suffering to the good news sections of our doctrines, we will always be incomplete and often feel defeated and confused in our Christian journey.

▪ Reasons Why God Wants You to Experience Suffering

1. God wants you to experience suffering because it pleases Him.

> **Yet it pleased the Lord to bruise him; he hath put him to grief:**
>
> **Isaiah 53:10**

Have you ever wondered why the sacrifice of Jesus on the cross was described as *sweet smelling* to God? "... as Christ also hath loved us, and hath given himself for us an offering and a sacrifice to God for a sweetsmelling savour" (Ephesians 5:2).

You would have thought that the sacrifice of Jesus on the cross would present a detestable, disgusting and repugnant scent to God. Yet He calls it a sweet-smelling savour.

Amazingly, it pleases God for you to experience some suffering. I thought of the verse, *"It pleased the Lord to bruise him"* and said to myself, "This must be a mistake. How could the Lord be pleased to bruise Jesus? How could God be happy when His Son is suffering? Which parent would be happy for his child to suffer?"

Yet I remembered when my children were going to boarding school. I knew they were going to encounter things they had never experienced before. I knew they were going to scrub, weed and work like never before. They would have to get up early and work to a certain routine. I also knew they were going to suffer at the hands of wicked seniors.

And yet, I was pleased to send them to this boarding school. Why was I pleased to send them to this school even though they were going to experience some hardship and suffering?

You see, there were lessons I had tried to teach them when they were at home. Somehow, they did not seem to grasp or imbibe some of the things I was telling them. There were lessons of life I wanted them to learn. They had learnt as much as they could learn from my nagging parental instructions. It was time for the hardships of unprotected life to step in and teach them what we as parents couldn't.

2. God wants you to experience suffering because it makes you perfect.

> **For it became him, for whom are all things, and by whom are all things, in bringing many sons unto glory, to make the captain of their salvation PERFECT THROUGH SUFFERINGS.**
>
> **Hebrews 2:10**

The word *perfect* means to make you complete. We are incomplete without suffering. A person who has had no problems in this life lacks something. He lacks the element that makes him complete and mature. Life on this earth includes suffering of all kinds. Once you have not experienced some kind of suffering there is a level of maturity that you simply lack.

3. God wants you to experience suffering because it will make you obedient.

> Though he were a Son, **yet learned he obedience by the things which he suffered;**
>
> **Hebrews 5:8**

The Bible teaches us that Jesus Christ became obedient through the things that He suffered. Jesus Christ was holy and without sin. Yet His obedience to God depended on him suffering certain things. You must also experience some suffering if you are to fully obey God.

Sometimes we think it is stubborn and bad people who need to suffer in order to make them obedient. But good people also need some suffering to prod them on into perfect obedience. When you experience hardships and suffering, ask yourself what the Lord is trying to get you to do. What does He want me to obey? What does He want me to do for Him?

Several people became obedient and served the Lord only because of certain hard experiences they went through. There are great men you know who only became ministers because they suffered certain experiences.

Maria Woodworth Etter

Maria Woodworth Etter, one of God's Lady-Generals was known for her supernatural ministry of signs and wonders. She had a vision of the harvest when she was thirteen years old and heard the voice of God tell her to "go to the highways and hedges and gather the lost sheep".

Somehow, she did not heed the call. Probably desiring to be like the average woman, she married a couple of years after she had had this vision. Eventually she had a large family with six beautiful children! Then tragedy struck and five of her six children died within a short space of time.

Maria herself became ill many times and often thought that she would die. Throughout the time of these different crises, she felt God calling her to preach to the lost.

Finally, she gave herself up to the Lord and became obedient to the call. She began ministering in her local area and began to see many conversions. This was the beginning of a great ministry that lay ahead of her. Maria suffered the loss of five children. What a terrible tragedy. Yet, it was this suffering that brought her to her ministry.

William Branham

William Branham, the famous prophet, also received a supernatural call to ministry. William Braham was a young boy when he started having visions and feeling the call of God on his life. When he was fourteen, he was involved in an accident in which he nearly lost both of his legs. As he lay there in a pool of blood, he saw a terrifying vision of Hell. He cried out to God for mercy promising to be a good boy if he lived. He lived, but forgot about his promise and about God.

One day as he walked by a church, he felt 'something' telling him to go into the church but he refused to obey and continued on his way. Soon after, he heard a voice saying, "I called you, and you would not go." He realized then that he had to approach the Lord since his life has been spared, but he did not know how.

One day he decided to tack a letter to a tree. He then went into a barn and prayed sincerely from his heart. When he opened his eyes he saw floating in front of him, a brilliant amber light, forming a perfect cross in the air. There, in that barn, he accepted the Lord Jesus Christ.

When God called him into nation-wide evangelism in 1934, he refused because his mother-in-law felt that he should not drag his new wife, Hope, around the country. He paid dearly for the mistake of not listening to the Lord by losing his wife, Hope, and daughter, Sharon Rose, to tuberculosis in the Flood of 1936.

After the death of his wife and daughter, he fell into a deep depression, feeling that God had abandoned him. He tried to commit suicide a few times but did not succeed.

Branham struggled over the next several years. One day he went to pray to seek God's will for him and repented of his decision not to go into nation-wide evangelism. He went on to minister and obey the call of God, having one of the most spectacular prophetic ministries ever recorded in history.

As you can see from these examples, many people do not obey the voice of God until they go through much suffering.

4. God wants you to experience suffering because it will bring you closer to Christ.

That I may know him, and the power of his resurrection, and the FELLOWSHIP OF HIS SUFFERINGS, being made conformable unto his death;

Philippians 3:10

Suffering creates a fellowship of like-minded sufferers who have experienced the same things. There is a bond that forms between people who have gone through certain experiences. In order therefore to be a part of certain fellowships you must suffer certain things.

You must suffer the seven years of medical school to be a part of the fellowship of doctors.

You must suffer the ridicule and rejection that people in full-time ministry experience in order to join a certain fellowship.

There is a closeness to God and to Christ that you have when you experience suffering. You will have a deeper understanding of who Jesus is and what He has done for you as you experience the sufferings of Christ.

5. God wants you to experience suffering because of the glory that will follow you.

Just as the day follows the night, the glory of God will come after the sufferings we experience. The glory of being a doctor comes after the sufferings of medical school. The glory of having a baby comes after the suffering of labour and childbirth. The glory of having a baby comes after the suffering and difficulties of adoption.

The good news is that the glory we will experience cannot be compared with the suffering we must go through. "For I reckon that the sufferings of this present time are not worthy to be compared with the glory which shall be revealed in us" (Romans 8:18). There are too many Scriptures that support these great truths and these are just a few:

For our light AFFLICTION, which is but for a moment, worketh for us a far more exceeding and eternal weight of GLORY;

2 Corinthians 4:17

Searching what, or what manner of time the Spirit of Christ which was in them did signify, when it testified beforehand the SUFFERINGS of Christ, and the GLORY that should follow.

1 Peter 1:11

But rejoice, inasmuch as ye are partakers of Christ's SUFFERINGS; that, when his GLORY shall be revealed, ye may be glad also with exceeding joy.

1 Peter 4:13

And if children, then heirs; heirs of God, and joint-heirs with Christ; if so be that we suffer with him, that we may be also glorified together. For I reckon that the SUFFERINGS of this present time are not worthy to be compared with the GLORY which shall be revealed in us.

Romans 8:17-18

6. God wants you to experience suffering so that you play your part in the completion of the sufferings of Christ.

Now I rejoice in my sufferings for your sake, and in my flesh I do my share on behalf of His body (which is the church) in filling up that which is lacking in Christ's afflictions.

Colossians 1:24 (NASB)

This is perhaps the most mysterious reason why we should suffer: to complete the sufferings of Christ. Does it mean that Jesus did not complete His work on earth? I think not. Jesus is the head and we are the body of Christ.

He told us to take up our crosses because the head had taken up the cross and the body of Christ must also take up its cross. If the head suffers and the body does not suffer then the sufferings of Christ are not complete.

7. God wants you to experience suffering so that you become humble.

Satan's nature is pride. Satan is the king and origin of pride. He is also the ruler and the overseer of all the children of pride.

> **... he *is* a king over all the children of pride.**
>
> **Job 41:34**

After the fall of man, Satan's nature of pride was somehow injected into mankind. This satanic nature is the source of all the evils in man. Even after our salvation, we constantly struggle with this demonic influence that seeks to dominate our character and personality.

After the Lord has called us and we begin to serve Him, this very nature carries us away from His will. A little confidence, a little success and we are changed into demonized, pride-filled brats who no longer listen to advice. We secretly mock at others we deem inferior.

This is the reason why the Lord leads us along a road that humbles us and causes us to trust in Him. Perhaps no Scripture is as clear as Deuteronomy 8:2 on this matter. Some so called faith people (I say this because I consider myself a faith person) would wish that this verse was not in the Bible. But it is and there is nothing you can do about it. God does lead us on journeys with the intention of humbling us.

Some of the things that are happening to you are just to humble you and make you cool, sober, mellow and gentle!

> **And thou shalt remember all the way which the Lord thy God led thee these forty years in the wilderness, TO HUMBLE THEE, and to prove thee, to know what was in thine heart, whether thou wouldest keep his commandments, or no.**
>
> **Deuteronomy 8:2**

The apostle Paul also confirmed this truth. He said that he had been given a messenger of Satan to buffet him so that he would not be lifted up in pride because of his numerous revelations. He interpreted his difficulties, persecutions, reproaches and distresses to be gifts from God which induced the gift of humility in his life. "And because of the surpassing greatness of the revelations, for this reason, to keep me from exalting myself, there was given me a thorn in the flesh, a messenger of Satan to buffet me--to keep me from exalting myself!" 2 Corinthians 12:7 (NASB).

■ Your Greatest Gift Is What Makes You Humble in This Life

If humility is the key to becoming the greatest in Heaven ("Whosoever therefore shall humble himself as this little child, the same is greatest in the kingdom of heaven," Matthew 18:4) then whatever brings you humility must be the greatest gift from God to you.

The suffering that makes you humble is therefore God's greatest gift to you.

If you have eyes to see you will count it all joy when you enter into various testings, trials and temptations (James 1:2).

What is it that has made you sad in this life and caused you to suffer?

It is the same thing that God has used to make you a humble person.

Is it your husband?

Is it the rejection you experienced?

Is it your wife?

Is it your marriage?

Is it your child?

Is it the child you didn't have?

Is it the husband you didn't have? Is it your poverty? Is it your sickness? Is it the death of your spouse? Is it your accusers? Is it your weakness? Is it your inferiority? Is it the colour of your skin?

The natural man would call these things your greatest misfortunes. Indeed, to an unspiritual person, these things may look like the calamities and bad luck of your life.

However, if you can receive it, you would recognize that your hardships and your sufferings are the greatest gifts of God to you.

Not Everyone Becomes Humble through Suffering

Don't make a mistake though. It is not everybody who experiences suffering that becomes humble. Some actually become even more hardened and resistant to God. You must allow God to work things out in you.

8. God wants you to experience suffering because He wants to test you.

> **And you shall remember all the way which the LORD your God has led you in the wilderness these forty years, that He might humble you, TESTING YOU, to know what was in your heart, whether you would keep His commandments or not.**
>
> **Deuteronomy 8:2 (NASB)**

Suffering is indeed a test. It brings out what is in you. When you rebuke someone or correct him his true nature is exposed.

The Angry Pastor

One day, a pastor did something wrong and was corrected for what he had done. He was then moved elsewhere to do another job. Because he was moved, he developed a bad attitude, threatening to leave the church. He felt his issues had not been fairly handled.

I said to my wife, "This fellow is proving to everyone that he was indeed rebellious." Before his correction it had been uncertain as to whether he was really rebellious, or just an innocent victim of circumstances.

His response to his difficulties revealed who he was.

This is how come marriage brings out your true character. Through marriage you will discover whether you are patient, kind, unreasonable, wicked, caring, unfeeling, hard, soft, flat or blank.

He Never Became Bitter

I attended the funeral of a great man of God. There were several comments passed by people who knew this man. There was, however, one comment that struck me. This comment was given by a seasoned minister.

He said, "Our brother has given us a good example in life. He showed us how to live and he has also shown us how to die. In life, he was cheerful, pleasant and full of faith. But in the years that run up to his death he was equally cheerful, pleasant and full of faith."

Then he added, "He never became bitter in spite of his sickness and suffering."

I think that was a powerful testimony of a man who successfully went through a test of suffering. He manifested faith and hope through his suffering.

Unfortunately, this is not what happens to everyone who goes through suffering. Some people become bitter because of the contradictory sufferings they experience after giving everything to God.

Don't Become Bitter Because of Your Suffering

For consider him that endured such contradiction of sinners against himself, lest ye be wearied and faint in your minds.

Hebrews 12:3

The Bible teaches about how Jesus Christ received the contradiction of sinners (Hebrews 12:3). What is the contradiction of sinners? It is experiencing something contrary to what you would expect.

After doing good deeds and serving the Lord you expect to receive a nice reward. After being a good husband, you expect to receive nice treatment from your wife. You do not expect to receive insults, accusations, bad food or bad sex. That would be a contradiction.

After being a good wife you expect to receive love, care and devotion from your husband. You do not expect to have an antagonistic, hateful, uncaring and unfaithful husband. That would also be a contradiction.

Be careful when you receive the contradiction of sinners.

Receiving the contradiction of sinners is one of the sufferings we are to experience on this earth. Do not turn against God when you receive the contradiction of sinners. Jesus experienced the contradiction of sinners and showed us how to endure it.

Do not become bitter.

Do not say that you need to be happy in this life.

Do not say that you need a break.

Do not say that you need to get away from all this.

You can never get away from the will of God!

The Swedish Missionary

One day, a European couple went to Belgian Congo as missionaries with their two-year old son. They laboured there for many years with no fruit.

During their stay there, the only person who had responded to the ministry was a little Congolese boy who used to bring them food. Imagine that! Your only convert after years of ministry is a little boy.

Finally his wife died a week after giving birth to their daughter. In despair, he left the Congo with his son but dumped the week-old baby girl on another Swedish couple. Sadly, this couple also died. An American missionary couple then adopted their daughter.

The Swedish missionary, thinking he was such a failure, turned to alcohol and completely forsook the ministry upon his return to Sweden. Indeed, he had received the contradiction of sinners in Congo.

But his daughter grew up in America and married a man who became the principal of a Bible school. On a trip to Sweden with her husband they stopped in London and whilst taking a walk stumbled on a congress being addressed by a Congolese missionary evangelist who was testifying of the great works of God in Zaire.

A conversation between her and the great evangelist revealed that he was the little native boy who had been her parents' only convert during their years in Belgian Congo. He had grown up to be a missionary evangelist to his own country. His ministry included one hundred and ten thousand Christians, thirty-two mission stations, several Bible schools and a one hundred and twenty-bed hospital.

The next day she travelled to Sweden to look for her father. She found him in a run-down building in an impoverished part of Stockholm. When they knocked on the door a woman let them in. Inside, liquor bottles lay everywhere. And lying on a cot in the corner was her father – the one time missionary. He was now seventy-three years old and suffering from diabetes. He also had a stroke and cataracts covered both of his eyes.

She fell to her father's side crying, "Dad I'm the one you left in Africa."

The old man turned and looked at her. Tears formed in his eyes. He answered, "I never meant to give you away. I just couldn't handle you both."

She answered, "That's okay Daddy, God took care of me."

Her father's face darkened at the mention of "God".

"God didn't take care of you," he raged.

"He ruined our whole family. He led us to Africa and then betrayed us. Nothing ever came of our time there. It was a waste of our lives."

She then told him of the black preacher she had met in London and how the Congo had been evangelized through him.

"It's all true, Daddy," she said. "Everybody knows about that little boy convert."

Her father was amazed. The Holy Spirit fell on him and he broke down. He had received the contradiction of sinners and it had turned him away from God. He had felt God was not real. He had felt that God had repaid him with evil after he had sacrificed his whole life for the Gospel.

Tears of sorrow and repentance flowed down his face and God restored him.

9. God wants you to experience suffering so that you can follow the example of Jesus Christ.

For even hereunto were ye called: because CHRIST ALSO SUFFERED FOR US, LEAVING US AN EXAMPLE, that ye should follow his steps:

1 Peter 2:21

Suffering will be part of our Christian lives because Jesus Christ set the example and asked us to follow Him. No matter how much faith we have we cannot have more faith than Jesus Christ.

Jesus had all the faith to raise the dead and to heal the sick and yet He set us an example of suffering.

Suffering is not a sign of weakness.

Suffering is not a sign of defeat.

Suffering is often a sign of God's hand actively working in your life.

10. God wants you to experience suffering so that the power of sin will be broken in your life.

When you suffer in the flesh you stop sinning. Because the Church is averse to suffering it has not ceased from sinning.

Forasmuch then as Christ hath suffered for us in the flesh, arm yourselves likewise with the same mind: for HE THAT HATH SUFFERED IN THE FLESH HATH CEASED FROM SIN;

1 Peter 4:1

He that has suffered in the flesh ceases from sin. Where there is no suffering you see the increase of sin. The church of God that emphasizes on prosperity, healing and success but has no component of suffering is setting itself up for a great deviation from the faith.

Suffering has the power to break the influence of sin on your life. When people love money they often love pleasure.

Money has power to prevent sufferings.

Money gives people the power to steer their lives away from anything that threatens to cause any kind of suffering. That is why money is the root of all evil.

Money has been able to change the course of the church. Money has steered it away from places that it is needed most.

Instead of the Holy Spirit leading the church to the mission fields, the church is being led by an unspoken policy of avoiding trouble, difficulties or hardships.

11. God wants you to experience suffering because it proves that you are a good Christian.

> **For therefore WE BOTH LABOUR AND SUFFER REPROACH, BECAUSE WE TRUST IN THE LIVING GOD, who is the Saviour of all men, specially of those that believe.**
>
> **1 Timothy 4:10**

Suffering is actually a sign that you are a good Christian. Paul said he was labouring and suffering reproach just because he trusted in the living God. When people are following the will of the Lord, they always encounter difficulties and hardships.

You must give up the notion that suffering is a sign of defeat or failure.

There is a notion that if you suffer, you are a failure. There is a notion that if you suffer, God does not like you. There is a notion that people experience difficulties because they are out of the will of God. Such thinking will not help you to be a good Christian.

Paul said Christians who want to live in a godly way will suffer. "Yea, and all that will live godly in Christ Jesus shall suffer persecution" (2 Timothy 3:12).

I want you to make up your mind to fight till the end of your life. Fight in every situation. Don't give up! Don't think that God is angry with you.

Those kinds of thoughts only weaken you. God is not angry with you! God is allowing you to encounter the sufferings and experiences that His generals and chosen ones go through.

When Jacob met up with Pharaoh he made a profound statement. He said, "... the years of my pilgrimage are a hundred and thirty. MY YEARS HAVE BEEN FEW AND DIFFICULT, and they do not equal the years of the pilgrimage of my fathers..." (Genesis 47:9, NIV).

Life on this earth has few and difficult years. You must accept this reality of suffering and brace yourself to go through it.

Do not live this life trying to be happy!

You must survive!

You must make it!

You don't *have* to be happy on earth!

All you need is to make it to the end of your course having obeyed the Lord in all that He told you to do.

If you try to be "happy" you will make a mistake and jump out of God's plan for your life!

12. God wants you to experience suffering because it goes along with your specific calling.

> Whereunto I am appointed a preacher, and an apostle, and a teacher of the Gentiles. FOR THE WHICH CAUSE I ALSO SUFFER THESE THINGS: nevertheless I am not ashamed...
>
> 2 Timothy 1:11-12

> But the Lord said unto him, Go thy way: for he is a chosen vessel unto me, to bear my name before the Gentiles, and kings, and the children of Israel:
>
> For I will shew him HOW GREAT THINGS HE MUST SUFFER FOR MY NAME'S SAKE.
>
> Acts 9:15-16

When people are immature they do not understand why certain ministers go through certain things.

One day, a minister of the Gospel heard me preaching about the trials of the work of ministry.

He said to me, "It seems you have really been through hell in your ministry."

I was surprised at his comment and said, "Really? Did you not have any of these experiences when you were building your church?"

He said, "No, I did not experience any such thing."

I felt silly to say the least. Perhaps the people I had preached to also felt that I had had all these experiences because I lived in Africa. But I later found out that that pastor had never founded a church. He had actually been made the senior pastor of a church that was already in existence.

The suffering and experiences that you go through to found a new church is different from the suffering and experiences you go through to grow an already existing church.

This pastor could not relate with what I had been through because he had not functioned as an apostle, giving birth to churches, but as a pastor growing a church.

There are certain things you will suffer just because you are functioning in certain callings. Paul said he was appointed an apostle and a teacher, and because of that he was suffering certain things.

Some people go through challenges in their marriages just because of their calling. If they were not functioning as pastors or apostles they may have had a happier and easier marriage. Do not despise them because of the suffering they seem to be experiencing in marriage.

The Spotted Tree

One day, whilst on the golf course I noticed a big tree that had lots of spots on it. After walking by it I turned back to look at this amazingly spotted tree. To my surprise there was not a single spot on the other side of the tree. Then I realized that it was not really a spotted tree but a normal tree that had been brutally assaulted by a thousand different golf balls. It only had those marks on it because of its position in the fairway of the golf course. If it was not positioned where it was it would never have any of those scars.

There are scars that people have just because of their callings and giftings. Most of the time ministers do not suffer because they have special weaknesses but rather because they have particular callings.

13. God wants you to experience suffering for the sake of righteousness.

But and if ye SUFFER FOR RIGHTEOUSNESS' sake, happy are ye: and be not afraid of their terror, neither be troubled;

1 Peter 3:14

But let none of you suffer as a murderer, or as a thief, or as an evildoer, or as a busybody in other men's matters.

Yet if any man SUFFER AS A CHRISTIAN, let him not be ashamed; but let him glorify God on this behalf.

1 Peter 4:15-16

There are different reasons for suffering. Many people suffer because of their own mistakes. This is what causes all the confusion when it comes to *why* people suffer.

Am I suffering because of my mistakes or I am suffering because I am in the will of God? Did so-and-so die because of his mistakes or did he die because he was in the will of God?

Unfortunately, we will not be able to answer all these questions now. If we try to answer all these questions now we will make mistakes. You must search your heart and believe that you are operating in the will of God.

Once you are certain that you are in the will of God, you must battle to survive and endure your sufferings.

14. God wants you to experience suffering because Christians must suffer affliction rather than enjoying the pleasures of sin for a season.

By faith Moses, when he was come to years, refused to be called the son of Pharaoh's daughter; choosing rather to suffer affliction with the people of God, than to enjoy the pleasures of sin for a season;

Hebrews 11:24-25

Brother, Why Do You Want to Be Happy?

Many years ago, a pastor mistakenly married an attractive young lady who was unknowingly bad tempered, argumentative and ill-natured. He suffered in his marriage for many years whilst this woman secretly tormented him.

He endured her cantankerous nature for many years never considering divorce. Perhaps, he secretly hoped that she would die but she never did. She seemed only to get stronger, healthier and fatter.

But one day, a new thought began to form in his mind; thoughts of leaving his wife and marrying someone else. The Scriptures on divorce were not strong enough to prevent him walking on his new road to divorce. I wondered what had brought about the change.

Sometime later, I made a discovery that seemed to explain the new drive towards divorce and remarriage. I found out that members of his family had been encouraging him to divorce, saying that he needed to be happy.

They urged him on, counselled him and impressed upon him that he could be happy, and that he needed to take steps so that he could have a new and happier phase of his life. "We want our dear brother to be happy," they said.

Perhaps this "call to happiness" was the stimulus that urged the pastor to his eventual divorce and remarriage.

I believe that the desire to be happy is one of the most dangerous desires that have entered the Body of Christ.

That I can be happy on earth and that I should be happy on earth is a delusion that drives Christians into error.

It is the same kind of dangerous delusion that drives Christians to desire riches.

Why Should I Suffer?

That I should suffer, go through and stay on in darkness and difficulty is the mentality that keeps Christians on the narrow path. That is the mind that the older generation of Christians and ministers had.

The mindset of modern Christians is "I must be happy! I can be happy! I will do everything I need to do so that I am happy on earth! I will do that even if it means breaking Scriptures that are crystal clear!"

Many great ministers endure tumultuous and truly difficult marriages in which they are tormented secretly by calm looking beautiful wives. No one really knows that these pretty wives are also pretty pretenders and secret tormentors.

Many ministers are able to endure and even have semi-successful homes until the thought of being happy occurs to them. Through this idea of "becoming happy" the enemy is able to destroy God's honourable servants.

But Why Do You Want to Be Happy?

But why do you want to be happy on earth? This is the key question you must keep in your spirit. Don't even try to be happy. Tell yourself it won't be long.

Dear friend, you will not live very long anyway. Your pursuit of happiness will cause you to wander into many temptations and snares.

You will sink and plunge into the mire of confusion as you seek for happiness on this earth.

This Must Be Your Prayer

"Help me to survive, O Lord" should be your prayer.

"Keep me alive. Help me to stay to the end of the road without letting you down. Strengthen me so that I can endure the pain, confusion, torment, difficulty, suffering, reproach, unhappiness, contradictions and depression that engulf my life."

Chapter

6

What You Will Accomplish through the Sufferings of Christ

CHAPTER SUMMARY

6.1 Enduring temptation is an accomplishment of the sufferings of Christ

6.2 Enduring pressure is an accomplishment of the sufferings of Christ

6.3 Enduring betrayal is an accomplishment of the sufferings of Christ

6.4 Enduring hours of prayer is an accomplishment of the sufferings of Christ

6.5 Enduring sleepless nights is an accomplish-ment of the sufferings of Christ

6.6 Enduring sorrow is an accomplishment of the sufferings of Christ

6.7 Enduring abandonment is an accomplishment of the sufferings of Christ

6.8 Enduring the contradictions of sinners against you is an accomplishment of the sufferings of Christ

6.9 Enduring accusations is an accomplishment of the sufferings of Christ

6.10 Enduring hatred is an accomplishment of the sufferings of Christ

6.11 Enduring envy is an accomplishment of the sufferings of Christ

6.12 Enduring rejection by man is an accomplishment of the sufferings of Christ

6.13 Enduring the disappointing ways of men of authority is an accomplishment of the sufferings of Christ

6.14 Enduring pain is an accomplishment of the sufferings of Christ

6.15 Enduring mockery is an accomplishment of the sufferings of Christ

6.16 Enduring the psychological torment of impending death is an accomplishment of the sufferings of Christ

6.17 Enduring weakness is an accomplishment of the sufferings of Christ

6.18 Enduring helplessness is an accomplishment of the sufferings of Christ

6.19 Enduring insults is an accomplishment of the sufferings of Christ

6.20 Enduring shame is an accomplishment of the sufferings of Christ

6.21 Becoming vulnerable is an accomplishment of the sufferings of Christ.

6.22 Enduring degradation is an accomplishment of the sufferings of Christ

6.23 Enduring cheating and robbery is an accomplishment of the sufferings of Christ

6.24 Enduring painful separation is an accomplishment of the sufferings of Christ

6.25 Enduring desolation and loneliness is an accomplishment of the sufferings of Christ

6.26 Enduring the moment of death is an accomplishment of the sufferings of Christ

> **After this, Jesus knowing that ALL THINGS WERE NOW ACCOMPLISHED, that the scripture might be fulfilled, saith, I thirst**
>
> **John 19:28**

In the ministry, most people view accomplishments as positive things they have done and achieved for the Lord. You will hear ministers of the Gospel say, "I have preached in ninety-six countries."

"My church has eight hundred members."

"I have built a building that seats three thousand people."

"We have four services every Sunday."

"I have established six Bible schools."

"I am in demand as a conference speaker."

"I had two thousand decisions for Christ in my crusade."

"I have crusades in different countries."

"I baptise five hundred people every Sunday."

"We have six choirs in our church and we have recorded two albums."

Indeed, these are great accomplishments. But they are only one aspect of the accomplishments that will be required from you.

There is another kind of accomplishment mentioned in the Bible. It is the *accomplishments of the cross* and the accomplishment of sufferings that are destined for servants of the Lord.

Jesus knew that He was accomplishing something by enduring and surviving the torment of contradictions, hatred, envy and wickedness unleashed against Him by sinful men. Read it for yourself:

> **Behold, we go up to Jerusalem, and all things that are written by the prophets concerning the Son of man shall be ACCOMPLISHED.**
>
> **Luke 18:31**

The accomplishments of Jesus on the cross are, however, in a completely different category. They concern the things you have been through and the things you have survived. Herein is birthed the saying, "What have you been through and what have you survived?"

What is accomplished when someone goes through suffering? What is the benefit of someone enduring such hardships, pain and affliction?

That is a good question because the conventional view of an accomplishment is always of something positive that is achieved.

But according to the Bible, suffering on a cross is an accomplishment. On many occasions Jesus' afflictions and experiences on the cross were described as accomplishments. Jesus Christ Himself said, "But I have a baptism to undergo, and how distressed I am until it is accomplished!" (Luke 12:50, NASB).

Jesus went through great suffering and there is some significance in the degree to which we experience similar sufferings. "But to the degree that you share the sufferings of Christ, keep on rejoicing; so that also at the revelation of His glory, you may rejoice with exultation" (1 Peter 4:13, NASB).

Derek Prince

I once read the book of an older world-renowned "man of God". He described how he was watching a young minister on television who had a large and thriving ministry.

As he watched this young man he thought to himself, "This young man is doing well. He is achieving many things for the Lord.

But one day, he will come to the place where he will discover that it is not about the things he has achieved. He will discover that it is more about what he can yield to. It is about what you can allow to happen to you. He will discover that it is more about what you can go through." Indeed, this was an experienced man of God.

What Have You Been Through?

On another occasion I met an older man of God who was complaining about young ministers who felt they were bigger and better than he was. He said to me, "These young men think that success is about how many members you have or how many cars you have."

He continued, "It's about what you've been through." He pointed his fingers at me and said, "What have you been through? What have you survived?"

"Enduring things" is an accomplishment just as "achieving things" is an accomplishment. "... Jesus knowing that all things were now accomplished, that the scripture might be fulfilled, saith, I thirst" (John 19:28).

Therefore, I exhort the elders among you, as your fellow elder and witness of the sufferings of Christ, and a partaker also of the glory that is to be revealed:

1 Peter 5:1, NASB.

The Grieving Missionary

A missionary who had preached to thousands of people all over the world was going through a super crisis in his personal life. He felt like giving up on God and the ministry and even ending his life.

A friend of his tried to console him saying, "God has allowed this for a purpose. God is in control. You must trust God."

But he answered, "God has no part in this. What would God gain by putting me through this terrible crisis? God does not need to speak to me by destroying my family.

He continued, "I do not serve a God who can allow such terrible things to happen."

A friend of his explained to him how the famous missionary Adoniram Judson had brought the gospel to India at great personal cost.

He explained to his grieving friend that Adoniram Judson had had the tragedy of burying two wives and four children even though he was serving God on the mission field.

This information did not seem to matter to the grieving missionary. He became more vociferous as suggestions were made that God could have had a hand in the terrible crisis. This healing evangelist then dropped a bombshell that revealed his understanding of the spiritual accomplishment of suffering.

He said, "God had better not have anything to do with this problem. I would prefer to become a Muslim than to serve a God who would allow anything like this to happen to me. If God has anything to do with this I will become a Muslim!" This missionary insisted that if the God of Christianity would allow these troubles to happen to him then he would change his allegiance to God to another and change religions.

But the apostle Paul recognized that it is possible for God to allow Satan to attack a minister of the gospel. Read it for yourself.

> **Even though I have received wonderful revelations from God. But to keep me from getting puffed up, I was given a thorn in my flesh, a messenger from Satan to torment me and keep me from getting proud.**
>
> **2 Corinthians 12:7 (NLT)**

It is time to look unto Jesus, who is the beginning and the end of everything for us. He came to this earth and ministered powerfully to thousands of people. Many were saved and healed through His ministry.

His successful field ministry was combined with the successful enduring of the cross. We must minister the Word of God powerfully with miracles, signs and wonders and we must also endure, tolerate and experience whatever God has planned for us. "For just as the sufferings of Christ are ours in abundance, so also our comfort is abundant through Christ" (2 Corinthians 1:5, NASB).

This will be our portion too as we follow the Lord ardently. Like the old and wise minister said, a time will come when it will not be about the positive things you achieve but about the things you can go through and the things you can allow to happen in your life.

> **Looking unto Jesus the author and finisher of our faith; who for the joy that was set before him ENDURED THE CROSS, despising the shame, and is set down at the right hand of the throne of God.**
>
> **Hebrews 12:2**

■ The Sufferings of Christ

> **Therefore, I exhort the elders among you, as your fellow elder and witness of THE SUFFERINGS OF CHRIST, and a partaker also of the glory that is to be revealed.**
>
> **1 Peter 5:1, NASB**

The things you can accomplish through your suffering are the things that Jesus accomplished with His sufferings. That is why it is important to know what the sufferings of Christ were. When Jesus knew that He had accomplished the necessary sufferings, He gave up the ghost and finished His ministry.

I want you to study the special accomplishments that Jesus achieved on the cross. They are the sufferings that we must also endeavour to accomplish if God so wills. Consider sufferings as accomplishments because that is what they are and that is what the Bible describes them as! Jesus Christ endured the cross and so must we. What exactly did Jesus Christ endure? He endured the sufferings I have listed below. Each of the sufferings was an accomplishment.

> **... who for the joy that was set before him ENDURED THE CROSS...**
> **Hebrews 12:2**

1. Enduring temptation is an accomplishment of the sufferings of Christ.

> **Being forty days tempted of the devil. And in those days he did eat nothing: and when they were ended, he afterward hungered.**
> **Luke 4:2**
>
> **He saved others; himself he cannot save. If he be the King of Israel, let him now come down from the cross, and we will believe him.**
> **Matthew 27:42**

Jesus Christ endured the suffering of temptation from the beginning of His ministry to the very end. In the wilderness, He was tempted to abort his ministry and prove that he was the Son of God. On the cross he was tempted again to come down and prove that he was the Son of God. It was exactly the same demon and exactly the same temptation that haunted Jesus throughout His ministry.

This is what explains the persistent temptations of ministers of the gospel. The temptation received at the beginning of your ministry is usually the same thing that comes again and again. If you analyse your life and ministry, you will find out that the same thing keeps coming up again and again although sometimes in different forms.

You must understand that you will suffer from temptation until you die.

If a pastor is tormented in his marriage this torment usually carries on to the very end.

It comes up again and again and the demon never stops trying to break up the marriage. Demons realize that persistence yields fruit and so they keep trying.

Often, the demonic pressure and the temptation is successful after many years. This could explain why some men of God get divorced twenty or thirty years after marriage. After twenty years of marriage you would have thought they would be tired of fighting each other.

The Temptation to Divorce

One day, an important minister of the gospel shocked the Christian world with an announcement of his divorce. He had been married for over thirty years and everything seemed rosy on the outside. Interestingly, I happened to meet someone who knew this divorcing pastor quite closely.

Full of hope, I asked the friend of this divorcing pastor whether their marriage couldn't be healed. He smiled wryly and shook his head.

"I don't think so."

Then he dropped a bombshell: "I am even surprised that they have stayed married so long."

"What do you mean?" I asked.

"O they've had a tempestuous marriage relationship for the thirty years they've been together. It's surprising that they've lasted so long."

He said no more and I realised he did not want to talk about it.

I was amazed that this divorcing pastor had been dogged with the same temptations for so many years.

He had quietly suffered the temptation to divorce for many years.

2. Enduring pressure is an accomplishment of the sufferings of Christ.

But I have a baptism to undergo, and how distressed I am until it is accomplished!

Luke 12:50 (NASB)

There was intense pressure on Jesus as He carried out His ministry. He spoke of a baptism of fire, temptation, stress and pressure that he felt as he approached Jerusalem. He knew he had to go through successfully without succumbing to the pressure of the demonic hordes that had gathered. He was mocked, tempted, rejected, despised and eventually murdered.

For we would not, brethren, have you ignorant of our trouble which came to us in Asia, that we were pressed out of measure, above strength, insomuch that we despaired even of life:

2 Corinthians 1:8

3. Enduring betrayal is an accomplishment of the sufferings of Christ.

And as they did eat, he said, Verily I say unto you, that one of you shall betray me.

Matthew 26:21

Jesus Christ endured betrayal and so will you. Young ministers of the gospel make fun of older people when they are betrayed.

I once heard a young minister of the gospel pass a comment about an older minister who had been betrayed by his associates.

He said, "People are turning against that Bishop because of his bad leadership." A few years later, this young minister of the gospel who thought he had good leadership skills experienced a worse betrayal by his associates. What he did not realise was that betrayal is one of the things that will come to all disciples of Christ. If you have not yet experienced it you will experience it one day. It is just a matter of time.

When you go through betrayals and let downs do not think that something strange is happening to you because you are in error. You may be in error and you may even have sinned. But remember also that betrayal is one of the things you will have to endure as part of your Christian service.

Relating with people who have experienced betrayal is different from relating with inexperienced fellows. Experienced people have a more mellow and mature approach to ministry. I have watched as ministers of the gospel have made fun of my books on loyalty, only to turn around and fall in love with them after they experience betrayal.

Honestly, maturity in ministry goes more by what you have been through than by the number of sermons you have preached.

4. Enduring hours of prayer is an accomplishment of the sufferings of Christ.

> **And he went a little further, and fell on his face, and prayed, saying, O my Father, if it be possible, let this cup pass from me: nevertheless not as I will, but as thou *wilt*.**
>
> **Matthew 26:39**

Praying for hours with no apparent response from Heaven is an experience you must endure if you are to have fruit in the ministry. There is suffering in praying for hours in a room where you can only hear your monotonous voice repeating the same words.

No wonder few people can pray for one hour. If you are not prepared to discipline yourself and stay indoors you will never accomplish the suffering of praying for hours. You must experience what it is like to pray continuously for one hour, three hours, six hours, ten hours and twelve hours.

Praying on your own for hours helps you to accomplish the same sufferings that Jesus accomplished.

Praying on your own for hours helps you to experience the suffering that Christ did in the Garden of Gethsemane.

5. Enduring sleepless nights is an accomplishment of the sufferings of Christ.

> **What, could ye not watch with me one hour?**
>
> **Matthew 26:40**

There is another kind of suffering that you must endure in order to watch and pray. Staying awake is no easy art. I thought you wanted to be a miracle worker like Jesus Christ and have a worldwide ministry? Jesus prayed through the night that the will of God be done. His disciples slept whilst he endured sleeplessness.

Within a few hours of the suffering of sleeplessness, he had borne fruit and had become the Lamb of God that taketh away the sins of the world.

Within a few hours, the disciples who could not stay awake had become betrayers and deserters of God!

6. Enduring sorrow is an accomplishment of the sufferings of Christ.

> **Then saith he unto them, My soul is exceeding sorrowful, even unto death: tarry ye here, and watch with me.**
>
> **Matthew 26:38**

Sorrow is another kind of suffering that God allowed Jesus Christ to go through. His soul was exceedingly sorrowful!

Are you experiencing sorrow?

Has your loved one died?

Has your family been ripped apart?

Has your world changed overnight with the departure of a dear cherished one?

What Kind of God Are You?

A pastor whose wife had died suddenly in the midst of her years said to me, "I would not wish that experience for my worst enemy." You see, his wife had been killed in a terrible car accident.

He described how he had just finished fasting for forty days.

"I grew so lean during the fast that my trousers were falling off my waist."

Right at the end of the fast whilst I was praying for God to move, my wife was killed in a freak accident.

He told me how he looked up into the sky and prayed a prayer he had never prayed before.

He told me, "I looked up, prayed and said: 'What kind of God are you? What kind of God are you? What kind of God are you?'"

He knew that his wife could not have died without the divine permission of the Lord.

He was wondering what kind of God would listen to him praying and fasting for forty days and then kill his wife.

But somehow he pulled through this tragedy and was able to continue serving God in the ministry.

But that is not the case for everyone. Some people become bitter and never successfully accomplish the enduring of the suffering of sorrow.

It is important to believe that nothing can happen to you unless God allows it. The devil is not in control of your life; God is.

You must successfully endure the sorrow, the darkness, the pain and the hopelessness that you have fallen into.

You must not become bitter! You must not threaten to become a Muslim because of your sorrows!

You must not threaten to leave the Lord or the ministry!

7. Enduring abandonment is an accomplishment of the sufferings of Christ.

> **Then began he to curse and to swear, *saying*, I know not the man. And immediately the cock crew.**
>
> **Matthew 26:74**

Being abandoned is another kind of suffering. You have to experience it to know what it is like to be abandoned by all and sundry. Jesus Christ was abandoned by His disciples. No one seemed to know Him anymore. Peter angrily rebuked anyone who tried to associate him with Christ.

"I don't know Him and I don't want to know Him! He is on his own now. If he insists on dying, it's up to him!

We tried to advise him but he called us Satan. We tried to save him in the garden but he would have none of it. He actually rebuked us in front of the soldiers. You can't really help a stubborn person when he wants to have his own way. Every man for himself!

You can't help a stubborn person if he doesn't want to be helped."

When I decided to leave my medical practice and go into ministry, I felt all alone and abandoned by men. People thought I was crazy. My father said I could do what I wanted to. My parents-in-law thought I was crazy. My classmates passed comments, muttering under their breath about me, as they took off one by one, leaving Ghana forever.

Indeed, I felt all alone in the ministry and in life. I knew that God had to save me otherwise I would become the laughing stock of the town. God helped me and He did not abandon me even though men may have abandoned me. Enduring abandonment is an important spiritual accomplishment. The suffering of the abandoned person is one of the sufferings of Christ.

8. Enduring the contradictions of sinners against you is an accomplishment of the sufferings of Christ.

> **For consider him that ENDURED SUCH CONTRADICTION of sinners against himself, lest ye be wearied and faint in your minds.**
>
> **Hebrews 12:3**

One of the most difficult things to endure is the contradiction of sinners. The contradiction of sinners speaks of bad negative and opposite responses that you receive in response to your good deeds.

Perhaps, because some ministers are no longer prepared to suffer the contradiction of sinners, they do not stay in the difficult and demonic marriages they find themselves in.

Pastors are saying to themselves as they get ready to divorce and end the contradiction in their homes, "Why should I suffer at the hands of this witch when I come home? Did I not minister the Word of God with all my heart?"

"Why should I not have food to eat after fasting the whole day and preaching for hours?"

"Why should I not have good exciting sex after I have kept myself pure from all the other women I meet?"

"Why should I stay at home with this contentious, ill-natured and accusative woman when there are so many ladies in the congregation who admire me and believe so much in my ministry?"

Indeed, many ministers of the gospel receive the contradiction of sinners in the privacy of their homes.

But that is exactly what Christ endured. After preaching the most beautiful sermons on love, meekness and joy and after healing their blind, deaf and dumb patients, the masses of Jerusalem overwhelmingly voted to execute him.

Actually, it gets even worse than that. After driving out thieves from the temple, healing madmen and raising the dead, Jesus was put up for elections and his only opponent was an armed robber who was also a hired assassin and a known murderer. Barabbas won the elections overwhelmingly and was pardoned and released from prison whilst Jesus Christ was sent over to be slaughtered for his good works. Jesus asked them, "For which of these good works do you seek to kill me?"

It is time to tell yourself, "I am ready to endure the contradiction of sinners." It is time to ask yourself, "Why do you want to be happy? Why don't you rather decide to be like Jesus Christ?"

Tell yourself: "I don't need to be happy in this life. I just need to be like Jesus Christ and endure the contradictions of sinners successfully."

9. Enduring accusations is an accomplishment of the sufferings of Christ.

And the chief priests accused him of many things: but he answered nothing.

Mark 15:3

Jesus was accused of things he never did. He successfully endured false accusations with all their implications. Accusations are some of the strongest pressures that can come on a minister of the gospel. Accusations tend to direct and guide people into error.

One day, a minister of the gospel said to me, "I cannot stand it when people talk about me and say bad things about me."

This pastor had a growing church but had never experienced a certain level of accusations. I assured the pastor that accusations would be part of the things to expect.

One day, whilst visiting a missionary in a foreign country, I remarked to him, "One day, someone will accuse you of stealing money."

"Me? Stealing money? After all I gave up to come here?"

I assured him that he was on the way of the cross and it was just a matter of time before someone accused him of stealing. Sometimes, when you are inexperienced, you just can't believe how certain accusations will be levelled against you.

10. Enduring hatred is an accomplishment of the sufferings of Christ.

Then Pilate said unto them, why, what evil hath he done? And they cried out the more exceedingly, crucify him.

Mark 15:14

> **But this cometh to pass, that the word might be fulfilled that is written in their law, they hated me without a cause.**
>
> **John 15:25**

It is difficult to live with people who hate you. This is one of the reasons why people divorce or separate; because they cannot bear to live in the same place with someone who obviously hates them. Jesus Christ endured the hatred of the Jews. They murdered him because they hated him.

One day, some men accosted me at a golf course. I was absolutely stunned as they railed at me and treated me with open hatred. Although I was entitled to play free of charge because I belonged to a sister club, they ganged up on me and made me pay fees to the club. I had to pay even though no one else in my category was ever made to do any such thing. They seemed to just dislike my presence at the golf course.

On another occasion, a golf club to which my pastors and I belonged actually changed their rules so that we would not qualify for certain discounts any more. These newly created rules affected only ourselves and one or two other players! It was not difficult to feel the hatred and dislike for our presence.

But hatred is something you must endure if you are to be a minister of the gospel of Jesus Christ. It is an accomplishment to thrive successfully in spite of hatred all around.

11. Enduring envy is an accomplishment of the sufferings of Christ.

> **For he knew that the chief priests had delivered him for envy.**
>
> **Mark 15:10**

Jesus Christ was crucified because of jealousy. O how jealous we are of each other! The demon of envy fills the hearts of many pastors. We look enviously across our shoulders, wishing to hear bad news about someone who is doing better than us.

"He will soon fall, he will soon die, he will soon have bad news", we say to ourselves because we are filled with the spirit of envy.

Do not be disheartened because you sense pretentious behaviour in the people around you.

Living with jealousy is part of our calling. Sometimes, people are nasty to you because they are jealous of you.

12. Enduring rejection by man is an accomplishment of the sufferings of Christ.

> **Then cried they all again, saying, Not this man, but Barabbas. Now Barabbas was a robber.**
>
> **John 18:40**

Hatred and envy often result in rejection. Before any one is accepted he first of all suffers rejection. Moses was rejected by the Israelites before he was eventually accepted. Jesus Christ was rejected by the Israelites and then accepted as Saviour by the whole world. The suffering of rejection must be experienced by all who want to be accepted.

You will never have great spiritual credentials if you have not been first rejected. You will be accepted after you suffer rejection.

13. Enduring the disappointing ways of men of authority is an accomplishment of the sufferings of Christ.

> **And from thenceforth Pilate sought to release him: but the Jews cried out, saying, If thou let this man go, thou art not Caesar's friend: whosoever maketh himself a king speaketh against Caesar.**
>
> **When Pilate therefore heard that saying, he brought Jesus forth, and sat down in the judgment seat in a place that is called the Pavement, but in the Hebrew, Gabbatha.**
>
> **John 19:12-13**

As you get higher in ministry you will relate with kings and other men of authority. The lack of truth and honesty in many of these men of authority causes great suffering. Jesus Christ suffered because neither Pilate nor Herod would stand up for the principles of truth and verity.

Lying, scheming and political motives guided both Pilate, Herod and the High Priest until they had put to death the Son of the living God. Successfully co-existing and living under such authorities is part of the suffering of Christ.

Jesus Christ was successful in enduring the nonsense and hypocrisy of secular leaders. You will need the grace of God to endure this kind of suffering.

Working under men of authority who are not good leaders can also lead to much suffering. It is difficult to work under someone who is incompetent, lazy and slow. Sometimes, God wants you to suffer hardship under the hand of authority.

Jesus Christ suffered under incompetent men of authority. He was never rude to any of them. He never insulted or threatened them. He meekly endured everything as though he was a common criminal.

Can you accomplish the suffering of living and working under incompetent and incapable leadership?

14. Enduring pain is an accomplishment of the sufferings of Christ.

> **So Pilate, anxious to please the crowd, released Barabbas to them. He ordered Jesus flogged with a lead-tipped whip, then turned him over to the Roman soldiers to crucify him.**
>
> **Mark 15:15 (NLT)**

Enduring physical pain is one of the sufferings of Christ. He went through much pain for us. Someone may ask, "What is the use of all these different punishments? What does it accomplish? Indeed, great things are accomplished in the Spirit when you suffer for Jesus Christ. Paul, speaking of the effect of sorrow said:

> **For behold what earnestness this very thing, this godly sorrow, has produced in you: what vindication of yourselves, what indignation, what fear, what longing, what zeal, what avenging of wrong! In everything you demonstrated yourselves to be innocent in the matter.**
>
> **2 Corinthians 7:11 (NASB)**

The suffering of pain and sorrow brings out the fear of God in you. Suffering makes you zealous and causes you to cleanse your soul.

15. Enduring mockery is an accomplishment of the sufferings of Christ.

> **And they smote him on the head with a reed, and did spit upon him, and bowing *their* knees worshipped him.**
>
> **And when THEY HAD MOCKED HIM, they took off the purple from him, and put his own clothes on him, and led him out to crucify him.**
>
> **Mark 15:19-20**

Suffering the scorn of mockers is one of the sufferings of Christ! Mockery is a terrible thing to endure. But Jesus endured it for all of us. Do not expect to fulfil your ministry without being mocked.

I have been mocked for starting a church. What are they doing? What are they building? It will amount to nothing!

I have been mocked for starting branches. "It will never work," they said in their hearts.

Men have mocked my preaching! Men have mocked my calling!

Miracle Days Are Here

I once started a TV programme and I called it "Miracle Days are Here". A fellow minister had a good laugh when he heard of the name of my TV programme.

He said to me personally, "Why did you call your TV programme Miracle Days Are Here? Where did miracle days go? Miracle days have been here all along."

"Ha ha ha! Maybe you have not had miracles in your ministry all this time." There was a lot of mocking laughter from this minister.

"Ha ha ha, he never had miracles in his ministry. Miracle days have been here all along."

"Ha ha ha. He thinks miracles have just begun to happen. But they've been here all along. We've been having miracles for years."

"Ha ha ha. You are a teacher and an administrator with no power for real ministry. Miracle days have always been here!"

I tell you, I felt silly about my TV programme.

Men have mocked at my branch churches. "You have only two or three people and you call it a church? They are not churches; they are cells," they laughed. People mocked at my books calling them nonsense. People mocked at my teachings calling them unnecessary.

But there is no need to be bitter against these people. God is using them to accomplish His will in your life. It is part of your destiny to be mocked at and also ridiculed. You are supposed to endure it as part of your great accomplishments in the ministry. Suffering the scorn of mockers is one of the sufferings of Christ!

16. Enduring the psychological torment of impending death is an accomplishment of the sufferings of Christ.

But we see Jesus, who was made a little lower than the angels for the SUFFERING OF DEATH, crowned with glory and honour; that he by the grace of God should taste death for every man.

Hebrews 2:9

The knowledge that you are going to die is one of the most disturbing and psychologically unsettling thoughts. We all know that we will die one day. But to have knowledge of its certainty and to be given a time to expect it is indeed one of the most difficult types of suffering a person can be given.

No one knows what Jesus Christ went through as He walked towards Jerusalem. He said, "I have a terrible baptism of suffering ahead of me, and I am under a heavy burden until it is accomplished" (Luke 12:50).

Sometimes God allows people to die slowly and become conscious of their end so that they become humble and open to Him. Sometimes a slow death is His grace at work so that we don't suffer loss in the final judgment.

In the book, *The Final Quest*, Rick Joyner makes reference to ministers who had been given slow deaths as a form of grace to humble them and bring them to repentance before they died.

Impending death may be the kind of suffering you are called upon to endure. Jesus Christ experienced this for us.

17. Enduring weakness is an accomplishment of the sufferings of Christ.

And as they came out, they found a man of Cyrene, Simon by name: him they compelled to bear his cross.

Matthew 27:32

Being seemingly weak is one of the sufferings of Christ.

One day, our church suffered attacks from elements in the community. We became the laughing stock of churches that felt we were sissies, unable to stand up for our rights and unable to defend ourselves.

A pastor visited us asking whether we had been prayerful. He could not see how such things could happen to us if we were spiritually powerful. He then told me of a pastor who had decreed that anyone who attacked them would pay with their lives.

That pastor had declared boldly, "One block for one life." This statement had been enough to stop all aggression against the church. I listened carefully to these exhortations.

But I only felt weaker and more inadequate. I had not been able to declare "one block for one life." Many of my blocks had been broken and taken away and none of our enemies had died. Actually, our enemies were getting stronger, healthier and fatter. I felt I was a weak and helpless pastor.

But weakness is a part of the suffering God intends for you. Jesus Christ was weak as he carried the cross. That is why Simon of Cyrene was called to help Christ.

All is not lost because you seem weak and helpless. Jesus Christ was weak and helpless at the cross. It is one of the sufferings of Christ and it may be one of the sufferings you may have to accomplish.

18. Enduring helplessness is an accomplishment of the sufferings of Christ.

He saved others; himself he cannot save. If he be the King of Israel, let him now come down from the cross, and we will believe him.

Matthew 27:42

We love to exercise authority and show ourselves capable of solving every problem. There is a place, however, where you are unable to do anything about anything any more. It is the place of helplessness. You may have been used to save many situations, but there are situations that you can do nothing about.

One night, in the midst of a season of helplessness, I drove around my city playing mournful music. At my side was a widow whose husband had just died. I was trying to talk to her and encourage her. Within me was a strong desire to bring back her husband and hand him back to her. I felt uselessly helpless as I rambled on, quoting Scriptures and telling her stories about how her husband would be enjoying the glories of Heaven at that time.

Time and time again I wanted to do something practical that would change everything for her. But I had no ability to change anything. I was simply helpless and incapable of changing what had happened.

God has appointed a place of helplessness so that we would experience what it is like to be unable to change anything. It is a place you must descend to and rise from again. The place of helplessness!

You must survive it! Suffering helplessness is one of the sufferings of Christ. May you be strong in the day of your helplessness.

19. Enduring insults is an accomplishment of the sufferings of Christ.

And those passing by were hurling ABUSE at Him, wagging their heads, and saying, "Ha! You who are going to destroy the temple and rebuild it in three days, save Yourself, and come down from the cross!"

In the same way the chief priests also, along with the scribes, were mocking Him among themselves and saying, "He saved others; He cannot save Himself.

Let this Christ, the King of Israel, now come down from the cross, so that we may see and believe!" And those who were crucified with Him were casting the same INSULT at Him.

Mark 15:29-32, (NASB)

Enduring insults is one of the things Jesus Christ suffered for us. Get ready to suffer the same things if you want to follow Him. Have you been insulted for what you believed? It is an accomplishment to receive insults on behalf of Christ.

One day, a young man lifted his hand and hurled insults at me. For several minutes he lifted his hand and gave me a good dressing down. I gave glory to God that I had experienced insults and abuse for Christ's sake.

On another occasion someone insulted me for about thirty minutes. That night, I received a good dose of insults, abuses and curses. I was simply amazed as this Christian friend insulted me for the stance I had taken for the Lord.

You may be counting the countries you have preached in. As you become more mature, you will also count the number of times you have been insulted for the sake of Christ. Enduring insults is one of the accomplishments you must achieve.

20. Enduring shame is an accomplishment of the sufferings of Christ.

Looking unto Jesus the author and finisher of *our* faith; who for the joy that was set before him endured the cross, DESPISING THE SHAME, and is set down at the right hand of the throne of God.

Hebrews 12:2

The shame of the cross is part of the sufferings of Christ. God may allow you to go through shame as part of the accomplishments he desires from you. Despising shame is an art you must learn. Accepting shame is one of the sufferings you may have to experience in order to fulfil your ministry.

Are you ashamed of the gospel?

Are you ashamed of Christ?

Are you ashamed of praying in tongues?

Do you feel silly when you pray in tongues?

Are you ashamed of the ministry? Do you think it is too small?

Are you ashamed of your church?

Are you ashamed of your circumstances?

Are you embarrassed by the work God has given you?

Do not forget: enduring shame and embarrassment is one of the sufferings of Jesus Christ.

21. Becoming vulnerable is an accomplishment of the sufferings of Christ.

They gave him vinegar to drink mingled with gall: and when he had tasted thereof, he would not drink.

Matthew 27:34

Becoming vulnerable is one of the sufferings of Christ. Many people do not enter the ministry because they don't want to be vulnerable. They don't want their lives to depend on tithes and free-will offerings.

Being in the ministry opens you up to people who can hurt you. People you love can turn against you and hurt you. In the ministry, you become, vulnerable because you expose yourself to people you would never have met.

When you preach, people get to know all about you, whilst you know little about them. Good preaching always makes you vulnerable because you share details of your life from the pulpit.

Jesus Christ became vulnerable to the Jews, the Romans and the wicked human race. He did it because he loved us. He came from Heaven to earth and exposed himself for our sakes. Becoming vulnerable is part of the call to sacrifice. Becoming vulnerable is one of the sufferings of Jesus Christ.

22. Enduring degradation is an accomplishment of the sufferings of Christ.

Then were there two thieves crucified with him, one on the right hand, and another on the left.

Matthew 27:38

Degradation is one of the sufferings of Christ. Jesus Christ endured the suffering of being degraded. Jesus Christ was reduced to a mere thief. His associations with thieves made everyone think that Jesus Christ was also a thief.

To do the will of God you will have to accept a lowering of people's impression or estimation of who you are. If you are very concerned about what people think, you will constantly reject the suffering of Christ.

I was trained as a medical doctor. I had great respect for being a part of this noble profession. Becoming a pastor made me lose the honour of that noble profession. I had joined a group that had a very questionable reputation in the community. I was now a pastor and many people think of pastors as thieves who start churches just to take people's money.

One day, I attended a big funeral in my city. Whilst I was parking my car, some bystanders began to have a discussion about me.

One of them said to his friend "I think I will also start a church."

Why is that? His friend asked.

"So that I can also have a car like the one he is driving."

He continued, "Church business is very lucrative. If I become a pastor I will also have a car like this."

I was amazed at the thought patterns of the gossiping bystanders. Obviously, they were clueless about what it really involved to be a pastor or to have a church.

Suffering degradation is part of the sufferings of Christ. I would not have had people making such comments about me if I was a well-known heart surgeon in my city. But you cannot maintain your high society airs if you really want to follow Jesus Christ.

23. Enduring cheating and robbery is an accomplishment of the sufferings of Christ.

Then the soldiers, when they had crucified Jesus, took his garments, and made four parts, to every soldier a part; and also his coat: now the coat was without seam, woven from the top throughout.

John 19:23

Being cheated is one of the sufferings of Christ. Enduring injustice, robbery and mistreatment is one of the sufferings Jesus experienced for our sake. Jesus Christ endured the suffering of being cheated and robbed. To be cheated and robbed is a type of suffering a Christian must go through. It is part of the sufferings of Christ. You will not amount to much in the ministry if you are not prepared to be cheated or robbed.

An attitude of standing up for your rights will constantly keep you away from true fruitfulness. An attitude of not wanting to be cheated will prevent you from ever being useful in the ministry.

24. Enduring painful separation is an accomplish-ment of the sufferings of Christ.

When Jesus therefore saw his mother, and the disciple standing by, whom he loved, he saith unto his mother, Woman, behold thy son!

Then saith he to the disciple, Behold thy mother! And from that hour that disciple took her unto his own *home*.

John 19:26-27

Through death, Jesus Christ was separated from His mother and from the people He loved. Separation from loved ones tears the heart apart. It is painful to send away people you love. Missionaries are not sent out because churches don't want to be separated from the nice people they know.

Without the pain of separation many new fruits never come into existence.

There are many ministries that are barren because they do not want to go through the pain of separation in order to bear fruits. Do not resist the suffering of separation. Through this kind of suffering you will accomplish the will of God.

25. Enduring desolation and loneliness is an accomplishment of the sufferings of Christ.

And at the ninth hour Jesus cried with a loud voice, saying, Eloi, Eloi, lama sabachthani? Which is, being interpreted, My God, my God, why hast thou forsaken me?

Mark 15:34

The suffering of loneliness is one of the sufferings of Christ. People leave the call of God because they are lonely. I have known single people to abandon their ministry and exchange it for a marriage because they can't take being alone anymore. Indeed, loneliness is a form of suffering.

Jesus was lonely on the cross. He looked across to see if His friends, the disciples, were also on crosses beside Him. But His disciples had run away and were nowhere to be found. They were having lunch in their various homes whilst He lay dying on the cross.

When Jesus looked to His right and to His left, he saw thieves. When He looked down, He saw wicked Roman soldiers casting lots for His clothes.

He was not used to this company. He was used to His disciples, His mother, Mary Magdalene and others.

The crucifixion had isolated him and separated him from everything and everyone he knew. Your call has a way of separating you and giving you a lonely existence in this world.

There are often very few people who understand what you are doing. Do not complain because you are lonely. It is part of the call of God on your life. The suffering of loneliness is one of the sufferings of Christ.

26. Enduring the moment of death is an accomplishment of the sufferings of Christ.

And Jesus cried with a loud voice, and gave up the ghost.

Mark 15:37

And being found in fashion as a man, HE HUMBLED HIMSELF, and became obedient unto death, EVEN THE DEATH OF THE CROSS.

Philippians 2:8

The moment of death comes with pain. Sometimes the pain is short-lived and sometimes it lasts longer. Whether you die by the electric chair, by hanging or by lethal injection, the moment of death is a frightening one.

Many people have endured this moment because of their beliefs in Jesus Christ. They held on to their faith and allowed their lives to pass away because of their faith. It is an accomplishment that is rewarded greatly by the Lord. You will not die for him in vain.

A Foolish Death?

I once had a soldier friend who travelled all over the world on military duties. He told me how peacekeeping soldiers in some West African countries had begun to do business – operating taxis and trading in diamonds. He told me that these soldiers were not keen on getting caught in the crossfire that raged between the two warring factions.

"I thought they were professional soldiers," I told him.

"Yes, they are but they don't want to die a foolish death," he answered.

"What is a foolish death," I asked.

"A foolish death is death for a foolish cause!"

I mused over the phrase "a foolish death".

I had also heard someone say, "All die be die!". This statement meant that all deaths are the same. Death is death, in other words!

But there is such a thing as a foolish death. Therefore all deaths are not the same.

Dying because of your faith in Jesus Christ is not a foolish death. It is an honourable death with many great rewards. You will be rewarded for the suffering you experienced at the moment of death.

Chapter

7

How Sacrifice Releases Power

CHAPTER SUMMARY

Every sacrifice releases some power! The preaching of the cross is the preaching of sacrifice. It is also the preaching of power. As Christians, we should preach boldly about the cross and what it means. The Bible tells us in the verse we read, that the preaching of Christ is foolishness to those that are perishing but unto us, it is the power of God.

> **For the preaching of the cross is to them that perish foolishness; but unto us which are saved IT IS THE POWER OF GOD.**
>
> **1 Corinthians 1:18**

Every Sacrifice releases spiritual power! This explains why many demonic rituals involve some kind of sacrifice. Various animals and sometimes human beings are sacrificed in rituals, to release power. Occultists make sacrifices. People seeking spiritual power are always asked to sacrifice something.

The king of Moab sacrificed his son when he saw that he was losing a battle with the Israelites:

> **And when the king of Moab saw that the battle was too sore for him, he took with him seven hundred men that drew swords, to break through even unto the king of Edom: but they could not. THEN HE TOOK HIS ELDEST SON THAT SHOULD HAVE REIGNED IN HIS STEAD, AND OFFERED HIM FOR A BURNT OFFERING UPON THE WALL. And there was great indignation against Israel: and they departed from him, and returned to their own land.**
>
> **2 Kings 3:26-27**

This sacrifice turned away the approaching armies. Power was released by sacrificing the king's son. This saved the king's life and the lives of his people. Sacrifice will always release power. Learn this principle - *sacrifice will always release power.*

The Israelites made God angry because they sacrificed their children to idols for power:

> **Yea, THEY SACRIFICED THEIR SONS AND THEIR DAUGHTERS UNTO DEVILS, And shed innocent blood, even the blood of their sons and of their daughters, whom they sacrificed unto the idols of Canaan: and the land was polluted with blood.**
>
> **Psalm 106:37-38**

Many pastors and leaders of churches are powerless because they make no sacrifices for the Lord and have no intention to do so.

Some years ago, the Church in Switzerland was very powerful. They sent missionaries to Ghana, even though they could not speak Ghanaian languages. One of these missionaries called Johann Riis translated the Bible into Twi, one of the most widely spoken dialects in Ghana. He also translated 6000 Twi proverbs into English. Today, there are still Swiss people who speak fluent Twi. They are descendants of the original missionaries.

If I were to send people to certain places for missionary work, there would be an outcry. That is why there is no power in our ministries. There is power only when there is sacrifice!

A lot of power is released, for instance, when you fast. This is because a sacrifice is made when you fast. Fasting is sacrificing your meals. When people give up something for the ministry, power is released.

The early church was so powerful. The more they were martyred, the stronger they became. However, when the Church was accepted officially in Rome, it lost its power. This acceptance removed the need for sacrifice and therefore weakened the Church.

The power of the Church is often increased where there is opposition and much need of sacrifice.

■ Three Types of Power Released through Sacrifice

a. The power to make people follow you

There is an aura around anyone who makes great sacrifices. He is respected and held in high esteem by people around him. People see this person doing things that *they* fear to touch. This inspires confidence and stirs up followers to do the same.

Let's face it: How many of the democratically elected politicians are prepared to die for what they believe? Some of them do not even believe in their own speeches. They read speeches that are written for them and make promises that are not true. I sometimes marvel at how unreal some of these people are. They rarely speak extemporaneously. Tell me, am I lying?

b. The power to convince people

Have you ever wondered why some people are so unconvincing? No one wants to hear what they have to say. Have you asked yourself why some pastors have very few members (followers)? Many politicians claim to love their countries. They talk about their concern for their countries at political rallies and news conferences. Unfortunately, many people do not believe them.

Think about Jesus. He never wrote a book and never published an article. He never campaigned for votes or support. In fact, He constantly told people not to publicize the good things He had done for them.

He never travelled more than two hundred miles from His hometown. He never preached on TV or on radio. He did not build any institutions to His memory! His picture was never on a billboard and He never owned a car.

Yet, the whole world has gone after Him. Two thousand years have gone by and millions still believe in Him. Thousands are converted to Him daily and there are volunteers who are ready to die for Him today.

What is the reason for the long-lasting effect of His ministry? The answer is simple. The sacrifice! The sacrifice of His life on the cross was the most significant spiritual thing that Jesus did on earth. He preached, He taught and healed the sick. However, the eternal fruit was borne when He gave up His life on the cross.

Have you ever wondered why Jesus did not stay around longer than 33 years? When He was threatened why didn't He travel to Morocco, Algeria, Macedonia or Egypt? Why didn't He preach for a few more years? Were there no more good works that He could do on earth?

What we need to learn here, is that obedience and sacrifice will bear more eternal fruit than any other good works we do. This one sacrifice for humankind has released so much power into the earth.

This is why millions from all nations believe and follow Him. This is why Jesus focused on sacrificing Himself on the cross. The sacrifice on the cross was the key that would release the power of salvation. No amount of preaching or teaching could replace what would be accomplished on the cross.

c. The power to make people committed

> **But what things were gain to me, those I counted loss for Christ. Yea doubtless, and I count all things but loss for the excellency of the knowledge of Christ Jesus my Lord: for whom I have suffered the loss of all things, and do count them but dung, that I may win Christ,**
>
> **Philippians 3:7-8**

Many great men and women have left all to follow Jesus. Kathryn Kuhlman had to leave her husband. Not many women would be prepared to leave their husbands.

In one of Kathryn Khulman's biographies, the author talks about how he had asked Kathryn about her marriage. He said they were alone in a room together when he asked about this chapter of her life. In a rare moment, she began to speak about her former husband and what it had cost her to leave him.

Suddenly, the power of God entered the office. The writer described how he could hardly stand. He said the presence of God came into the room so powerfully that he had to leave. *A sacrifice always releases power.* Sometimes even talking about the sacrifice releases the power.

I once had an uncanny experience when the holy presence of God walked into my office. I was in conversation with two other pastors when the anointing walked into the room. The three of us suddenly knew that someone had walked in.

Everyone there could feel that He was standing by us. These things are real. I had never had an experience like that.

We have so much knowledge and so little sacrifice. There is power ready to break forth in our lives the moment we make the sacrifice. You will be surprised at how many people will become committed to your cause when you make the sacrifice.

Do People Take You Seriously?

I once asked some pastors, "You preach the same messages that I do, don't you?" Then I asked them, "Is the impact of your message felt?" They stared at me silently.

I continued, "Because you have not given up anything for what you believe, people do not take you seriously. You may say the same things that I do but if you do not pay the price, you will never make the impact you need to."

Many preachers are not taken seriously. Many of their statements are ignored. But everything changes when someone pays the price. Every situation changes in the moment that blood is shed.

There was a time when our church was attacked. The people in the community were hostile to us. My young men wanted to fight back and kill the invaders. They wanted us to arm ourselves and launch counter-attacks. But I knew that if someone was killed in the confrontation, the intensity and seriousness of the conflict would change forever. We did not want to shed blood. This is the reason why we did not fight back when our church was attacked. Macbeth said, "Blood will have blood!" Jesus said, "He that comes by the sword will go by the sword."

You see, the gravity of every situation changes as soon as a sacrifice of someone's life is made. Where there is no sacrifice, there will be no power. You may have many doctrines and ideas, but without sacrifice you will have no power in your ministry.

You should come to the Lord and ask Him if there is anything He wants from you. You must give yourself as a living sacrifice to Him. There can be no power without a sacrifice. Sacrifices release the power of God in your life.

When there is sacrifice, there is power. This is why suicide bombers are making such an impact in the world today. You would think that these terrorist acts would drive people away from their religion. On the contrary, it stirs up more commitment. Sacrifice attracts more followers.

God told me that He called me to start churches. He has asked me to send people to the corners of the world to start churches. The Lord told me that there are several people who will respond to this call. He told me not to worry about people's lives but to sacrifice my best sons and daughters on the harvest fields. I tell you, many have responded and are doing great things for the Lord.

God is going to make you sacrifice. He may change your life and change everything about you. He is going to ask you to give up certain things, and as you do, you are going to see His power. When you speak, your words will be taken seriously because of the sacrifices you've made.

Chapter

8

The Enemies of Sacrifice

CHAPTER SUMMARY

8.1 The Antichrist is the first enemy of sacrifice

8.2 Judas Iscariot is the second enemy of sacrifice

8.3 Satan is the third enemy of sacrifice

Since sacrifice releases so much power, the enemies of God have historically fought against the concept of sacrifice. When you make a sacrifice to the Lord, it often looks as though you are doing something stupid. You go down in pain but you comc up in victory.

Not surprisingly, the devil has succeeded in keeping believers as far from sacrificing as possible. The Anti-Christ, Pharaoh and Satan himself, all get involved to prevent you from having any such ideas. It is time for Christians to know that power lies just beyond the cross.

■ The Three Enemies of Sacrifice

> **And out of one of them came forth a little horn, which waxed exceeding great, toward the south, and toward the east, and toward the pleasant land. And it waxed great, even to the host of heaven; and it cast down some of the host and of the stars to the ground, and stamped upon them.**
>
> **Daniel 8:9-10**

The Prophet Daniel prophesied about a little horn, which rose to defile the temple. This refers to the reign of Antiochus Epiphanies. He made himself an enemy of the Jews. He profaned the temple, entered the sanctuary, and took away the golden altar. He stopped the daily sacrifice and set up the abomination of desolation upon the altar (an idol), and called Solomon's temple the temple of Jupiter Olympius. This man, a type of Anti-Christ, did not want God's people to sacrifice to their God.

1. The Antichrist is the first enemy of sacrifice.

> **And an host was given him AGAINST THE DAILY SACRIFICE by reason of transgression, and it cast down the truth to the ground; and it practiced, and prospered.**
>
> **Daniel 8:12**
>
> **And arms shall stand on his part, and they shall pollute the sanctuary of strength, AND SHALL TAKE AWAY THE DAILY SACRIFICE, and they shall place the abomination that maketh desolate.**
>
> **Daniel 11:31**

Notice right here that, one of the things the Antichrist will do is to stop the daily sacrifice. He will stop people from sacrificing to God. Get this clear! The enemies of God are against you obeying God and laying down your life for Him.

The Antichrist will prevail by peace. He will be cast in the mould of Hitler but will be even wiser. He will prosper not by war but by peace. He will win and succeed. He will come in the name of peace; talk about peace, and everybody will think that he is God. But the most significant thing he will do is to stop people from sacrificing to God.

> **And his power shall be mighty, but not by his own power: and he shall destroy wonderfully, and shall prosper, and practise, and shall destroy the mighty and the holy people. And through his policy also he shall**

> **cause craft to prosper in his hand; and he shall magnify himself in his heart, and BY PEACE shall destroy many: he shall also stand up against the Prince of princes; but he shall be broken without hand.**
>
> **Daniel 8:24-25**

When the spirit of antichrist is at work, it stops you from sacrificing to God.

Antichrist is anti-God and anti-God is anti-sacrifice! One of the devil's goals is to stop you from sacrificing to God! The antichrist spirit is against you going to church, giving your money, your time and your life to the work of God. That voice in your life is the voice of the Antichrist. The Bible says that the Antichrist will come and stop the people from sacrificing to God.

I want you to know that when God is calling on you to give up something or to do something for Him, *the spirit of the Antichrist* will tell you not to do it.

Desolation in Ministry

> **Then I heard one saint speaking, and another saint said unto that certain saint which spake, How long shall be the vision concerning the daily sacrifice, and the TRANSGRESSION OF DESOLATION, to give both the sanctuary and the host to be trodden under foot?**
>
> **Daniel 8:13**

The taking away of the sacrifice is described as the sin of desolation. Desolation means: *destitute, barren, empty, forgotten, dark, rejected and dejected.* The sin of desolation is what comes when sacrifice is taken away from the church.

We cannot build more churches if people are not prepared to sacrifice. People have made sacrifices for us to be Christians today. They made it possible for us to know the Lord.

Where there are no sacrificial people, the church is desolate.

Our church looked very odd when we sent out missionaries to Africa. It looked as though we were destroying the lives of young promising couples. Parents fought against it with all their might. Yet, these same parents would not mind if the United Nations gave their children a job in a war zone.

Struggling in the Sun

One day, I was praying in the presence of God. I was also expecting an important phone call so I had my phone on. (I usually do not have my phone on when I am praying). Then the phone rang. It was one of my lay pastors.

Immediately after speaking to him, I had a vision. I saw the same person walking in a hot desert. He was sweating profusely and struggling in the heat of the shining sun. I knew immediately that he was distressed by his secular job. The Lord showed me that this lay pastor was not where he was supposed to be. So I called him and told him, "Pastor, you are in the wrong place. It is time to give it all up for Jesus. You are called to serve in the house of the Lord. You are a priest."

He responded, "Bishop, it's true, I struggle everyday at work. I know I am lost. I'm coming." That was the end of his secular career. Today he is fruitful in full-time ministry.

It was not easy for me to talk to this lay pastor. I felt very intimidated because he had a good job that was giving him a lot of money. Both Satan and the Anti-Christ were against my talking to this young man about full-time ministry.

Your life will be desolate when you hold back the sacrifice that you must make for God!

May desolation and barrenness be removed from your church and ministry!

2. Judas Iscariot is the second enemy of sacrifice.

Remember that it was no other person than Judas Iscariot who criticized the woman with the alabaster box. This woman poured out her expensive perfume on Jesus. It was the most valuable thing she had. Women spend hours doing their hair. They know what their hair means to them. A woman's hair symbolizes her beauty. Mary sacrificed her beauty and her valuable things for Jesus.

> **Then took Mary a pound of ointment of spikenard, very costly, and anointed the feet of Jesus, and wiped his feet with her hair: and the house was filled with the odour of the ointment. Then saith one of his disciples, JUDAS ISCARIOT, Simon's son, which should betray him, WHY WAS NOT THIS OINTMENT SOLD FOR THREE HUNDRED PENCE, AND GIVEN TO THE POOR?**
>
> **John 12:3-5**

It is true that this woman had been living in sin. However, she gave what was most precious to her - her hair, her perfume, her tears to Jesus. But Judas Iscariot, the honourable treasurer of the team (your treasurer is usually the most trusted person in the organization) didn't like it. Even though it wasn't his alabaster box, his life or his hair that were being sacrificed, he was against it.

The appearances of people who are antichrist or anti-sacrifice, can be very deceptive. The *anti-sacrifice, anti-give-up-everything, anti-do-a-lot, anti-give-a-lot* spirit is the spirit of the Antichrist. These people often present themselves as being very decent, very logical, very organized, and dignified. *But it is still the spirit of the Antichrist.*

3. Satan is the third enemy of sacrifice.

> **From that time forth began Jesus to shew unto his disciples, how that he must go unto Jerusalem, and SUFFER MANY THINGS of the elders and chief priests and scribes, AND BE KILLED, and be raised again the third day. Then Peter took him, and began to rebuke him, saying, Be it far from thee, Lord: this shall not be unto thee. BUT HE TURNED, AND SAID UNTO PETER, GET THEE BEHIND ME, SATAN: thou art an offence unto me: for thou savourest not the things that be of God, but those that be of men.**
>
> **Matthew 16:21-23**

When Jesus explained that He had to die on the cross, one of His pastors, Pastor Peter, took Jesus aside and began to rebuke Him.

"Be it far from you." Pastor Peter said.

"Never! As long as we are here, it will not happen."

Jesus turned and addressed the person who was against His sacrifice and said, "Get thee behind me *Satan*." Jesus spoke directly to Satan, as the person who was preventing His sacrifice.

We can all understand Peter's love for Jesus. In the natural, the people who love you will often oppose your decision to take up your cross. Peter did not know that the devil was using him. Our Lord Jesus exposed the devil for who he really was. We all know the story of how Peter rebuked Jesus for suggesting that He would die on the cross. Peter did this in the name of love, care, and concern for his Lord. What he did not know was that, this *love and concern* was actually the voice of Satan trying to prevent Jesus from sacrificing Himself.

I qualified as a medical doctor on the 10th of March, 1989. After working for a year, I decided to go into full-time ministry. Many caring relatives were against this idea. My father-in-law was so concerned that he offered to help me get a posting to another medical department. He felt I had lost interest in medicine because I had been posted to the Pathology (dead people's) Department. My dear mother-in-law also was deeply concerned about my situation. She constantly spoke about it.

One day, I said to her, "Please-Teacher (she was a teacher, so all her children called her 'Please-Teacher'), please do not talk about this any more. I have decided to go this way and God will keep me." From that time onwards, she never spoke about my decision to quit practising medicine.

You see, they were concerned about my welfare. Wouldn't you be concerned if your daughter was married to some wild young man who did not want to work any more? Of course, you would be concerned! My mother-in- law loved me just like Peter loved Jesus. In the natural, this is a sign of great concern.

However, in the spirit, it is opposition to the sacrifice. The enemy knew that if I sacrificed this treasured and noble profession, power would be released for ministry. I was about to take up my cross and follow Jesus.

To take up your cross does not mean to build a wooden cross and walk up to Mount Calvary. It means following the example of Christ Jesus. It means sacrificing your life for Jesus. And truly, much power for ministry has been released since I took that step. Ministry is far more honourable than medicine. In comparison to Christ, everything else is dung.

Jesus came into the world to save sinners. In the famous temptation of Christ in the wilderness, Satan showed Jesus the kingdoms of the world.

He said, "I've got a plan. I know your goal is to save the whole world. I have a plan that will avoid pain. This plan will give the same results. There will be no anguish, no torment, and no forfeiting of anything." Satan continued, "Just bow down and worship me and all these kingdoms will be yours."

But Jesus knew better. He said, "The sacrifice must come on! I have to suffer. I have to die! I have to pay the price!" Jesus was not fooled by Satan's easy plan.

Please do not be fooled by Satan's trouble-free plan. There are no shortcuts or easy-jets to the will of God.

Sometimes as pastors, we are nervy when we call on people to make sacrifices. That is the devil at work! I have learnt not to back down. I have learnt to boldly lead people into sacrificing for the Gospel.

Chapter

9

The Substitute for Sacrifice

CHAPTER SUMMARY

History shows us that there were people who opposed the offering of sacrifices to God. Not only were they against God's sacrifice but they had a substitute. In place of sacrificing to God, the Antichrist will put an "abomination that maketh desolate".

> **And arms shall stand on his part, and they shall pollute the sanctuary of strength, and shall take away the daily sacrifice, AND THEY SHALL PLACE THE ABOMINATION THAT MAKETH DESOLATE.**
>
> **Daniel 11:31**

History shows us that there were people who opposed the offering of sacrifices to God. Not only were they against God's sacrifice but they had a substitute. In place of sacrificing to God, the Antichrist will put an "abomination that maketh desolate".

This has happened before. Antiochus made the Jews sacrifice pigs in the temple. These pigs were the substitutes for the real sacrifice.

King Antiochus built an idol altar upon God's altar and slew swine upon it. He offered sacrifices which were not according to the law or to Jewish religious practices. Antiochus compelled the Jews to forsake the real worship and sacrifice pigs every day.

This incorrigible behaviour of King Antiochus shows us how people substitute the real sacrifice with other things. Everybody is sacrificing something. Everybody *will* sacrifice something. But the question is what will be sacrificed, and to whom will this sacrifice be made?

The Israelites were constantly worshipping images and sacrificing to idols. They sacrificed their sons and daughters to other gods and made them pass through fire.

> **But he walked in the way of the kings of Israel, yea, AND MADE HIS SON TO PASS THROUGH THE FIRE, according to the abominations of the heathen, whom the LORD cast out from before the children of Israel.**
>
> **2 Kings 16:3**
>
> **YEA, THEY SACRIFICED THEIR SONS AND THEIR DAUGHTERS UNTO DEVILS, And shed innocent blood, even the blood of their sons and of their daughters, whom they sacrificed unto the idols of Canaan: and the land was polluted with blood.**
>
> **Psalm 106:37-38**

Today, people are not prepared for their sons and daughters to be in ministry. But these same people would love their children to work in risky environments for money.

In 1 Corinthians 10:20, the Bible declares that the sacrifices the unbelievers make are made to devils.

> **But I say, that the things WHICH THE GENTILES SACRIFICE, THEY SACRIFICE TO DEVILS, and not to God: and I would not that ye should have fellowship with devils.**
>
> **1 Corinthians 10:20**
>
> **Amon was two and twenty years old when he began to reign, and reigned two years in Jerusalem. But he did that which was evil in the sight of the LORD, as did Manasseh his father: FOR AMON SACRIFICED UNTO ALL THE CARVED IMAGES which Manasseh his father had made, and**

> **served them; And humbled not himself before the LORD, as Manasseh his father had humbled himself; but Amon trespassed more and more. And his servants conspired against him, and slew him in his own house.**
>
> **2 Chronicles 33:21-24**

Do not deceive yourself. Sacrifices are made all the time. If you do not do it for one cause, you will do it for another. Sacrifices are made constantly. The Gentiles do make sacrifices but to the devil.

The Sacrifice of Doctors

Medical doctors sacrifice very much for their profession. Medical school lasts seven years and postgraduate medical school lasts another five years.

I recently asked a doctor about how many years he had studied medicine. Amazingly, he had been in medical school for more than twenty years. Is it not amazing! If someone had said he was going to sacrifice two years of his life in a theological school, people would say that he was wasting his time.

If you are in university for twenty years, it means you have a student's income for that long. No one seems to mind a low income for twenty years for the sake of medicine. But a low income for the sake of ministry is not acceptable to most people. Many people would not like to work in a church because they fear they would have a low income.

Near Death Experiences for Christ

I risked my life for medicine, now I risk my life for Christ. I used to sacrifice my "pig in the temple" but now I sacrifice my life to the Lord. My life has been at risk because of the ministry. There was a time my life was threatened for the ministry. I almost died in a car wreck while on a missionary journey to the north of Ghana. A pastor even said to me, "I wonder why you bother to start churches in such places." I have almost died in near plane crashes. More than once, I almost died while fasting. It may seem I am involved in a very high risk job.

But what about the risks that doctors take all the time? I remember one night; I was working in the accident centre of Korle Bu Teaching Hospital in Accra, Ghana. I was suturing an accident victim when the needle slipped and accidentally pierced my gloves and finger. My patient's blood and my blood were well and truly mixed together that night. I tell you, I heard the voice of God clearly, "You can die of HIV in disobedience, as you continue to do your own thing."

Doctors are at risk all the time. I know doctors who have contracted the Hepatitis B virus from their work. I could go on to tell you many more risks that doctors take. But no one seems to mind if they die for the cause of medicine. There is a deep disrespect for God and the ministry. It is not seen as something worth dying for.

Dear friend, I would rather die on the mission field serving Jesus than die in the hospital looking after patients.

> **But I say, THAT THE THINGS WHICH THE GENTILES SACRIFICE, THEY SACRIFICE TO DEVILS...**
>
> **I Corinthians 10:20**

■ Seven Sacrifices of Unbelievers

1. The Sacrifice of Immigrants

Many people travel to distant lands and live as second-class citizens in foreign countries. This sacrifice is okay as long as the purpose is to get money. If this were to be done for the sake of missionary work, eyebrows would be raised.

It seems to be acceptable to many. But not for the ministry! I know people who walked across the Sahara Desert to get to Switzerland.

One man told us, "There were three of us who walked through the Sahara Desert. Two of us died and I survived." Is it not amazing that people, who can walk across the Sahara Desert, cannot come to church?

The Stowaway

Once, in Amsterdam, I was counselling a brother to come to church.

He told me, "I tried four times to come to Europe from Ghana. Four times I stowed away on a ship. Once the captain threw us overboard into shark-infested waters and we swam to the shore."

He said, "When I got to the shore, I found out that I was in Liberia. I went back to Ghana and stowed away again. I did this four times until I finally succeeded in coming to Holland."

He smiled proudly and declared, "I am a Dutch citizen today."

Then I asked, "Why don't you come to church regularly?"

He laughed and mumbled some lame excuse about his work. Surprisingly, this man would not make any effort to be in church but he was prepared to die to be in Holland. This young man risked his life four times to become a Dutch citizen but he wouldn't bother to become a citizen of Heaven.

But I say, THAT THE THINGS WHICH THE GENTILES SACRIFICE, THEY SACRIFICE TO DEVILS…

1 Corinthians 10:20

I know of people who have sacrificed their lives in a bid to live in Europe. I know of people who hid inside petrol tankers for a drive across the Sahara desert. Many of them died from the intolerable heat within the petrol tanker. Oh what sacrifices people make for the things they want. Yet people are prepared to do nothing for Jesus.

2. The Sacrifice of Pilots

Pilots and other airline crew make great sacrifices for money. In this era of terrorism it is amazing that these people continue to do the work they do. They come up with all kinds of statistics to show that flying is safe.

No one can discount the fear that exists today in airline travel. Nevertheless, there are wives who happily see their pilot-husbands off to the plane and don't think twice about it. These same wives would not allow their husbands to work in the ministry.

What you must see is that the sacrifice to God has been replaced by a "pig in the temple". When you are going on a journey for the Kingdom, you will be asked, "Do you have to go, is it necessary?" Yet, this same sacrifice is done regularly and effortlessly by thousands in the airline industry.

> **But I say, THAT THE THINGS WHICH THE GENTILES SACRIFICE, THEY SACRIFICE TO DEVILS…**
>
> **1 Corinthians 10:20**

3. The Sacrifice of Bankers and Accountants

These people spend many hours at work. Some of them come home after nine p.m. every night. They hardly see their families. *But this is okay if it is for the bank.*

One day, one of my pastors had his mother-in-law visiting. She began to complain about the time that he came home. He reacted, "Mummy, please don't complain about my work. It is because I am in the ministry that you even speak this way."

He reminded his mother-in-law, "What about your son who works at the bank? You know he comes home much later than I do. Yet, you have no complaints about that because you think his work is important enough for him to stay that long."

Unfortunately, the ministry is seen as a second-rate job not worth sacrificing for. "Sacrifice to the devil but don't sacrifice to God!" This is the unspoken message of our friends and relatives.

> **But I say, THAT THE THINGS WHICH THE GENTILES SACRIFICE, THEY SACRIFICE TO DEVILS…**
>
> **I Corinthians 10:20**

4. The Sacrifice of Businessmen

Businessmen risk their lives all the time for the sake of money. They travel up and down constantly trying to make deals. Many businessmen come under such pressure and strain that they develop high blood pressure, ulcers and other stress-related diseases. That is the price they pay for acquiring great wealth.

Many businessmen lose their families in the quest for more money. They are hardly at home with their children. They take on the risk of travel and endorse it all in the name of money.

Do you think top executives do not risk their lives? They do, and sometimes pay a high price for it. People are sacrificing all the time. They will sacrifice their God, their church and their families. They will do anything for more money.

They will change their lives, they will live anywhere, and they will travel to obscure places and make all kinds of sacrifices in order to make some more money or achieve their life's goals.

When ministers of the Gospel give themselves to the ministry it is always seen as unnecessary. What is more fleeting than the making of money and the building of houses on this earth?

We in the ministry have given ourselves to the highest and most worthy calling.

Take a country like Angola. They have had a civil war for more than twenty years. Yet, you will find the British, Americans, and Europeans living there and drilling oil!

In the midst of the war in the Democratic Republic of Congo, a Congolese diamond mine was listed on the London Stock Exchange. This means that active business was being conducted in the midst of war. It's amazing what people will do even in the midst of war!

All kinds of British, Dutch and American people are prepared to go to these war-torn African countries and risk their lives if it is for money. They are prepared to go where there is fighting and danger. They are prepared to die for oil, for gold and for diamonds.

Nigeria, well known for its dangerous cities and high crime rate is home to many white people who will sacrifice anything for money. In search of more money, British Airways flies to Nigeria several times a week.

Yet, were I to ask someone to start a church in certain African countries, the person's family would develop hysteria. There would be all kinds of reasons making me out to be an unreasonable and heartless leader.

This is the point: People are sacrificing, but they are sacrificing to the devil! The sacrifices are being made, but they are being made to the devil. The legitimate sacrifice to God has been replaced by the sacrifice of a pig in the temple.

5. The Sacrifice for the Dead

Many can give much more for the work of God but they won't. This money would rather be spent on a house, a car or even a funeral.

People attend funerals every weekend in different towns and villages but they can't come to church.

I know of someone who spent thousands of pounds to buy a shroud. It is not common to see people giving a thousand pounds offering, but people will give it for the dead.

6. The Sacrifice of Journalists

Reporters and journalists make sacrifices all the time and risk their lives in war zones. Many journalists were killed when America invaded Iraq.

I watched a beautiful one-eyed lady on TV. One eye was covered with a black patch. She was a journalist who had lost her eye while covering a conflict for one of the news networks. As I stared at this one-eyed woman, I marvelled at what people are prepared to do for their jobs. These journalists are honoured for their bravery in covering wars.

Men will honour scientists, doctors, beauty queens, boxers and athletes but they will not honour preachers. God has however promised that when we set our love on Him, He will honour us. I am looking for the honour of God.

> **Because he hath set his love upon me, therefore will I deliver him: I will set him on high, because he hath known my name. He shall call upon me, and I will answer him: I will be with him in trouble; I will deliver him, AND HONOR HIM.**
>
> **Psalm 91:14-15**

Seek the honour of God and not the honour of men!

7. The sacrifice of medical doctors

There are many doctors who give up their lives in the line of duty. I know of institutions that are named after doctors because they died while experimenting on cures for dangerous viruses.

Do not tell me that doctors do not sacrifice. In 1928 Noguchi, a Japanese bacteriologist, travelled to Africa to confirm his theories about yellow fever. The purpose of this field work was to test the hypothesis that yellow fever was caused by spirochaete bacteria instead of a virus. While working in Accra, Gold Coast, he died of this same yellow fever on May 21st 1928. His last words were, "I don't understand." Today, the Noguchi Institute in Accra is named after this Japanese bacteriologist who gave his life for his research. Indeed, everyone is sacrificing something for what he believes!

Chapter

10

Sacrifice is the Key to Fruitfulness

CHAPTER SUMMARY

Sacrifice is the missing ingredient. It is the master key that will take the average Christian from barrenness to fruitfulness. Sacrifice is the key that will transform a reverend minister from an official with a title to a truly fruitful minister.

> **And Jesus answered them, saying, The hour is come, that the Son of man should be glorified.**
>
> **Verily, verily, I say unto you, Except a corn of wheat FALL into the ground and DIE, it abideth alone: but if it die, it bringeth forth much FRUIT.**
>
> **John 12:23-24**

A Readiness to Die

The missing ingredient in some good churches is this - a readiness to die. Many of our churches are going to be small until we have people ready to sacrifice. There comes a time when what is needed is sacrifice. Many Christians can do more but they don't. It's because they don't want to sacrifice or give up anything.

Not a Lack of Knowledge

Many people do not lack information or knowledge. They know a lot! If you have read my books, you will know a lot of what I know. However, knowledge is not enough! You may not have the fruits that I have even if you have the knowledge that I have. For you to have what I have, you must pay the price. There is a price for everyone to pay. The price of glory is the same for everyone!

This Scripture says that unless a corn of wheat disappears into the ground and dies, it will be alone. The "corn of wheat" symbolizes the man of God. To be "alone" means "to be fruitless". It means to be without members or followers. The dying process in the man of God will eventually bring out much fruit.

Jesus would not have borne the fruit He did if He had not died on the cross. He would have been alone in Heaven with His Father. He could not have saved us if He had not died and gone to Hell for us. To win followers for Himself and His Father, He had to fall into the ground and die. The corn of wheat has to fall into the ground and die. When the seed falls into the ground, it disintegrates and decomposes.

This is what we call "dying". The seed actually goes through a process before it comes out as fruit.

There are many sincere leaders who know many things. They have heard much and think they are high up in God. Knowledge unfortunately breeds pride.

> **... knowledge puffeth up, but charity edifieth.**
>
> **1 Corinthians 8:1b**

The Kingdom is more than a school of history and doctrines. It is more than acquiring numerous certificates of Bible knowledge. Knowledge without this process will yield nothing. Have you noticed that some of the most learned and scholarly Bible expositors are very ineffective at real ministry? In fact, sometimes, the more scholarly they become the more faithless and godless they are.

A single seed will become a big tree with many fruits if it falls into the ground and dies. There are three processes for the corn of wheat to go through when it falls into the ground.

1. The Falling of the seed
2. The Dying of the seed
3. The Bearing Fruit of the seed

1. The Falling of the Seed

The falling into the ground speaks of a period in a man of God's life in which he is unknown and hidden from the view of the general public. It also speaks of a period of rejection and negative responses to himself. Concerning John the Baptist, the Bible declares that he was hidden in the wilderness until the time of his showing unto Israel. Every pastor must realize that God has a time when He hides you. Do not be in a hurry to be exposed. Premature exposure leads to destruction.

Jesus Christ was hidden for thirty years before He was exposed to public ministry. His appearance in the ministry surprised those who didn't know that a seed had been in the ground for thirty years.

Moses experienced this falling into the ground. He was utterly rejected by his brethren when he first tried to minister to them. He ended up in the wilderness for forty years. After years of rejection and isolation, he was ready to minister.

Joseph had this same experience of falling into the ground. His visions and dreams were utterly rejected. Then he himself was utterly rejected and dispensed with. He found himself first working as a slave and then as a prisoner in Egypt. After several years of separation from his brethren he was finally ready for a great ministry.

These are just a few examples of this pattern of falling into the ground. I tell you, no true minister is truly accepted until he has been first rejected.

I Don't Sow Amongst Thorns

I have experienced this falling into the ground myself. When I started out in ministry, I was utterly and totally rejected by the ministers of the day. One minister that we had a good relationship with, refused to minister to our group any more. When I asked why he wouldn't preach to our group any more, he said, "I don't sow amongst thorns."

He and other pastors claimed I was not called by God and had no business starting a church. They felt I was a medical student who should concentrate on his schooling. They told my assistant not to associate with me because it was dangerous to work with someone who was not called by God.

Which Bible School Did You Attend?

I told another senior minister with whom I had a good relationship, that I had started a church. I simply received a rebuke! Then I was queried as to which Bible school I had attended. Unfortunately, I had not been to Bible school. In discouragement, I went away with my "tail between my legs".

This pastor then decided to hold a campaign right where our church was meeting. He held a big programme and showed a very powerful video of his national and international programmes. It was one of the best presentations of that ministry I had ever seen.

Our ministry looked like a group of jokers, dwarfs and midgets together in one place. A powerful invitation to join this great ministry was made that night. After they had left, I asked myself, "Who would want to be with us when there are such powerful and established ministries in the city?"

Are You Mocking Me?

I also remember another incident where I met one of these great pastors of our city. It was at a wedding being held on the university campus. This pastor and his associate had spoken out against my ministry from their pulpit. They had spoken against people like myself whom they felt were not "called". In their eyes, I could never be a pastor!

I went up to him to say hello and he said, "Oh, hello Dag," Then he paused, looked at me and said, "Pastor!"

As I stood before him, I felt in my heart that he was mockingly referring to me as a pastor. I almost asked him, "Sir why are you mocking me? Why do you call me 'pastor' when you don't believe that I am a pastor?"

I don't know how I managed to keep those words from coming out of my mouth. The only thing I felt in that era of my life was rejection.

I went through a period of utter rejection and continued the ministry work in virtual separation from most of the ministers I had known prior to this period.

However, as a result of this separation, God taught me many things.

Don't be worried because you are not accepted or wanted. Don't bother if no one invites you. Your day of showing forth will come.

And the child grew, and waxed strong in spirit, and was in the deserts till the day of his shewing unto Israel.

Luke 1:80

2. The Dying of the Seed

When the seed falls to the ground, it disintegrates and decomposes. It utterly changes in its character and appearance. Allow the dying process to occur. Except the seed dies, it abides alone. Unless these qualities that God is going to bring forth in you are allowed to develop, you will never fulfil your ministry. Two things develop when you fall into the ground and die.

A Personal Relationship with God

When men reject you, your relationship with people is minimized. During this period of alienation, you have your best chance to develop a relationship with God. This is the principle that works on people in prison. Their relationship with the outside world is cut off. Many prisoners reflect on the Lord and develop a relationship with God. This is a time when important spiritual traits will be birthed in you. Developing a personal relationship with God is one of the most important things that you will learn when people reject you. Every true minister derives his strength from the Lord directly.

Many will come in that day and say, "I cast out demons in your name and I did great works in your name." But the Lord will say, "I never knew you."

"I never knew you," means that I never had a relationship with you. Rejection is sometimes the only way to this all-important relationship.

Developing Humility

Rejection is a humbling experience. The rejection by man is intended to make you develop humility and humility is the highest mantle a minister can wear.

The more humble a minister is, the higher his standing before the Lord.

One common deception is that the larger your church is, the higher your standing before the Lord. That is not the case. Jesus made it clear that the greatest pastor will be the most humble and childlike amongst us.

> **At the same time came the disciples unto Jesus, saying, Who is the greatest in the kingdom of heaven? And Jesus called a little child unto him, and set him in the midst of them, And said, Verily I say unto you, Except ye be converted, and become as little children, ye shall not enter into the kingdom of heaven. Whosoever therefore shall humble himself as this little child, the same is greatest in the kingdom of heaven.**
>
> **Matthew 18:1-4**

John the Baptist Was Humble

John the Baptist's humility was evident. He made it clear that he was not worthy to unlace the shoes of Jesus. He deferred to the Lord and stated that Jesus must increase and he must decrease. How many pastors today want others to increase while they decrease?

> **He must increase, but I must decrease.**
>
> **John 3:30**

Jesus Humbled Himself

The humility of Jesus was evident. He humbled Himself and became obedient even to the death of the cross.

> **And being found in fashion as a man, he humbled himself, and became obedient unto death, even the death of the cross.**
>
> **Philippians 2:8**

Moses Was Humbled

Moses lost all confidence in himself. The Bible calls him the meekest man on earth. Wouldn't you be meek after forty years in the wilderness as one of the ten most wanted men in Egypt?

When you read about the call of Moses, you see how Moses had zero confidence in himself. He was a great man but his opinion of himself was genuinely very low because he had suffered rejection. Notice the low esteem that Moses had of himself.

*The Ten Complaints of Moses

1. And Moses said unto God ...**Who am I?** Exodus 3:11
2. And Moses said unto God ...**what shall I say unto them?** Exodus 3:13
3. And Moses answered ... **they will not believe me** ... Exodus 4:1
4. And Moses said ... **I am not eloquent ... I am slow of speech, and of a slow tongue.** Exodus 4:10
5. And he said, **O my Lord, send, I pray thee, by the hand of him whom thou wilt send.** Exodus 4:13
6. And Moses ... said, **Lord ... why is it that thou hast sent me?** Exodus 5:22
7. And Moses spake ... **the children of Israel have not hearkened unto me** ... Exodus 6:12
8. And Moses said ... **I am of uncircumcised lips** ... Exodus 6:30
9. And Moses cried unto the LORD ... **they be almost ready to stone me.** Exodus 17:4
10. And Moses said unto the LORD, **Wherefore hast thou afflicted thy servant?** ... Numbers 11:11

Joseph Was Humbled

Joseph, after being a prisoner for some years did not think of vengeance when he saw his brothers. He could see through it all, that God had meant it for good.

> **Now therefore be not grieved, nor angry with yourselves, that ye sold me hither: for God did send me before you to preserve life. So now it was not you that sent me hither, but God...**
>
> **Genesis 45:5,8**

Joseph had so matured in the things of God that he felt his brothers had done nothing wrong. In fact, he felt his brothers were used of God.

After going through all that I have been through, I have come to love and appreciate the people who once rejected me. I feel that God used them to train me in the ministry. I bear none of them a grudge and I value their ministries greatly. Even the bitterest of experiences have worked out for my good.

■ 3. The Bearing Fruit of the Seed

Bearing fruit is a very spiritual thing. Most men of God think that if you have a large church, you have borne much fruit and are pleasing to the Lord.

However, you will notice that Jesus was pleasing to His Father even before He preached His first sermon. He pleased God long before He was publicly known. You can please God even when you are not famous.

> **And lo a voice from heaven, saying, This is my beloved Son, in whom I am well pleased.**
>
> **Matthew 3:17**

---

* Excerpt from Dake's Annotated Reference Bible, page 66.

You don't have to have a church for the Heavenly Father to say: "This is my beloved son in whom I am well pleased." You don't even have to be a pastor. You don't have to write a book. You don't have to preach a sermon to hear the words, "This is my beloved son in whom I am well pleased."

You don't need to be famous to hear the words, "This is my beloved son in whom I am well pleased." Jesus was not famous when this happened. This Scripture shows us that pleasing God is not based on our works per se. Any fruits we bear are actually gifts that are given by the Lord.

Have you wondered at the immense fruit that Christ Jesus bore? Two thousand years have gone by and He has more fruit than He has ever had before. What did He do that brought about so much fruit? He did six things:

1. Preaching. 2. Teaching 3. Healing 4. Humility 5. Obedience 6. Sacrifice on the cross.

Significant among these things was His sacrifice on the cross that opened the door for our salvation. By far, the greatest thing that Christ did for us was to die on the cross for our sins. Jesus bore much fruit after His sacrifice.

Chapter

11

Sacrifice Brings You to the Anointing

CHAPTER SUMMARY

How close do you want to be to the innermost place of power and anointing? How desperately do you want this anointing? I do not know of any great man of God who climbed to heights in ministry without paying a high price of sacrifice.

> **But now in Christ Jesus ye who sometimes were far off ARE MADE NIGH BY THE BLOOD (sacrifice) of Christ.**
>
> **Ephesians 2:13**

■ Understanding the Road to the Anointing

It took me many years to understand the wonderful symbolism of the tabernacle.

Years ago, I heard a man of God preaching about steps to the anointing. I listened to this message over and over again but I could not understand what he was talking about.

He was teaching about the tabernacle of Moses, the laver, the altar of sacrifice, the door to the Holy Place, the tent, the pegs, the poles, the white linen, the badgers' skin, the table of incense, the table of shewbread, the candlesticks and the Holy of Holies.

Honestly, I listened with all my heart trying hard to see how it was all connected to the anointing.

With time however, I found out that the Holy of Holies was considered to be the seat of God's power, God's anointing and God's presence. Taking steps to the Holy of Holies was therefore the same as taking steps to God's presence and God's power.

A study of the tabernacle of Moses reveals that there was always a sacrifice to be made at the door of the tabernacle before the priest could progress to the Holy of Holies. A sacrifice had to be made right at the entrance of the tabernacle.

This position of the altar of sacrifice (at the door) signified that there was the need to first offer a sacrifice if you wanted to go deeper into the things of God.

The Holy of Holies, the place of anointing and power, was the innermost room in the tabernacle. Without walking through the place of sacrifice, you could not come to this place of power and anointing.

> **... thou shalt kill the bullock before the lord, by the door of the tabernacle of the congregation.**
>
> **Exodus 29:11**

Many people know the Scriptures and the doctrines, but many are not prepared to pay the price of ministry. Therefore, they remain powerless and empty-handed in the face of a lost and dying world.

This is why we need to bring the concept of sacrifice back to the house of the Lord. As we make sacrifices, we get nearer and nearer to the inner place of power and anointing. We are brought near to the anointing by the blood. It is the blood and the sacrifice that enables us to come near to the anointing!

Without the sacrifice, without the pain and without the shedding of blood we cannot approach the Holy Place where the presence and power of God is.

■ Old Testament Sacrifices

In the Bible times, you could not even think of worshipping God without making a sacrifice. You simply had not worshipped God until a sacrifice was made.

Poor people sacrificed little birds like pigeons and turtledoves. They could not afford to bring sheep, goats and cows. You were required to sacrifice whatever you had. *But there had to be some sacrifice!* Can we say we worship God, if we present no sacrifice?

You may say, "Christ has sacrificed for us. No further sacrifices are needed." No one is asking you to die on the cross again! Nevertheless, Jesus told us to *take up our crosses and follow Him*, didn't He? This means that even though Christ has made the ultimate sacrifice, we are still to follow His example of self-sacrifice.

There are lessons to be learnt from the Old Testament system of sacrifices. The Old Testament is a treasure house of teaching for New Testament Christians.

■ Why Old Testament Sacrifices Are Relevant

Anyone who doubts that the Old Testament is very relevant today should just read on. The following are a number of reasons why Old Testament Scriptures can be used to teach us on important subjects like "sacrifice".

1. Christ Himself expounded the things in the Old Testament Scriptures concerning Himself in the Law, the Psalms, and the Prophets.

Ought not Christ to have suffered these things, and to enter into his glory?

And beginning at Moses and all the prophets, he expounded unto them in all the scriptures the things concerning himself.

And he said unto them, These are the words which I spake unto you, while I was yet with you, that all things must be fulfilled, which were written in the law of Moses, and in the prophets, and in the psalms, concerning me.

Then opened he their understanding, that they might understand the scriptures,

Luke 24:26-27, 44-45

2. The things that were written aforetime in the Old Testament Scriptures were written for our learning, that we through patience and comfort of the Scriptures might have hope.

For whatsoever things were written aforetime were written for our learning, that we through patience and comfort of the scriptures might have hope.

Romans 15:4

3. Jesus Himself came to fulfil the Law and the Prophets.

Think not that I am come to destroy the law, or the prophets: I am not come to destroy, but to fulfil. For verily I say unto you, till heaven and earth pass, one jot or one tittle shall in no wise pass from the law, till all be fulfilled.

Matthew 5:17-18

4. Jesus said that the Law and the Prophets prophesied.

For all the prophets and the law prophesied until John.

Matthew 11:13

5. The Old Testament prophets spoke of the sufferings of Christ and the glory that should follow. It was revealed to them that their utterances did not just concern their own generation but another.

Of which salvation the prophets have inquired and searched diligently, who prophesied of the grace that should come unto you: Searching what, or what manner of time the Spirit of Christ which was in them did signify, when it testified beforehand the sufferings of Christ, and the glory that should follow.

Unto whom it was revealed, that not unto themselves, but unto us they did minister the things, which are now reported unto you by them that have preached the gospel unto you with the Holy Ghost sent down from heaven; which things the angels desire to look into.

1 Peter 1:10-12

6. The things, which happened in Old Testament history in Israel, were for types and examples and these things are written for our admonition upon whom the ends of the ages are come.

Now these things were our examples, to the intent we should not lust after evil things, as they also lusted. Now all these things happened unto them for ensamples: and they are written for our admonition, upon whom the ends of the world are come.

1 Corinthians 10:6,11

7. The writer of the book of Hebrews said, "In the volume of the book it is written of Me", that is, of Christ.

Then said I, Lo, I come (in the volume of the book it is written of me,) to do thy will, O God.

Hebrews 10:7

> **Sacrifice and offering thou didst not desire; mine ears hast thou opened: burnt offering and sin offering hast thou not required. Then said I, Lo, I come: in the volume of the book it is written of me, I delight to do thy will, O my God: yea, thy law is within my heart.**
>
> **Psalm 40:6-8**

8. The Scripture speaks of, "first the natural and afterwards that which is spiritual", and this is a principle which may well be applied in this study.

> **Howbeit that was not first which is spiritual, but that which is natural; and afterward that which is spiritual. The first man is of the earth, earthy: the second man is the Lord from heaven.**
>
> **1 Corinthians 15:46-47**

All these points I have enumerated show us that the Old Testament can and must be used as sound teaching material. We cannot afford to ignore the revelation that we receive from Old Testament sacrifices.

Chapter

12

Sacrifice Eliminates Pharaoh

CHAPTER SUMMARY

This chapter talks about the elimination of Satan and his demonic chains from your life and ministry.

Pharaoh is a biblical "type" of Satan. Satan keeps the people of God in bondage and refuses to let them go. Pharaoh struggled with the children of Israel until they finally got out of Egypt and were on their way to the Promised Land. Even then he did not give up. He was bent on recapturing the Israelites. Satan will do almost anything to keep you in bondage. He chased the people of God until the Lord eliminated the Egyptians Himself.

How will Pharaoh finally be eliminated from your life? What will break satanic strongholds in your life? All you have to do is to follow the example of the Israelites and you will be free forever.

Walking through the Red Sea

"Walking through the Red Sea" speaks of walking into certain death. It signifies walking away from safety into a realm where you can only trust God. In the New Testament, walking through the Red Sea stands for the dying process.

Sometimes, walking by faith seems destructive. Walking through the Red Sea is a powerful tool that God uses to eliminate enemies. Walking through the Red Sea is an action in which you rely on God's grace. When you walk through the Red Sea, you do not depend on money, friends, family, or natural forms of assistance.

Pharaoh Could Not Go through the Red Sea

Satan can chase you and harass you. But there are certain places he cannot go to. The devil is not all-knowing and all-powerful. To escape from Pharaoh and his agents you need to go where he cannot follow. When you sacrifice to the Lord, you go through the Red Sea.

When you walk through the Red Sea, you sacrifice your future and place yourself in the hands of God. I am sure you know that it is not a normal thing to walk upon the seabed with a wall of water to your right and a wall of water to your left. What if you get stuck in the middle? What if the water came tumbling down?

> **Speak unto the children of Israel, that they turn and encamp before Pi-hahiroth, between Migdol and the sea, over against Baal-zephon: before it shall ye encamp by the sea. For Pharaoh will say of the children of Israel, They are entangled in the land, the wilderness hath shut them in. And I will harden Pharaoh's heart, THAT HE SHALL FOLLOW AFTER THEM; and I will be honoured upon Pharaoh, and upon all his host; that the Egyptians may know that I am the LORD. And they did so.**
>
> **Exodus 14:2-4**

Pharaoh's (Satan's) aim is to keep you from Christ. Pharaoh failed in his attempt to keep the people from knowing their God. However, Pharaoh does not give up easily. He says, "Chase him, and track him down. Prevent him from going too far."

The devil aims at keeping you away from the ministry. Have you wondered why you have undergone such a struggle since you decided to serve the Lord? It is because Pharaoh is chasing hard on your heels.

The Baptism of Death

Paul teaches us that going through the sea was a baptism for the children of Israel. It was a symbolic baptism. They entered into the depths of the sea and came out again.

> **Moreover, brethren, I would not that ye should be ignorant, how that all our fathers were under the cloud, AND ALL PASSED THROUGH THE SEA; AND WERE ALL BAPTIZED UNTO MOSES IN THE CLOUD AND IN THE SEA;**
>
> **1 Corinthians 10:1-2**

You can compare this to what the Bible says elsewhere:

> **Know ye not, that so many of us as were baptized into Jesus Christ were baptized into his death? Therefore we are buried with him BY BAPTISM INTO DEATH: that like as Christ was raised up from the dead by the glory of the Father, even so we also should walk in newness of life.**
>
> **Romans 6:3-4**

By baptism, we are symbolically buried with Jesus. Baptism is therefore a symbol of sacrifice and death. When you walk through the Red Sea you eliminate Pharaoh and his agents. When you die to yourself, your desires, your needs and your wants, you eliminate Pharaoh and all other enemies.

This is how the children of Israel got rid of their enemies: by sacrificing their lives in the Red Sea. God began to fight for the Israelites only when they entered into the Red Sea.

When we're not afraid to sacrifice ourselves and walk into the Red Sea; when we allow ourselves to die in Christ, our enemies perish behind us!

If the Israelites had stayed out because of fear, Pharaoh would have recaptured them. They would have been killed in the desert. Many people die of the things they fear. The things that many of us are afraid of eventually happen. Death in the Red Sea is better than being killed in the desert.

Discussion by the Red Sea

I have observed people who have shied away from full-time ministry. Mostly, people stay away from the ministry because of the fear of poverty and ridicule. They fear that they will perish in the Red Sea. I have watched these same people stand at the shore of the Red Sea and discuss how they intend to eventually, one day, go through this sea.

They say things like, "Oh, that is my ultimate goal. As for full-time ministry, I know that I will by all means do it."

They carry on, "By all means, I will get to that point. I know in my heart that is what I want to do one day."

They explain, "We all get to that point at different times."

Then I have watched Pharaoh descend upon these people. Suddenly, their lives become one long battle as they try to ward off Pharaoh and the world's system. Soon these people who were just about to go through the Red Sea don't even have time to go to church. They are fully entangled with Satan and the world's system. Are you stuck on the shores of the Red Sea?

I Can't Believe He Is Going Through

When you give your precious life to God, you walk through the Red Sea. When you give your future to God, you walk through the Red Sea.

The enemy stands at the shores of the sea and says, "I can't believe he's going in!! I can't believe he's giving up his life. I tried to frighten him about the dangers of the Red Sea ministry." The devil knows that he can't follow you through your sacrifice.

Satan remembers how he perished when he tried to follow Moses. He laments: "I can't believe it! I've had this experience before! I remember what happened to me at the Red Sea and I do not want to go into the sea again." The devil will lose his control over you when you give up everything for God.

It is true. He will lose his control. The devil does not lose his control because of the message you heard. He does not go away after we anoint you with oil, and pray for you. Until you go through the Red Sea, the world still has control over you. As long as you stand there and refuse to enter, Pharaoh has access to you! As long as you refuse to die and give up what you're supposed to give up, the world's system will dominate you.

Pharaoh, Dirty Daniel and Freaky Freda

*A beautiful young lady called Freaky Freda gave her life to Jesus Christ and was gloriously born again. She had had several boyfriends in the past. Slappy Jay, Ricky Zee, Kweku Killer, Big Bobo were all part of the squadron. Zee!**

Her current and steady lover whom she was planning to marry was none other than the swanky toe-tapping, cool-rapping Dirty Daniel, a favourite with the ladies.

However, she had attended a breakfast meeting and given her life to Christ. To say the least, Pharaoh was very angry at the loss of one of his slaves.

Pharaoh thought this young lady would return to Egypt. But her commitment to the things of God grew. At an emergency session, Pharaoh decided to get her back at all costs or to kill her. Pharaoh hatched up a plan to kill Freaky Freda with HIV. Pharaoh knew that Freaky Freda could not resist Dirty Daniel. One night, Satan ensured that Dirty Daniel was fully loaded with HIV from his other girlfriend, Slippery Susie.

Pharaoh smiled confidently as he charged Dirty Daniel to infect and destroy Freaky Freda for her unfaithfulness to him.

Dirty Daniel called Freaky Freda, "Hi baby, I miss you baby."

He continued, "Where have you been? I've been calling your number all weekend.

"Oh, I was at a camp meeting," she answered.

---

*The expression zee is the author's colloquial exclamation.

"Camp meeting," he retorted. "What on earth is that?"

"It is a meeting for Christian leaders in my new church," she informed him.

"Oh, I see. Anyway, I miss you. Do you miss me? Can I come to your place tonight?"

"Yes, I've wanted to see you myself. There is something I need to tell you," she answered. "I'll be home early."

Pharaoh and his legions began rejoicing in advance. "The plan is working; we will end this rebellion."

But that night, Dirty Daniel had the shock of his life.

Freaky Freda said, "No! I am sorry I cannot continue this relationship with you."

"Don't you love me?" he asked. "Don't you want to marry me?"

She told him tearfully, "It's not been easy for me, I've been crying all day. But I have decided to sacrifice this relationship so that I can serve the Lord."

In the moment that Freaky Freda sacrificed her relationship with Dirty Daniel, she walked through the Red Sea and went out of the reach of Pharaoh.

Pharaoh and legions stood by the shore in shock. They said, "We can't believe she's going in!! We can't believe she's doing it! We are losing control over Freaky Freda."

The devil knows that he can't follow you through your sacrifice. As you sacrifice your profession for the Lord, Satan loses his influence over your life.

Chapter

13

Sacrifice Gives You a Place in the Ministry

CHAPTER SUMMARY

You need to pay the price to occupy your room of ministry. Your gift and sacrifice is what will make room for you.

> **... and Elisha the son of Shaphat of Abel-Meholah shalt thou anoint to be prophet IN THY ROOM.**
>
> **1 Kings 19:16**

God has called many of us. However, you have to pay the price in order to take your place in the ministry. Your place in the ministry is also called your "room" of ministry. Everybody has a room or position that he occupies in ministry.

This room of ministry defines your standing before God. It also identifies and classifies you among God's numerous servants.

> **A man's gift MAKETH ROOM FOR HIM, and bringeth him before great men.**
>
> **Proverbs 18:16**

One day, when you get to Heaven, you will either have a room waiting or not. This will depend on your obedience to the Lord. The gift you give creates a space, and makes room for you.

I occupy a particular spiritual position in my country. At the spiritual gates of the country and among the spiritual elders, I occupy a particular chair. It may not be a very great position but it is a position anyway. That is the room God has given me.

Perhaps, God has given you a place in the ministry. God has prepared a place for you among the ministers.

Do you want that place?

Do you like that place?

Will you take your place or will someone else have to take it?

You Can Be Replaced

Even while in your room of ministry, you can be replaced by someone else. Elisha was given Elijah's room of ministry. He complained about the ministry. He felt he had sacrificed so much for the Lord. He erroneously thought that he was the only one doing something for the Lord. God told him, "There are seven thousand pastors and churches you don't know about."

> *Many years ago, I had a strange vision. In the vision, I saw a man sitting on a chair. I did not know who the man was. Suddenly, a hand appeared and this hand picked the man by his collar and lifted him out of his chair. The hand then lifted me by my collar and placed me in that chair. The Lord revealed to me that I was replacing someone. He said to me that I was to occupy a chair that someone else had occupied before.*

There are many reasons why God may replace you. You can be replaced if you do not sacrifice to take your room. There is a place among the Christian heroes for you.

I've known people who failed to stand in the room that God gave them. It wasn't long before somebody else took up that room. If you fail to take the step when you should, others will be brought in to replace you.

Are You Worthy of the Room?

Jesus was placed in a position of honour. He is the only one who sits at the right hand of God the Father. He was the one who was allowed to open and to read the book. He was found worthy to do these things because He is the "lamb that was slain". "Thou art worthy to take the book and to open the seals because thou art the lamb that was slain."

> **And I wept much, because NO MAN WAS FOUND WORTHY to open and to read the book, neither to look thereon. ...And they sung a new song, saying, THOU ART WORTHY TO TAKE THE BOOK, and to open the seals thereof: for thou wast slain, and hast redeemed us to God by thy blood out of every kindred, and tongue, and people, and nation;**
>
> **Revelation 5:4, 9**

The Famous Evangelist

When you listen to an evangelist preaching, you may think that you could preach better than he does. You could probably preach circles around him. However, that does not qualify you to stand in his room of ministry. You may actually know more than he does and have a better character than he does. But God gives him the room of ministry.

There are many questions and speculations about successful ministers. Many wonder why such people are so successful. Why does anyone listen to this person? Why does anyone come for his crusades? This person is occupying a room of ministry given to him by the Lord.

> *One day, as I observed a famous evangelist preach at a crusade, I thought to myself, "I could probably preach this message better." I marvelled that so many thousands had gathered to hear such a message. When it was time to pray for miracles, there were hardly any healings. Yet the crowds kept coming, night after night.*

As I mused over this, I knew that if this were my crusade, no one would attend to hear my "good preaching". The Lord spoke to me and said, "I have given this man of God a room.

He occupies a position that he did not create for himself. He has paid a price to be in that room. It is not by his preaching, organization or even healings, but by the room that I have placed him in."

What Have You Been Through?

I once formed an association of pastors.

One senior minister asked me, "What do you think you're doing? Do you know what it means to form an association of churches and pastors?" Then he asked me a question: "What have you been through, what have you suffered, what have you survived?"

What he was asking was, "Have you paid the price to be the leader of an association of churches and pastors?"

He continued, "I have contended with the prince of this nation. What have you been through, what have you suffered, what have you survived?"

Later on, I discussed with this pastor about how the government was persecuting me. He already knew about how the government of the day had broken our walls and attacked us in the night.

But I told him, "That is not all. After breaking our walls, they sent the Internal Revenue Service to hound us. All my pastors came under investigation. Then they turned their attention on me personally."

I had to fill various forms and I was interrogated at their offices. They questioned me extensively and wanted to know about my car, home, money etc. I sent my Chief Accountant but they refused to see him. They insisted that I came myself; they wanted to see me. Someone who had won an award for being the best tax expert for that year interrogated me.

As I narrated my woes to this senior minister, he laughed and shook my hand. Surprised, I asked him why he was giving me a "pat on the back".

He answered, "Congratulations. I have filled that form five times. I have been through that process five different times."

He went on to commend me, saying that I was maturing and paying the price to be in the high place of ministry.

So you see, before you can occupy certain positions, you have to pay a price. When you pay the price, you enter the room that God has prepared for you.

Elisha Paid the Price for Elijah's Room

Elisha paid the price to take Elijah's room. When Elijah came to Elisha, he just threw his mantle on him. Elisha was surprised. He knew Elijah was calling him. Elijah himself was so sad about it. He knew that Elisha was going to make a great sacrifice.

"What have I done to you? What have I done?" Elijah asked.

Elisha told his business partners that he was quitting. He took his oxen and ended his business in one stroke. He divided up his business and walked away from it. He told himself, "It is over, I can't go back." He was going to follow Elijah. Elisha paid the price to stand in Elijah's room.

Joshua paid the price to take over from Moses. Peter, James and John paid the price to be apostles.

How many are going to live and sacrifice for Jesus? How many are going to stand in their rooms and pay the price?

Get in there. God has a room for you. God had a room for me and I believe that He has one for you. I believe that there are more rooms to occupy and I intend to be there. You must determine to be in the room that God has for you.

Chapter

14

Sacrifice Brings the Glory into Your Ministry

CHAPTER SUMMARY

Do you want to see the glory of God in your life? Then do not shy away from the sacrifice that God has placed before you. A minister who has the glory of God on his life has paid the price.

■ Moses Brings the Glory through Sacrifice

> **And the breasts and the right shoulder Aaron waved for a wave offering before the LORD; as Moses commanded.**
>
> **And Aaron lifted up his hand toward the people, and blessed them, and came down from offering of the sin offering, and the burnt offering, and peace offerings.**
>
> **And Moses and Aaron went into the tabernacle of the congregation, and came out, and blessed the people: and THE GLORY OF THE LORD APPEARED unto all the people.**
>
> **And there came a fire out from before the LORD, and consumed upon the altar the burnt offering and the fat: which when all the people saw, they shouted, and fell on their faces.**
>
> **Leviticus 9:21-24**

As you can see in this account, when the Israelites offered sacrifice, the glory of God came down. Do you want to see the glory of God in your life? Then do not shy away from the sacrifice that God has placed before you. A minister who has the glory of God on his life has paid the price.

Solomon Brings the Glory through Sacrifice

> **...then the house was filled with a cloud, even the house of the LORD; So that the priests could not stand to minister by reason of the cloud: for the glory of the LORD had filled the house of God.**
>
> **2 Chronicles 5:13-14**

In this account, Solomon sacrificed thousands of bullocks. Solomon made many sacrifices to the Lord. Suddenly, the glory filled the temple and no one could stand to minister. God was apparently moved by the sacrifice. God is still moved by your sacrifice.

The Price of Glory Is the Same

I have noticed that there is no successful minister who does not have a story of suffering and difficulties.

Recently, a visiting minister, whose ministry I knew little about, came to speak in our church. As he shared his life testimony, I marvelled at how this principle is played out in everyone's life. He had been through many things.

He had gone hungry on many occasions; he had encouraged his wife on several occasions. He had been without money and food many times. This man was a very successful minister in his country but the story of sacrifice was the same. The story is the same everywhere. There is a sacrifice that brings the glory of God!

David Brings the Glory through Sacrifice

And it was told king David, saying, The LORD hath blessed the house of Obed-edom, and all that pertaineth unto him, because of the ark of God. So David went and brought up the ark of God from the house of Obed-edom into the city of David with gladness. And it was so, that when they that bare the ark of the LORD had gone six paces, he sacrificed oxen and fatlings.

2 Samuel 6:12-13

This story shows us how King David made innumerable sacrifices as he brought in the ark of God. The ark of God represents the anointing. The ark represents the glory of God. After every six steps, they would sacrifice oxen and fatling. Can you imagine how many sacrifices they must have made from Obed-edom's house to the City of David?

This journey of David symbolizes how the sacrifice brings in the glory.

It is time to believe in His glory. Expect glory as you serve the Lord. Expect glory on earth and in Heaven.

Give yourself to Him. The glory of God is worth your sacrifice!

Chapter

15

The Cross – The Symbol of Death

CHAPTER SUMMARY

The cross of Jesus Christ is the symbol of Christianity and it stands for many truths. Every time you see the cross, you must be reminded of what it symbolizes. The symbol of Christianity is not an umbrella, an elephant, a fruit or a bird. The symbol of Christianity is the cross of Jesus Christ. This symbol has important meanings that must be understood by all Christians.

The Old Rugged Cross

On a hill far away, stood an old rugged cross
The emblem of suffering and shame,
And I love that old cross where the dearest and best,
for a world of lost sinners was slain

Chorus:

So I'll cherish the old rugged cross, Till my trophies
at last I'll lay down
I will cling to the old rugged cross, and exchange it some day for a crown.
Oh that old rugged cross, So despised by the world
Holds a wondrous attraction to me,
for the dear Lamb of God left His glory above
to bear it to dark Calvary

In that old rugged cross, stained with blood so divine
a wondrous beauty I see
For t'was on that old cross Jesus suffered and died,
To pardon and sanctify me

To the old rugged cross, I will ever be true
It's shame and reproach gladly bear,
Then He'll call me some day
To my home far away, Where His glory forever
I'll share.

George Bennard

The cross of Jesus Christ is the symbol of Christianity and it stands for many truths. Every time you see the cross, you must be reminded of what it symbolizes. The symbol of Christianity is not an umbrella, an elephant, a fruit or a bird. The symbol of Christianity is the cross of Jesus Christ. This symbol has important meanings that must be understood by all Christians.

The cross is the true symbol of Christianity. I keep a cross in my room because it is the symbol of Christ, the symbol of Christianity and the symbol of the Church!

I remember meeting one of the politicians in my country. He was one of the most senior ministers of the government and was attending a wedding in our church.

After the ceremony he came to my office to meet me. As he sat down, I noticed that he was wearing the emblem of his political party on his lapel. I was amazed at this politician's boldness. He was wearing his party symbol even at a wedding!

Even though his political party had become unpopular, he boldly sported their symbol. His party had led the country into difficult times but he was not ashamed of it.

If unbelievers are not ashamed of their empty and temporary jobs, we cannot be ashamed of the cross of Jesus Christ.

It is our symbol; it is the symbol of obedience and sacrifice! Below are a few of the meanings of this wonderful symbol.

1. The cross is the SYMBOL OF DEATH you must experience.

> **But we see Jesus, who was made a little lower than the angels for the SUFFERING OF DEATH, crowned with glory and honour; that he by the grace of God should taste death for every man.**
>
> **Hebrews 2:9**

> **And he said to *them* all, if any *man* will come after me, let him deny himself, and take up his cross daily, and follow me.**
>
> **Luke 9:23**

The cross of Jesus Christ is a symbol of many things but most of all it is a symbol of death. A person found carrying a cross was on his way to his death. When Jesus told us to carry our cross he was telling us to go to a place where we would die and lose our lives.

Christianity is all about dying so that we may live a new life through Jesus Christ. Preachers of success, good living and prosperity are forced to ignore these "dark and brutal" parts of the Scripture.

And yet, there are so many references to losing, suffering, sacrificing and dying in the Bible. The death we speak about when we speak of the cross is not the physical termination our lives. It is the disappearance of yourself, your dreams, your visions, your plans, your future, and the emergence of God's plans, dreams and vision for your existence on Earth.

Indeed it is a painful experience to lose everything and to give up everything for the gospel of Jesus Christ.

Paul spoke of his life declaring that he had suffered the loss of all things.

Why You Must Die

You must "die" for Jesus because the old life you were going to live is not worth living. There is a new life that God has in store for you. Everyone who is used by the Lord undergoes a dying process in which his old life disappears and a brand new one appears.

One day, my mother sat in church and commented that she could not recognize her own son who was preaching. "Is that my boy, my son?"

Most Christians live out their lives on earth never dying to themselves and therefore never becoming what God wanted them to be. You must die for Jesus so that you can experience a life of living by faith. "I am crucified with Christ: nevertheless I live; yet not I, but Christ liveth in me: and the life which I now live in the flesh I live by the faith of the Son of God, who loved me, and gave himself for me" (Galatians 2:20).

Living by faith is the most exciting adventures you can have on earth. It's a life of trusting God. It's a life of trusting God for everything in the present, the past and the future. The Apostle Paul described how he had died to everything in the past. He was completely cut off from his past. You will also be completely cut off from the past things in your life when you follow Jesus.

2. The cross is the SYMBOL OF THE PRICE Christians must pay.

There is a price for becoming a Christian. It is the greatest deliverance for a human being to become a Christian. It was not free, neither was it easy for Christ to purchase our salvation with his blood. Every time you see the cross you must remember the price that was paid for our salvation. Jesus paid the price and *you* will also have to pay a price to follow Him.

> **For ye are bought with a price: therefore glorify God in your body, and in your spirit, which are God's.**
>
> **1 Corinthians 6:20**

3. The cross is the SYMBOL OF THE LOVE OF GOD you must emulate.

Through the cross of Jesus Christ we discern the love of God and recognize His compassion for the lost. The cross is the symbol of God's love for mankind.

> **Hereby perceive we the love of God, because he laid down his life for us: and we ought to lay down our lives for the brethren.**
>
> **1 John 3:16**

4. The cross is the SYMBOL OF OBEDIENCE.

Through the cross, we see how Jesus Christ was obedient even onto death. The cross of Jesus Christ is therefore the greatest symbol of obedience.

> **And being found in fashion as a man, he humbled himself, and became obedient unto death, even the death of the cross.**
>
> **Philippians 2:8**

5. The cross is the SYMBOL OF THE SACRIFICE.

The cross of Jesus is the symbol of the sacrifice all of us must make to serve the Lord.

> **And walk in love, as Christ also hath loved us, and hath given himself for us an offering and a sacrifice to God for a sweetsmelling savour.**
>
> **Ephesians 5:2**

6. The cross is the SYMBOL OF HUMILITY.

In the cross, Jesus Christ humbled himself to the uttermost. He made himself of no reputation and allowed himself to be shamed, disgraced and belittled by sinful men. Indeed the cross is a symbol of humility.

> **And being found in fashion as a man, he humbled himself, and became obedient unto death, even the death of the cross.**
>
> **Philippians 2:8**

7. The cross of Jesus Christ is a SYMBOL OF THE BLOOD of Jesus Christ.

The cross of Jesus Christ was the instrument that was used to take the life of the Son of God. The wooden cross broke the body of Jesus Christ and shed His blood. When we ask people to come to the cross we are asking them to come to the shed blood of Jesus Christ.

> **And, having made peace through the blood of his cross, by him to reconcile all things unto himself; by him, *I say*, whether *they be* things in earth, or things in heaven.**
>
> **Colossians 1:20**

Chapter

16

Why You Must Preach the Cross

CHAPTER SUMMARY

The cross of Jesus Christ is the greatest secret of power in the ministry. The power of the cross is far-reaching. The power of the cross is diverse in its application and effects. You must preach the cross of Jesus Christ because it will bring back the power of God.

> **For the preaching of the cross is to them that perish foolishness; but unto us which are saved it is the power of God.**
>
> **1 Corinthians 1:18**

Some years ago, I read a book by a well-recognized prophet in which he described an encounter with the Apostle Paul in a vision. I was stunned by the account of his reported interaction with Paul. In this interaction, Paul said to him, *"Except for in a few places in the world, we can hardly recognize the ministry or the message that is being preached today."*

He continued, "When we served, being in the ministry was the greatest sacrifice that one could make and this was reflected in the message of the greatest sacrifice that was made - the cross."

Some months later, I was walking on a golf course in England with a pastor friend of mine. As we walked and talked, the Lord spoke to me.

He said to me, "Preach about sacrifice."

I said, "Lord, I do not know anything about sacrifice. I have never preached about it." Nevertheless, I had to obey Him.

I believe in the prophet's vision of the Apostle Paul. I also agree that the message and the ministry of the church today are quite different from that of the early church. The concept of sacrificing anything to God is foreign to most Christians today.

The focus of Christianity today is money, prosperity, establishment, safety and self-preservation. The goals of most Christians are to get more money, houses, cars, and security. Even pastors measure their success by the amount of money they have, and by the size of the offerings in their churches.

Preaching the Cross vs. Preaching Successful Living

The message of the church has become a teaching about how to have a better life on earth. The message of prosperity has become the message of the church.

Church members are postured as receivers - "Yes Lord, I receive!" This is the catchphrase of the church! But it is time for us to present ourselves before the Lord as people who have something to give. The church must be seen as a group of people who sacrifice for the Kingdom and not as a group of people who only receive blessings.

You will notice that whenever the church has a miracle service, the attendance is different from when there is a teaching service. Any meeting that calls for some kind of work like witnessing or prayer is poorly attended. The crowds however gather when they expect to receive miracles. But the church is supposed to be a place where we "take up our crosses and follow Him".

Money has never been a measure of God's approval of our lives and never will be. The Bible clearly teaches that in the last days, some will suppose that gain is godliness.

> **Perverse disputings of men of corrupt minds, and destitute of the truth, supposing that GAIN IS GODLINESS: from such withdraw thyself.**
>
> **1 Timothy 6:5**

"Sacrifice" means "giving up something". It is a central theme of the Bible. Many of us first heard of the word *sacrifice* from the Bible. We read about Abraham's sacrifice, Isaac's sacrifice and Jacob's sacrifice. Throughout the Old Testament, we see the Israelites making sacrifices to God continually. You could not think of a prophet of God in the Bible without thinking about sacrifices. You could not think of Elijah, without thinking of his experience with the four hundred prophets of Baal.

Yet, today, *sacrifice* is one of the most hushed topics. Today, the theme of our preaching is prosperity, miracles and blessings. The church has totally abandoned the original message of sacrifice. The church has become a phantom of the original church; fearful and powerless. Other religions constantly demonstrate to us the essence and practice of sacrifice. The message of sacrifice is very relevant for all of us today. The teaching of sacrifice must return to the church otherwise we will continue to be a phantom of the real church!

Your Heart Follows Your Sacrifice

> **But lay up for yourselves treasures in heaven, where neither moth nor rust doth corrupt, and where thieves do not break through nor steal: FOR WHERE YOUR TREASURE IS, THERE WILL YOUR HEART BE ALSO.**
>
> **Matthew 6:20-21**

Your heart will be where your treasure is. When I became a pastor, the Lord asked me to put a lot of my own money into the ministry. The Lord made me make many sacrificial donations to help the fledgling church. You see, when you put your money in the church, your heart follows suit.

Let your heart be with God! When your heart is with God, you will be ready to sacrifice; you will be ready to die for what you believe! Not because you have some special calling, but because you believe what you say you believe!

Anything for Christ

> **But Christ has shown me that what I once thought was valuable is worthless. Nothing is as wonderful as knowing Christ Jesus my Lord. I have given up everything else and count it all as rubbish. All I want is Christ.**
>
> **Philippians 3:7-8 (Contemporary English Version)**
>
> **But what things were gain to me, those I counted loss for Christ. Yea doubtless, and I count all things but loss for the excellency of the knowledge of Christ Jesus my Lord: for whom I have suffered the loss of all things, and do count them but dung, that I may win Christ**
>
> **Philippians 3:7-8**

Paul made many sacrifices for his faith and was glad about it. There is nothing like living for God without paying the price. Jesus said that unless a corn of wheat falls into the ground and dies, it abideth alone.

The seed must always die if it is to bear fruit. Some people want to be pastors without paying the price. Be honest with yourself and accept the reality of sacrifice.

In the Foxe's Book of Martyrs, there are several accounts of how people were killed for their faith. They died in droves. Some were eaten by lions.

I would not like to be eaten by a lion. I have been bitten by a lion before and it was not an easy experience. I've seen a lion having lunch before and I certainly wouldn't like to be its supper.

Some of the early Christians were hanged on crosses. Some thought they were not worthy to be crucified in the same way as their master Jesus. So they asked to be crucified upside down.

Take up Your Cross Daily

By him therefore let us offer the sacrifice of praise to God CONTINUALLY, that is, the fruit of our lips giving thanks to his name.

Hebrews 13:15

I beseech you therefore, brethren, by the mercies of God, that you present your bodies A LIVING SACRIFICE, holy, acceptable unto God which is your reasonable service.

Romans 12:1

In the days of the temple, sacrifices were made to the Lord everyday. It was part of their service and worship to God. It was a daily thing they did for the Lord. There is nothing like a one-time sacrifice that you make for life.

God asks you to present your body as a *living sacrifice!* This type of sacrifice is an undying sacrifice, something that goes on and on. *It is unending!*

One martyr said, "Eighty and four years have I served the Lord. Why should I deny my Lord at this time? What evil has He done to me?" Someone with faith will never deny the Lord!

Chapter

17

Why You Must Take Up Your Cross

CHAPTER SUMMARY

17.1 You must take up your cross because the cross has the power to put away sins.

17.2 Taking up your cross has the power to make you die to sin and live to righteousness.

17.3 A cross releases power that is able to make people not live for themselves.

17.4 A cross releases the power that enables people to crucify the world to themselves.

17.5 Taking up your cross will enable you to enter into a new life of faith and ministry.

17.6 A cross creates an unusual group of people.

17.7 A cross defines the true standards of Christian service.

17.8 You must take up your cross because it destroys the power of death.

17.9 A cross takes away the curse that is due rebellious people.

17. 10 A cross demonstrates great love.

17. 11 A cross gives off a sweet-smelling offering which is pleasing to God.

17. 12 A cross reconciles people to God.

17. 13 A cross brings true life.

17. 14 Taking up your cross can give you a worldwide ministry.

17. 15 A cross can deliver many from punishment.

17. 16 A cross will bring glory and honour.

17. 17 A cross enables you to receive power, riches, strength, wisdom, honour, glory and blessing.

Which cross are we talking about? *Your* cross or *His* cross? Well, we are talking about both. We are talking about the cross of Jesus Christ and the effect that it has.

We are studying the effect that the cross of Jesus Christ has had on the world. We are deducing therefore that *your* cross will also have a great effect on the world.

The cross is a symbol of something that both Jesus and His followers partake of. Jesus told his followers to take up *their* crosses.

This extends the experience of the cross from Christ alone to His followers. Because the experience of the cross is extended to Jesus' followers the powers that the cross releases are also extended to the followers who take up their crosses. In this chapter, you will learn about your cross and the powers that it can release in your life.

1. You must take up your cross because the cross has the power to put away sins.

> **For then must he often have suffered since the foundation of the world: but now once in the end of the world hath he appeared TO PUT AWAY SIN BY THE SACRIFICE of himself.**
>
> **Hebrews 9:26**

When someone makes great sacrifices, his flaws seem to fade away.

When Christians make great sacrifices for the Lord's work, people tend to ignore their weaknesses.

Everyone knows you are an imperfect being. But when you make sacrifices for the Lord, these sacrifices stand out and minimise your imperfections. The great sacrifices tend to set aside your obvious weaknesses.

The cross of Jesus Christ took away the sins of the whole world. Similarly, your great sacrifices for the Lord will cause your sins and weaknesses to become insignificant in comparison to what you have done for the Lord.

2. Taking up your cross has the power to make you die to sin and live to righteousness.

> **Who his own self bare our sins in his own body on the tree, that we, being dead to sins, SHOULD LIVE UNTO RIGHTEOUSNESS: by whose stripes ye were healed.**
>
> **1 Peter 2:24**

The cross of Jesus Christ made many people die to sin and live to righteousness. In the same way one person who makes sacrifices, inspires many people to die to sin and to live to righteousness.

Often, one person inspires many others to do something for the Lord. Mother Theresa inspired many people to live for righteousness. By taking up her cross and dying to herself she lived a life of faith in God. The life she would have lived as an ordinary woman was different from the life she lived as a nun. She died to herself and lived by faith.

3. A cross releases power that is able to make people not live for themselves.

> **And that he died for all, that they which live SHOULD NOT HENCEFORTH LIVE UNTO THEMSELVES, but unto him which died for them, and rose again.**
>
> **2 Corinthians 5:15**

Although your cross is not the same as the cross of Jesus Christ, it will have the same effect as the cross of Christ. The cross of Jesus Christ makes people not live for themselves. *Your* cross also makes people *not* live for themselves!

Most people live for themselves doing what they please and what makes them happy. Most of us do not think of giving up anything for the Lord. But Jesus Christ died for us and released the power that inspired people not to live for themselves but for a higher purpose.

This is one of the clearest effects that the cross of Jesus Christ has had, thereby creating an army of zealous followers.

If you do take up your cross you will also release power that can make people live for a higher reason. I never expected other medical doctors to give up their professions to follow Jesus. I have been surprised by the effect that setting aside my medical practice has had on other medical doctors.

Today, I can count more than ten other medical doctors who similarly gave up their lives as medical doctors and chose to be ministers of the gospel

Your cross will surely inspire people not to live for themselves but for a higher purpose. Perhaps you may preach the same sermons as someone else always wondering why it doesn't seem to have the same effect of inspiring them to change their lives.

Dear friend, a good message with a good power point presentation is no substitute for taking up *your* cross. It is the absence of the power of the cross that makes your sermons and ministry ineffective.

4. A cross releases the power that enables people to crucify the world to themselves.

> **But God forbid that I should glory, save in the cross of our Lord Jesus Christ, BY WHOM THE WORLD IS CRUCIFIED UNTO ME, and I unto the world.**
>
> **Galatians 6:14**

Today, people that belong in the world are found mingling freely in the house of the Lord. Unbelievers feel at home in the church because the church makes no demands for sacrifice or for change.

The desires of the world and the goals of worldly people have become the desires and goals of the church.

Pastors desire to be rich executives like managers of worldly companies. Women desire to dress and look like the models they see on television. The prevalence rates of immorality, fornication and HIV in the world are the same as in the church. Why is this?

Why is the world apposed to the church?

Why are the aims, goals, aspirations dreams of the average Christian the same as the goals and aspirations of demonized unbelievers in the world? Why have we become so worldly?

Because the cross has been thrown out of the church and has been replaced with flowers, decorations and projectors.

The cross of Jesus Christ released the power through which separation from the world could take place. Through the teaching of sacrifice and death to the world and its pleasures, Christians will once again rise up with the power to be separate from the world, its desires, its attractions and its ideals.

Through the power of a cross, a Christian will not mind being the odd one out in a crowd of unbelievers.

Through the power of a cross, a young boy or girl will not mind being a virgin when everyone around him has had numerous sexual experiences.

Through the powers of a cross a young man will not mind giving up a life of wealth and success to pursue the humble career of a minister of the gospel.

Through the powers of a cross a lady will not mind wearing unfashionable things if that is what it takes to be decently dressed.

Jesus Christ gave Himself on the cross to save us from this present evil world.

> **Who gave himself for our sins, that he might deliver us from this present evil world, according to the will of God and our Father:**
>
> **Galatians 1:4**

It is because the cross is absent from the church that the world and the Church look so similar. That is why we can hardly tell the difference between Christians and worldly non-Christians.

5. Taking up your cross will enable you to enter into a new life of faith and ministry.

> **I am crucified with Christ: nevertheless I live; yet not I, but Christ liveth in me: and the life which I now live in the flesh I live by the faith of the Son of God, who loved me, and gave himself for me.**
>
> **Galatians 2:20**

There is a new life waiting for anyone who is ready to take up his cross. You will never experience this life until you take up your cross.

There is a new American life and an American dream waiting for anyone who is able to catch a flight to the United States. You will never have this American life or dream until you get on that plane.

Similarly, you will never experience what God has for you until you take up your cross and die for Him.

Paul said he was crucified with Christ and we all have to be crucified with Christ. It is not only Christ who must be crucified on a cross. We must all be crucified on a cross. When you are crucified with Christ you will not become what you would have been in the natural. You will become something else. Paul described it as "the *life* I now live".

Some people had childhood dreams to be doctors or lawyers. But when God called them and chose them, they refused to give up these childhood dreams. They insisted on being doctors and lawyers instead of allowing those dreams to be crucified on the cross. Obviously, the Lord allows many people to do what they want because He does not force anyone to obey Him!

If they had crucified their lives in the natural and given their lives to Him, they would have become something else and lived a completely different life.

I cannot say it would have been a life of riches and earthly rewards but it would certainly have been a life of faith and adventure. It would have been a life of faith and trusting God! These doctors and lawyers would have been able to say with Paul "the lives we now live, we live by the faith of the Son of God".

Indeed, there is no resemblance between the life I now live and the life I would have lived. That life is gone forever. I would have lived the life of a doctor and had the friends and colleagues of a doctor. Today, I live the life of a pastor and a servant of the Lord. What a life I would have missed if I had refused to be crucified with Christ. O what a life I would have missed if I had refused to take up my cross!

6. A cross creates an unusual group of people.

> **Who gave himself for us, that he might redeem us from all iniquity, and purify unto himself a peculiar people, zealous of good works.**
>
> **Titus 2:14**

Through the cross of Jesus Christ an unusual group of people, zealous of good works have been released into the world. The whole world recognizes the presence of this unusual people, zealous of good works. All over the world, Christians go about preaching, teaching, healing and showing compassion to the poor, blind, naked, sick and hungry. Through Jesus' sacrifice, this unusual group of zealous people have been released into the earth.

When you also take up your cross you will create an unusual group of people zealous for good works. One person who lays down his life inspires others to do the same. Indeed, it has a domino effect and everybody wants to be the next.

In the era when missionaries were sent from Europe to Africa, there were young men and women ready to leave their lives in Europe and come to die from malaria in West Africa. Although several of them perished they kept coming. Wave after wave of missionaries landed on the shores of dark Africa to bring the gospel of Jesus Christ. The cost didn't matter any more. Death or no death they were ready. They wanted to come.

In response to a ship captain who tried to turn back a missionary to the cannibals of Fiji Islands, the missionary said, "We died before we came here".

Stories like these, of missionaries exploring the jungles of Africa, finding natives and preaching to savages, only inspired more people to throw in their lives.

But when the era of sacrifice ended, and the phase of prosperity, safety and successful living was born, there were no more leaders who inspired missionaries to lay down their lives. There were no more people to inspire others to become peculiar people zealous of good works.

The missionary movement died when the concept of young Christians going to the furthermost parts of the earth to sacrifice their lives for the cause of the gospel became absurd, far-fetched and out of the question! Peculiarity and zeal are products of the cross of Jesus Christ. Once the cross is chucked out of the church, zeal dries up.

Where is our zeal? Where is the unusual group of people who are ready to do anything for God?

7. A cross defines the true standards of Christian service.

> **And he that taketh not his cross, and followeth after me, is not worthy of me.**
>
> **Matthew 10:38**

Jesus Christ never lowered the standards for anyone who wanted to follow Him. The standard was the same – give up everything and follow Me. When the young rich man came to Jesus He did not lower the standards for him. He gave him exactly the same conditions. He said to him, "You must give up everything and follow me.

Do you remember that these are the same conditions He gave to Peter, James and John by the sea when He said to them, Follow me and I will make you fishers of men.

They had to leave their fishing boats and their fishing professions to follow Him. The rich young ruler equally had to leave behind his valuables. This is the standard everyone must meet for following Jesus Christ. The cross sets a standard for service in the kingdom of God. The cross of Jesus Christ was the price and cost of His ministry. Your cross will be the price and cost of your ministry. There is no change in standard for you.

The price for a real ministry is the cross and not a degree. Some people have great degrees but they are unable to have a great ministry! The price for having a real powerful ministry is not money; it is the cross, *your* cross! Some people have a lot of money but they are unable to have a great ministry!

The price for having a real ministry is not a good family pedigree. Some people come from families that are well known for ministry. The fact that your father was famous in the ministry does not mean *you* will have a great ministry. The price that your father paid will be the price that you will also pay. The price for a real ministry is always the cross. The cross is the standard set for all ministries and all service to God.

8. You must take up your cross because it destroys the power of death.

> **Forasmuch then as the children are partakers of flesh and blood, he also himself likewise took part of the same; that THROUGH DEATH HE MIGHT DESTROY HIM THAT HAD THE POWER OF DEATH, that is, the devil; and deliver them who through fear of death were all their lifetime subject to bondage.**
>
> **Hebrews 2:14-15**

Through the cross of Jesus Christ, death was defeated. Jesus relentlessly pursued His appointment with Calvary. He was fearless in the face of death. He showed Satan that he was not intimidated by soldiers, pain or any hardship that could be inflicted on him. He said to himself, it is just a matter of time and I will breathe my last. Soon, I will no longer suffer this torture. I will be in glory with my Father. His bravery dissolved the defences of the enemy and eliminated the fear of death forever!

People who shy away from sacrifice are controlled by the fear of death. People who shy away from the death of the cross live their lives constantly trying to protect themselves and create safe environments for themselves. Such people must live in countries where there are no dangers. They must always eat the right food and drink the right kind of water to avoid any shortening of their lives.

They dare not step on the mission or harvest fields because of the dangers of bad drinking water. Their entire ministry is redirected and refashioned by the fear of death.

Today, large parts of the church stay away from God's perfect will. They build shells around themselves and protect themselves from dangerous ventures into the "wild" and "dangerous" harvest fields of the world.

Is it safe, they will ask, when you invite them to come preach to the hungry souls? Today, the absence of the cross and the domination of the church by the fear of death have given rise to a multitude of health programmes on Christian television.

All kinds of capsules and vitamins are sold to the safety and health-conscious Christian world that want to live forever on this earth and are no more conscious of Heaven, eternity and judgment.

The fear of death has also spawned a host of television broadcasts to the world. Many churches have an ever-increasing number of channels that they air their programmes on.

Could it be that these programmes have become a convenient substitute for any one going to the mission or harvest fields? You can reach more people through TV, they say. We reach one hundred and sixty million people with this broadcast, they say.

Meanwhile, the masses of poor, hungry and desperate souls who have neither electricity nor television, eagerly await the arrival of the missionaries and evangelists.

But potential missionaries and evangelists are now very conscious of their health, their lives and their personal safety. And they will not come! How sad it is when the greatest examples of Christianity today have set aside the cross of Jesus Christ and given us a weakened and powerless version of the great faith.

It is time to take up the cross again and show a renewed fearlessness of death. The cross of Jesus Christ demonstrated His fearlessness of death and His willingness to obey God and fulfil His calling. Your cross will demonstrate your fearlessness of death and show how willing you are to fulfil God's call.

9. A cross takes away the curse that is due rebellious people.

> **Christ hath redeemed us from the curse of the law, being made a curse for us: for it is written, Cursed is every one that hangeth on a tree:**
>
> **Galatians 3:13**

Through the cross of Jesus Christ, the curse that is due the rebellious human race is broken. God has broken through to us with His power and His love. This love from God came to us through the big sacrifice that Jesus made for us.

When you take up your cross and lay down your life, there are rebellious and accursed groups of people who will receive the love of God and the power of God. Never underestimate the power of the sacrifice of your life.

I spoke to a tearful young man who was grateful that I had sent a missionary to him on a remote island in Africa. He described how he would have been lost, worshipping idols and following the demonised and crazed traditions of his island. I listened to him and was grateful for the young men who had volunteered to go as missionaries to this poor African island.

You must never underestimate the power of your cross that is able to break a curse and release rebellious people from the curses that they live under.

10. A cross demonstrates great love.

> **For scarcely for a righteous man will one die: yet peradventure for a good man some would even dare to die. But God commendeth his love toward us, in that, while we were yet sinners, Christ died for us.**
>
> **Romans 5:7-8**

In our legal courts everyone expects the murderer to plead "not guilty". No one is ever guilty and no one ever did the crime. I am told that the first thing you must get used to when you work in a prison is the fact that every single prisoner claims innocence and has a long story of how he did not commit the crimes he was convicted of.

"I love you", they say, but no one believes it any more. The hardened cynical human race does not believe any more in love and peace.

A legal register is signed at every wedding because no one believes the promises the couple make to each other. Often, it is all a meaningless show.

Politicians wave their hands and say, "We love you and God bless you." But everyone knows it is not true.

"You don't love us; you just want our votes," they say in their hearts.

You can't blame them. If you have lived long enough you will know that men rarely tell the truth.

Why Jesus Died on the Cross

That is why Jesus Christ did not just tell us that He loved us. He died on a cross for us. Lots of people claim to have love for others. But Jesus Christ commended His love to us in that while we were yet sinners, He died on a cross for us.

This is the difference between Jesus Christ and other people who claim to love us. It is this love and sacrifice that has won the hearts of millions of people around the world. Two thousand years have gone by, but the story of the love of Jesus continues to win the hearts of millions. Indeed, God commended His love to us through the death of Jesus Christ on the cross.

Perhaps your ministry is weak and unconvincing. Few people respond to your preaching and your superbly prepared sermons. Jesus Christ did not win us to himself through perfect doctrines. *He won our hearts through His love that was shown on a cross.*

Dear friend, a cross has great power to demonstrate great love. Don't shy away from the sacrifice that comes through fasting, praying, visiting and counselling people. The love you demonstrate to your followers will win their hearts more than a thousand doctrinally correct sermons.

11. A cross gives off a sweet-smelling offering which is pleasing to God.

> **And walk in love, as Christ also hath loved us, and hath given himself for us an offering and a sacrifice to God for a sweetsmelling savour.**
>
> **Ephesians 5:2**

The sacrifice that Jesus made for us became a sweet-smelling offering to the Lord. Every boss' heart is warmed towards an employee who makes great sacrifices to please his master. It is easy to see those who have gone the extra mile. Through the cross, Jesus Christ impressed His heavenly Father.

The beautiful sermons of Jesus such as those about "the prodigal son" and "the man on the road to Jericho" did not evoke such responses from the heavenly Father. *It was the sacrifice of Jesus on the cross that was described as a sweet-smelling offering.*

Dear Christian brother, your sacrifice for Jesus Christ will never go unnoticed. It will invoke a powerful response from your heavenly Father.

What you need is the cross!

The cross makes the difference between a powerless ministry and a powerful ministry.

A cross makes a difference between a ministry that is sweet smelling to God and one that is foul smelling!

12. A cross reconciles people to God.

> **For if, when we were enemies, we were RECONCILED TO GOD BY THE DEATH of his Son, much more, being reconciled, we shall be saved by his life.**
>
> **Romans 5:10**

Through the cross of Jesus Christ many people were brought near to God. People were reconciled to God because of the cross. They were not reconciled to the Lord because of the good sermons of Jesus Christ.

It is our duty to bring people to God.

The whole world lies in wickedness and most men live their lives far away from God.

Unless we also take up our crosses and become evangelists and missionaries people will not hear the gospel as they should. Today, many souls are perishing and going to Hell. Thousands of people go to Hell every minute. But they will not go to Hell because Jesus did not take up His cross. People are going to Hell now because we are not taking up our crosses.

Christ has done His part. Read it for yourself. "For Christ also died for sins once for all, *the* just for *the* unjust, in order that He might bring us to God, having been put to death in the flesh" (1 Peter 3:18, NASB).

It is our turn to do something. When we take up our crosses, many will be saved. Many will be healed! The cross of Jesus Christ works with our crosses to bring salvation and reconciliation to the world.

13. A cross brings true life.

> **For if we have become united with Him in the likeness of His death, certainly we shall also be in the likeness of His resurrection,**
>
> **Romans 6:5 (NASU)**
>
> **It is a faithful saying: For if we be dead with him, we shall also live with him:**
>
> **2 Timothy 2:11**

Contrary to all expectations, the cross of Jesus Christ that seems to promise death actually brings life. After the cross brought death to Jesus Christ He entered into the resurrected life which is the real and permanent life that we all seek.

The only way to this life is through death. The darkest door leads to the brightest glory. Do not be afraid of the dark door that is presented to you. Just as Jesus entered the new resurrected life through the cross, you will also enter a new phase of life in your ministry when you pay the price God wants you to.

14. Taking up your cross can give you a worldwide ministry.

> **And this spake he not of himself: but being high priest that year, he prophesied that JESUS SHOULD DIE FOR THAT NATION; And not for that nation only, but that also HE SHOULD GATHER TOGETHER in one the children of God that were scattered abroad.**
>
> **John 11:51-52**
>
> **And other sheep I have, which are not of this fold: them also I must bring, and they shall hear my voice; and there shall be one fold, and one shepherd.**
>
> **John 10:16**

Jesus Christ has a worldwide everlasting impactful ministry that still changes lives by the millions, years after He walked this earth. No one has ever equalled this kind of influence. *The secret to Jesus' worldwide ministry was His death on a cross!*

Occasionally, God raises up people like John Wesley who seem to have a worldwide impact long after their death. Most people have community or regional ministries. Few people have national ministries and fewer still have worldwide ministries. It is all well and good to desire the worldwide ministries that great men have. But these things are not given to people on a silver platter. They have paid a price for any kind of worldwide influence they may have.

Today, you can have a worldwide ministry. This ministry will cost the same price that Jesus Christ paid for His calling. God wants to raise up many people with worldwide influence, worldwide churches and worldwide movements. The secret to this worldwide ministry is the cross! A cross can give rise to a worldwide ministry!

Believe in the power of a cross!

15. A cross can deliver many from punishment.

> **So Christ was once offered to bear the sins of many; and unto them that look for him shall he appear the second time without sin unto salvation.**
>
> **Hebrews 9:28**

Through the cross of Jesus Christ, multitudes are delivered from the punishment they deserve. The blood of Jesus that was shed on Calvary is the key to the salvation and the mercy shown to the whole world.

Today, our crosses are lying on the ground, waiting to be taken up. When we do so, this great mercy and love shown by the Father will extend to the whole world.

If we fail to take up our crosses, salvation will be limited to the cities and the comfort zones of the world.

16. A cross will bring glory and honour.

> **But we see Jesus, who was made a little lower than the angels for the suffering of death, crowned with glory and honour; that he by the grace of God should taste death for every man.**
>
> **Hebrews 2:9**

> **But made himself of no reputation, and took upon him the form of a servant, and was made in the likeness of men: ...Wherefore God also hath highly exalted him, and given him a name which is above every name:**
>
> **Philippians 2:7, 9**

These beautiful Scriptures show how glory and honour came to Jesus Christ for the *same* reason. He took up His cross!

Jesus Christ was crowned with glory and honour as you will be crowned with glory and honour if you take up *your* cross.

Jesus Christ was not crowned with glory and honour because He travelled from the north to the south of Israel.

He was not crowned with glory and honour because He preached in so many synagogues.

He was not crowned with glory and honour because He crossed the Sea of Galilee to preach.

He was crowned with glory and honour because of *the suffering of death.*

The lamb that was worthy to receive honour is *the lamb that was slain.* The lamb that was grazing peacefully in the fields did not get any such glory and honour.

It is *the lamb that was slain* that received glory and honour.

"Worthy is the Lamb that was slain to receive power, and riches, and wisdom, and strength, and honour, and glory, and blessing" (Revelation 5:12).

Jesus Christ humbled Himself and became of no reputation, dying humbly and quietly on a cross. Because of this, God highly exalted Him.

Have you ever wondered why God is not highly exalting you? It is important for you to humble yourself, become of no reputation and take up your cross. I see you being exalted in ministry as you take up *your* cross.

17. A cross enables you to receive power, riches, strength, wisdom, honour, glory and blessing.

> **Saying with a loud voice, Worthy is the Lamb that was slain to receive power, and riches, and wisdom, and strength, and honour, and glory, and blessing.**
>
> **Revelation 5:12**

Here comes the big surprise! Through the cross of humiliation, pain, suffering, loss and death comes the exact opposite of what we all expect: Power, riches, glory, strength, honour and blessing.

Is it not amazing that he who loses his life will gain it and he who keeps his life will lose it? Do not be surprised if you become rich and powerful after giving up everything for the Lord.

I once stood in a foreign country with a surprised missionary who had given up everything to come to the mission field.

He said to me privately, "I have become wealthier than when I was an active businessman."

"Really?" I asked.

"Yes", he continued. "Can you believe that my wealth has increased in this poverty-stricken part of the world?

I thought I would lose everything but it's turned out differently."

Initially, he had rejected the idea of becoming a missionary and actually run away from the opportunity. Eventually though, he surrendered everything to the Lord and abandoned himself to the mission field.

Amazingly, this Scripture had been fulfilled in his life: by dying to himself, he had received power, riches, wisdom, strength, honour and glory!

Instead of spending your life searching after riches, glory and power, seek to take up the cross of Jesus Christ. Seeking after money in this life will only lead you to numerous temptations, snares, foolish and harmful desires and error.

Choose the way of the Master.

The way of the Master is the way of the cross.

It is time for you to take up *your* cross!

Section

2

The Art of Ministry

To develop an art is to develop an ability or a skill. The Bible states that favor comes to men of skill. The work of ministry demands great ability.

This section, "The Art of Ministry" is a much-needed resource for all who desire to do the work of ministry. It clearly presents what is the right and wrong thinking about ministry, what is the work of ministry, what is required of you as a worker in ministry and how to perform the tasks of a minister.

Have you wondered about how to do your work in the ministry? This will challenge you to walk worthy of the call of God and guide you into giving yourself wholly to the work of ministry.

Chapter

18

The Gifts and Calling of God are without Repentance

CHAPTER SUMMARY

God is a God of mercy! He will give you a second chance to obey Him. Jonah is an example of someone who had a second chance to hear and obey. Sometimes we have only one chance!

■ The First Call

> **Now the word of the LORD came unto Jonah the son of Amittai, saying, Arise, go to Nineveh, that great city, and cry against it; for their wickedness is come up before me.**
>
> **Jonah 1:1-2**

■ The Second Call

> **And the word of the LORD came unto Jonah THE SECOND TIME, saying, Arise, go unto Nineveh, that great city, and preach unto it the preaching that I bid thee.**
>
> **Jonah 3:1-2**

■ The God of a Second Chance

Perhaps, God has always wanted you to work in a church and that is why He created you. Perhaps you have been running away from God's call. But God is speaking to you again. God spoke to Jonah twice. In between the first and second calls, Jonah had many experiences. He experienced the storms of life and the prison of the whale's belly. Perhaps after many hard experiences, you are ready to listen to God.

Perhaps as you hold this book, God is giving you a second chance to work in His house. It is time to join the army for the last battle.

■ No Change in the Call

You will notice that the first call and the second call were identical. In both the first and the second calls, Jonah was sent to the same city (Nineveh) with exactly the same message. The gifts and calling of God are without repentance (Romans 11:29).

God does not change His mind with the passage of time. Even after you have experienced the pain of storms and whales; bellies, He can still use you. Ten years may have passed since God first began to call you. It is not too late to obey Him. I am glad I serve the God who never changes His mind.

Accepting the call of God is accepting to be made into something that you are not. Jesus offered to make Peter into what he was not - a fisher of men!

Coming into the ministry is not about making some great contribution to the kingdom of God. Nothing depends on you and nothing will be destroyed by you neglecting the ministry. We are all expendable and dispensable.

> **For we can do nothing against the truth, but for the truth.**
>
> **2 Corinthians 13:8**

This Scripture teaches us that there is nothing we can ever do that will go against the truth of God's Word. Our greatest mistakes will not hinder the truth of the Gospel. Greatly neglecting our call cannot change the course of God's triumphant army. It is our privilege to be called to this work. It is our honour to be involved. It is time to stop thinking that you are going to do something unusual for God.

Being in the ministry is a humbling experience in which you actually learn about God and receive mercy. Jesus told His disciples to follow Him and He would make them into something. In full-time ministry, you will be moulded into a vessel God can use.

> **And Jesus said unto them, Come ye after me, and I WILL MAKE you to become fishers of men.**
>
> **Mark 1:17**

In full-time ministry, you will be transformed by the renewing of your mind and by the numerous humbling experiences that await you. Full-time ministry is actually the beginning of a journey that brings you closer to God. It changes you and makes you a humble person. The very nature of this despised work and the interaction with other Christians in ministry will surely break you down and make you a better person! Also, the interaction with outsiders who do not understand what full-time ministry is about will drive you deeper into God.

What Full-Time Ministry Is Not

Being in full-time ministry is when Jesus makes you into "fishers of men". Being paid by the ministry does not necessarily make you a full-time minister.

Switching your source of salary from the bank to the church does not mean you are in full-time ministry. Full-time ministry is an all-encompassing step in which you follow the Lord absolutely. Your following Him will mean many things, including some of the points listed below.

Full-time ministry is not as simple as switching jobs. It is a lifetime commitment. It will swallow your whole being and you will be transformed by the power of God.

Full-time ministry is not any of these:

- Full-time ministry is not a convenient job option.
- Full-time ministry is not an easier job option.
- Full-time ministry is not a retirement plan for the elderly.
- Full-time ministry is not an arrangement for redeployed workers.
- Full-time ministry is not a refuge for mothers of little children.
- Full-time ministry is not a last-minute death wish for people who have spent their better years doing other things.
- Full-time ministry is not a camouflaged business plan. Some people want to use full-time ministry to ensure a regular salary whilst they do their businesses on the side. Business is business and ministry is ministry!
- Full-time ministry is not an activity for people in between jobs.

- Full-time ministry is not a springboard for men with secular ambitions.
- Full-time ministry is not a poverty alleviation scheme. Sometimes it is financially better to work in the ministry.
- Full-time ministry is not the same as transferring your profession from the secular world to the church. The fact that you were an accountant in the world does not mean that you must be an accountant in the church.
- Full-time ministry is not just about switching your source of salary.
- Full-time ministry is not a vacation job. Full-time ministry is not something for students to do to whilst on holiday.

Delusions about Full-Time Ministry

There are common current state delusions that plague people in different circumstances. People in full-time ministry are not spared their share of delusions. Some of the delusions that afflict a full-time minister are:

1. Because I am in full-time ministry I am special.
2. Because I am in full-time ministry I will have a good salary.
3. Because I am in full-time ministry I have taken the highest spiritual step and there are no more spiritual steps to be taken.
4. Because I am in full-time ministry I am better than lay ministers.
5. Because I am in full-time ministry I will travel to foreign countries.
6. Because I am in full-time ministry I will have a big house.
7. Because I am in full-time ministry I will have a car.
8. Because I am in full-time ministry I will be rich.
9. Because I am in full-time ministry I have become spiritual.
10. Because I am in full-time ministry I will have a better marriage and a better family life.
11. Because I am in full-time ministry I will have more time to pray, worship and study the Word.
12. Because I am in full-time ministry God is very pleased with me.
13. Because I am in full-time ministry I am walking in love.
14. Because I am in full-time ministry my judgment will be easy.
15. Because I am in full-time ministry I am anointed and protected.
16. Because I am in full-time ministry my children will turn out very well.

17. Because I am in full-time ministry I will go to Heaven by all means.

18. Because I am in full-time ministry I am loyal.

None of the things listed above are necessarily true. They may be true, but many of them may not be true in your case. And they are definitely not things that will happen automatically. You must seek God in full-time ministry so that all His plans will come to pass.

Chapter

19

The Difference between Secular Work and Ministry Work

CHAPTER SUMMARY

There is a difference between working for God and working for the world. Amassing wealth in this fading world cannot be compared with the high calling of God. To build an eternal city with real foundations is the highest privilege for mortal man. Most men spend their lives building temporary things which have no future. The average man is simply a builder of temporal sandcastles.

■ There Is a Difference

> **But they will become his slaves so that they may LEARN THE DIFFERENCE between My service and the service of the kingdoms of the countries.**
>
> **2 Chronicles 12:8, NASB**

When Rehoboam rebelled against God, the prophet sent him a chilling message. He told him he would show him the difference between working for God and working for the nations of the world.

■ Who Is Pharaoh?

Pharaoh is a "type" of Satan. Egypt is a "type" of the world and Israel is a "type" of God's people. Pharaoh afflicted God's people with hard labour and made them build treasure cities. This clearly depicts secular work today.

Most of the time spent in the secular world is spent building the cities of this world. By the time we are dead and gone, we have only added more beautiful buildings to the skyline of this world's cities.

The work of this world is with much rigour, much tension and much sweat. We are made to work harder and harder without realizing that we are actually building the treasure cities of this world. New York City, Paris, London, Accra, Lagos and Nairobi were built with the sweat of hard-working human beings.

These human beings are dead and gone but the treasure cities remain. Their life's work may be summed up as a contribution to the development of the treasure cities of the world. Mind you, Satan said to Jesus when he showed Him the nations of this world:

> **All this power will I give thee, and the glory of them: for that is delivered unto me; and to whomsoever I will I give it.**
>
> **Luke 4:6**

This shows us that it is actually Satan who exercises power over the cities of this world. The devil is the god of this world (2 Corinthians 4:4). It is Satan who has given the sons of men much hard labour and guided them to build the cities of this world.

Christians simply join the army of builders and contribute their quota to build these treasure cities.

> **Now there arose up a new king over Egypt, which knew not Joseph.**
>
> **And he said unto his people, Behold, the people of the children of Israel are more and mightier than we:**
>
> **Come on, let us deal wisely with them; lest they multiply, and it come to pass, that, when there falleth out any war, they join also unto our enemies, and fight against us, and so get them up out of the land.**
>
> **Therefore they did set over them taskmasters to afflict them with their burdens. And they built for Pharaoh treasure cities, Pithom and Raamses.**

> **But the more they afflicted them, the more they multiplied and grew. And they were grieved because of the children of Israel.**
>
> **And the Egyptians made the children of Israel to serve with rigour:**
>
> **Exodus 1:8-13**

Just as Pharaoh controlled Egypt, Satan controls the world and its cities. That is why the entropy and confusion of this world is increasing steadily to its climax.

When you work in the financial institutions, banks and other secular organizations of this world, you can be compared to the Israelites working for Pharaoh; there is much rigour, much tension and much sweat about building sandcastles.

Moses requested that the people of Israel be set free so that they could serve the Lord. Anyone desiring to come into full-time ministry finds himself requesting a departure from the world system. Full-time ministry is service to the Lord! It is like going away from Egypt and into the desert to sacrifice to the Lord and build Him a tabernacle!

God wants His people to spend their time building Him a tabernacle and worshipping Him.

Of course, escaping from the world system is not going to be easy. It was not easy for Moses and the children of Israel to leave Egypt. It was only through a determined struggle that the people of God finally escaped from Pharaoh.

Dear friend, it will not be easy for you to escape from secular work. If it happens it will be through much struggle.

Four Stages for Escape from Pharaoh

> **And it came to pass, when PHARAOH WOULD HARDLY LET US GO...**
>
> **Exodus 13:15**

Pharaoh was not pleased to let the children of Israel go free. There are four stages that every Christian may go through in order to break out into full-time ministry. You must recognize each of these situations when you are presented with them.

Stage 1: *Pharaoh does not want you to leave his employment.*

> **And Pharaoh said, Who is the Lord, that I should obey his voice to let Israel go? I know not the Lord, NEITHER WILL I LET ISRAEL GO.**
>
> **Exodus 5:2**

Pharaoh wants you to work for him until you are dead. He wants you to sweat and toil until you die. Satan knows that many people will never reach the retirement age. He deludes them into working towards an imaginary retirement which will never materialize.

Stage 2: *Pharaoh will allow you to serve God but wants you to remain with him.*

> **And Pharaoh called for Moses and for Aaron, and said, Go ye, sacrifice to your God IN THE LAND.**
>
> **Exodus 8:25**

In this next stage, Pharaoh yields to some pressure. He agrees that you should serve God but you must remain in Egypt. You must continue to build Pharaoh's pyramids. This form of service is politely called the lay ministry. Serving God, but well fastened to the world system of earning money!

Pharaoh will prescribe when you can go to church and when you cannot. Once you are in his land, you belong to him and he decides everything you do. He decides when you wake up and when you go to bed. He decides what you do everyday of the week. He leaves you with only Sundays to relax but sometimes he will take even that from you.

Why should Pharaoh tell you to serve God only on Sunday afternoons and Wednesday evenings? Why can't you serve God on Monday mornings as well? Why should Pharaoh control what I do on Tuesdays, Wednesdays, Thursdays and Fridays? When Moses led the people of Israel to the wilderness, they were free to serve the Lord exclusively.

This is the ultimate desire of God for every one of His children. Sadly though, very few ever get to this state of perfect liberation from Pharaoh and all that he represents.

Stage 3: *Pharaoh does not want you to go too far.*

> **And Pharaoh said, I will let you go, that ye may sacrifice to the LORD your God in the wilderness; ONLY YE SHALL NOT GO VERY FAR away: intreat for me.**
>
> **Exodus 8:28**

In stage three, you are warned not to go too far with God and the ministry. Many Christians side with Pharaoh at this stage.

Good and moral Christians will warn of the dangers of extremism. Today's church is full of "Mr Good" and "Mrs. Perfect" who are neither hot nor cold. It is a church of "mature," moral, never-do-wrong Christians who neither go too far nor too near! "Mr. Clean" is neither hot nor cold!

Something in between will do! When you suggest the idea of full-time ministry, they say you should not go too far.

Stage 4: *Pharaoh does not want you to risk your finances in ministry.*

> **And Pharaoh called unto Moses, and said, Go ye, serve the Lord; ONLY LET YOUR FLOCKS AND YOUR HERDS BE STAYED: let your little ones also go with you.**
>
> **Exodus 10:24**

Today's lukewarm Christians want to serve God without risking anything. They fully agree with Pharaoh's suggestion about serving the Lord without risking their businesses or their earthly possessions.

The modern church, including the modern pastor, is amazed at the idea of professionals leaving their vocations for the ministry. What a glorious honour it is to receive an invitation of the Lord to build His tabernacle!

Yet, the voices of the ones who are neither hot nor cold drown the voice of the Spirit. They say, "Don't risk your life, don't risk the flocks, and don't risk your resources on a crazy adventure. Don't follow this crazy man."

Dear friend, there is no higher calling than to serve the King of Kings. Fight your way out of prison. Make it your life's ambition to follow the pillar of cloud and the pillar of fire. Make it your life's work to build His tabernacle rather than building the treasure cities of Pharaoh.

Chapter

20

What it Means to Walk Worthy of Your Calling

CHAPTER SUMMARY

- **Understand Why You Must Walk Worthy**

20.1 You must walk worthy because it is a privilege to be chosen

20.2 You must walk worthy because you have a limited season of opportunity

20. 3 You must walk worthy because the grace of God has worked for you

20. 4 It is more natural to live the life of an unbeliever than to serve God

■ Twenty Ways to Walk Worthy

20. 5 **Be humble in full-time ministry**

20. 6 **Gentleness in full-time ministry**

20. 7 **Patience in full-time ministry**

20. 8 **Tolerance for one another in full-time ministry**

20. 9 **Staying united in full-time ministry**

20. 10 **Ensure peace in full-time ministry**

20. 11 **Please God in full-time ministry**

20. 12 **Be fruitful in full-time ministry**

20. 13 **Increase in the knowledge of God in full-time ministry**

20. 14 **Become stronger spiritually**

20. 15 **Be steadfast in full-time ministry**

20. 16 **Become happy in full-time ministry**

20. 17 **Be thankful that you are in full-time ministry**

20. 18 **Do not lose heart in full-time ministry**

20. 19 **Renounce hidden things of dishonesty**

20. 20 **Do not be crafty**

20. 21 **Do not adulterate the Word of God**

20. 22 **Commend yourself to the conscience of men**

20. 23 **Commend yourself to men in God's sight**

20. 24 **Make sure the Gospel is not hidden because of us**

> **...walk in a manner worthy of the calling with which you have been called,**
>
> **Ephesians 4:1, NASB**

The Apostle warns us all to walk in a manner worthy of the calling. I became a medical doctor in 1989. I had been in medical school for seven long years. It was a strange feeling to suddenly be a "respected" medical doctor. I had been a student for so long.

For the last twenty-five years of my life, I had been treated as a "young" student. Now, I was a "prestigious" doctor. I couldn't do some of the things I did before. I had to live up to the new and esteemed image of a medical doctor.

So it is with ministry. God wants you to live up to your new vocation of full-time ministry. You must endeavour to accomplish all that God has desired for you.

■ Understand Why You Must Walk Worthy

1. You must walk worthy because it is a privilege to be chosen.

> **Therefore seeing we have this ministry, as WE HAVE RECEIVED MERCY, we faint not.**
>
> **2 Corinthians 4:1**

It is truly a privilege to be chosen by the Lord. To be saved is the highest privilege a human being could have. When I consider the millions of people who live and die, never knowing the Lord, I consider it my greatest blessing to be saved.

When I consider my friends and relatives who do not know the Lord, I am eternally grateful for my salvation. What more could I ask for? Yet there seems to be something higher that God is giving to some of us - a call to full-time ministry! This truly is the mercy of God. That is why you must walk worthy. To work for God is the opportunity very few people in this world will ever have.

2. You must walk worthy because you have a limited season of opportunity.

This is what applies to the Levites: from twenty-five years old and upward they shall enter to perform service in the work of the tent of meeting.

> **But at the age of fifty years they shall retire from service in the work and not work any more.**
>
> **Numbers 8:24-25, NASB**

From the Scripture above, a short period is allotted for the work of ministry. Some people delay unduly and lose their opportunity to work for God. It is a blessing if you responded to this call in time. It takes the grace of God to respond in time or even to respond at all!

If you find yourself working in a church, be thankful and behave yourself wisely because it is a privilege.

3. You must walk worthy because the grace of God has worked for you.

> **By the grace of God I am what I am...**
>
> **1 Corinthians 15:10**

It takes the grace of God to even hear the call. It takes the grace of God to respond appropriately to the call of God. Most human beings do not respond appropriately to the call. Jonah messed things up and had to be swallowed by a whale. Moses could not accept his call until Aaron was brought into the picture.

Many people stay away from ministry because they do not know what their calling is. Some simply do not have the opportunity to work in a church. Paul said, "I am what I am by the grace of God." How true that is!

Coming into full-time ministry can be very complicated. Parents and friends are likely to oppose the ministry. I struggled to enter full-time ministry. I tried business and other ventures. I tried to go to America to be close to a man of God so I could learn from him. None of these things worked out. When my father found out that I was not planning on becoming a specialist doctor, he warned me and told me I was on my own. Through the financial help of my sister I was able to launch out into full-time ministry.

Many people are also encumbered with debts and other burdens. These things effectively keep people out of full-time ministry. Very few people are able to actually respond to the call of ministry.

If therefore you have been able to enter into full-time ministry, walk worthy of it because it was the grace of God that brought you in.

4. It is more natural to live the life of an unbeliever than to serve God.

> **So this I say, and affirm together with the Lord, that you WALK NO LONGER JUST AS THE GENTILES also walk, in the futility of their mind, being darkened in their understanding, excluded from the life of God because of the ignorance that is in them, because of the hardness of their heart;**
>
> **Ephesians 4:17-18, NASB**

The life of an unbeliever (a Gentile) follows a fixed pattern. Paul described this fixed pattern of living in Ephesians 4:17. There are three main characteristics of a Gentile's (unbeliever) life:

a. To live as an unbeliever is to walk in the futility of your mind.

Generally speaking, the life of an unbeliever is spent on futile and empty pursuits. It is a life of never-ending quests and useless ventures. Unbelievers spend their days building sandcastles, which are soon to be washed away by the sea. Everyone in full-time ministry could have spent his life chasing useless projects and imaginary goals. Sadly, the futility of all that men do is not obvious to them.

The heaping up of money, bank accounts and earthly treasures come to nothing but it is not easy to see. Most people never ask themselves why they are alive and why they are doing the things they do.

> *One day, a bank manager came to my house and left a complimentary card with the security man. When I woke up, the security man gave me the business card. As I studied this card, the Spirit said to me, "This lady is the manager of a sandcastle."*

I was surprised at this statement coming from the Holy Spirit. But as I pondered over it, I realized that it was very very true. The bank is nothing but a sandcastle of imaginary wealth. It will perish and pass away with all its glory. I would rather be a door attendant in the permanent house of the Lord Jesus than to be the manager of a sandcastle organization.

The thinking of the Gentile mind is towards futility. Anybody who points out this futility looks strange. People would look at you strangely for calling the manager of a prestigious banking institution the manager of a sandcastle. In the world system, useless things are placed on a pedestal. They are feared and revered by one and all. It takes a man of the Spirit to see through the futility and the uselessness of it all. Surely, only a man of the Spirit can see and agree with the ancient Wisdom of Solomon: "...vanity of vanities; all is vanity" (Ecclesiastes 1:2).

b. To live as an unbeliever is to be darkened in understanding.

The life of an unbeliever is lived out through his darkened (limited) understanding. Darkness imposes limitations on all activities. There are many things we cannot do in the night. Movement is restricted and most workplaces are closed. Nightfall and darkness therefore impose severe limitations on those experiencing it.

A Gentile, someone whose understanding is darkened, is therefore operating with a severely limited understanding. His thinking has been greatly reduced (darkened). He cannot see beyond this life.

Working in full-time ministry is only possible if limitations on your mind are lifted and you can see beyond this life. People in full-time ministry are seeing beyond this life. My eyes are fixed on eternal rewards.

I recently heard of how a very young executive of a billion dollar company died. It was sad because he was at the peak of his career. He had achieved many things older people could not achieve. However, he was struck with cancer and had to die sooner than he expected.

For whom shall be the things he had acquired? Where will they be stored? How long will they last? Will he be coming back to enjoy them? Will the people he left behind eat his millions while he is in the grave? Will his successors be wise or foolish? These are the questions someone with a darkened understanding is unable to answer. His mind is too limited to even think of these issues. These issues are too heavy for a darkened mind!

c. To live as an unbeliever is to be excluded from the life of God.

Unbelievers are excluded from the life of God. It is easy to exist on this earth without ever experiencing the life of God. Exclusion from the life of God is living without God's involvement and direction! You live by the uselessness of your own thinking.

You may create happiness in your myopic world but the absence of God in your life will lead to your eventual destruction.

Adam and Eve lived happily in the garden where God visited them. They had a job given to them by the Lord. After the incident with the tree of the knowledge of good and evil, they died and began to experience death. They were condemned to an existence of sweating and toiling for mere food. Their life was destroyed. They were no more living. They were existing and surviving to gather food for themselves. Life had lost its meaning because they were excluded from God.

Without the life of God, all your labour is to provide food, drink, clothing and shelter. With the life of God, you live for a higher purpose. You live to fulfil God's plan for your life. You live to obey His Word. That is the life of God!

The millionaires of this world do not know why they are alive. For whom do they labour? When will they get the chance to eat up all their treasures? Will they take these treasures away from this earth? What will happen to them when they die?

Exclusion from the life of God takes place because of ignorance of the Word. Born-again Christians must ensure they are not excluded from the life of God through ignorance. Constantly studying the Word of God will change you and bring you deeper into the life of God.

Throughout my years in ministry, I have learnt some things about handling God's privileges. Perhaps the most important thing to do in your privileged position is to walk worthily and carefully. God's grace must motivate you to walk worthily.

Don't Offer Strange Fire!

Live and conduct yourself carefully in this ministry. Nadab and Abihu are examples of priests who did not walk carefully in their calling. They died whilst walking in their calling of full-time ministry. They did not die because they were thieves or murderers. They died because they did not practise their ministry in the right way. They offered strange fire to the Lord. They did not walk worthy of their calling.

> **Now Nadab and Abihu, the sons of Aaron, took their respective firepans, and after putting fire in them, placed incense on it and offered strange fire before the LORD, which He had not commanded them.**
>
> **AND FIRE CAME OUT FROM THE PRESENCE OF THE LORD AND CONSUMED THEM, and they died before the LORD. Then Moses said to Aaron, "It is what the LORD spoke, saying, 'By those who come near Me I will be treated as holy, And before all the people I will be honored.'" So Aaron, therefore, kept silent.**
>
> **Leviticus 10:1-3, NASB**

We want to study how to offer God the kind of service and sacrifice He loves. We want to practise full-time ministry in a way that pleases God.

There are many Scriptures that exhort us to walk worthy of our calling. I was surprised to find that walking worthily involves developing important spiritual virtues like humility and patience. God's idea of how to walk worthy is probably different from yours. Notice these three Scriptures that exhort us to walk worthily in the ministry.

> **Therefore I, the prisoner of the Lord, implore you to WALK IN A MANNER WORTHY OF THE CALLING with which you have been called, with all humility and gentleness, with patience, showing tolerance for one another in love, being diligent to preserve the unity of the Spirit in the bond of peace.**
>
> **Ephesians 4:1-3, NASB**

> **So that you will WALK IN A MANNER WORTHY OF THE LORD, to please Him in all respects, bearing fruit in every good work and increasing in the knowledge of God; strengthened with all power, according to His glorious might, for the attaining of all steadfastness and patience; joyously**
>
> **Colossians 1:10-11, NASB**
>
> **Therefore, SINCE WE HAVE THIS MINISTRY, as we received mercy, WE DO not lose heart, but we have renounced the things hidden because of shame, not walking in craftiness or adulterating the word of God, but by the manifestation of truth commending ourselves to every man's conscience in the sight of God.**
>
> **2 Corinthians 4:1-2, NASB**

■ Twenty Ways to Walk Worthy

1. Be humble in full-time ministry.

> **...walk in a manner worthy...with all humility...**
>
> **Ephesians 4:1-2, NASB**

The most important way of walking worthy is to walk in humility.

Recently, whilst writing a book, I had a revelation about a great ministry that had gone down from its former glory. The Lord showed me in a flash that those people had not walked in humility when their ministry grew. This church had publicly criticized other ministries and ridiculed ministers from their pulpit. At the peak of their ministry, they would ask people who came from other churches to stand up for cleansing (from the contamination of other ministries).

There are many ways to respond to God's promotion in ministry.

When the Lord gave Solomon the blessing of building a mega temple, he did not praise himself or think more highly of his achievements than he should. He actually demeaned his own achievements. He declared that the temple he had built was nothing. He knew that his great temple was simply a human attempt to do something for the Lord.

Notice the prayer of Solomon:

> **But will God indeed dwell on the earth? Behold, heaven and the highest heaven cannot contain You, how much less this house which I have built!**
>
> **1 Kings 8:27, NASB**

When you accomplish something for the Lord, you must see it in the right light. You have done nothing! God did not need you or me. It is His grace that makes it possible for us even to be around.

2. Gentleness in full-time ministry

...walk in a manner worthy...with gentleness...

Ephesians 4:1-2, NASB

To be gentle means to do things gradually. When you are in full-time ministry you must do things gradually. If you try to achieve certain heights in a hurry, you will have disaster. There are new ministers who want to be on television and radio in the first part of their ministry. Others want to write books because everyone is writing a book.

When you are not gentle, you push others around and you become frustrated about your apparent lack of success in the ministry.

3. Patience in full-time ministry

...walk in a manner worthy...with patience...

Ephesians 4:1-2, NASB

You must be patient in full-time ministry. You will not succeed overnight. Most of the casualties of full-time ministry were impatient. They could not wait to be bishops. They were not content with little things they were given to do. They wanted to hurry to the top. They drove faster and faster until there was a terrible accident.

4. Tolerance for one another in full-time ministry

...walk in a manner worthy...showing tolerance for one another...

Ephesians 4:1-2, NASB

It is necessary to be tolerant of others in the church. Working in a church involves working with others. You need to accept others as you work with them. Just like any other workplace, the church is full of human beings.

As soon as there is strife in the church, the anointing of the Lord is hindered. Let nothing be done through strife (Philippians 2:3). Full-time ministry must not be practiced through strife. Quarrels in the ministry should be treated as emergencies. They should be dealt with and the atmosphere of love must be maintained.

5. Staying united in full-time ministry

...walk in a manner worthy...to preserve the unity of the Spirit...

Ephesians 4:1, 3 NASB

Staying united is very important to the Lord. Whatever you do in the church, do not create division. If you create divisions, you are not walking worthy of the privilege of ministry. There is one body and we will not allow anyone to divide us into groups based on tribe, nationality or any other idea.

6. Ensure peace in full-time ministry.

...walk in a manner worthy...to preserve...the bond of peace.

Ephesians 4:1, 3 NASB

Peace is essential for building. King Solomon was able to build many things because he had peace. Solomon's armies were used for building instead of fighting. Any ministry which fights within itself will not build much for God.

7. Please God in full-time ministry.

...walk in a manner worthy...to please Him...

Colossians 1:10, NASB

Surprisingly, not everybody in full-time ministry pleases the Lord. It is important to please God in whatever you do. Like Nadab and Abihu, God may be displeased with you even though you spend most of your time in the church. Endeavour to please God even in full-time ministry. For instance, I know of only one thing that causes a stir in Heaven - soul winning. When you win a soul, you make the Father happy. Soul winning is one of the many activities a full-time minister can pursue. I assure you, it is one thing that will please the Father.

8. Be fruitful in full-time ministry.

...walk in a manner worthy...bearing fruit...

Colossians 1:10, NASB

There are differences in employees. Some members of staff are very fruitful and contribute greatly to the efforts of the ministry. Others are more of a burden. Ensure that you are one of those whose presence is beneficial to the work of God. The fact that you are paid by the organization does not mean that you are fruitful.

9. Increase in the knowledge of God in full-time ministry.

...walk in a manner worthy...increasing in the knowledge of God;

Colossians 1:10

One interesting phenomenon is that some people actually backslide when they are in full-time ministry. They actually pray less and read less than when they were lay people. The fact that you work in a church does not mean that you will be automatically full of the Word. Endeavour to increase in the knowledge of God even as you serve God in full-time ministry.

10. Become stronger spiritually.

...walk in a manner worthy...strengthened...

Colossians 1:10-11, NASB

You must become stronger spiritually now that you are in full-time ministry. Pray more and wait on the Lord. God will bless you.

11. Be steadfast in full-time ministry.

...walk in a manner worthy...attaining...all steadfastness...

Colossians 1:10-11, NASB

You must be steady and unmovable in the ministry. Financial pressures and job offers must not be able to move you away from your calling. As you work in full-time ministry, you will attain steadfastness. Steadfastness is the ability to stay on course. Steadfastness is also the ability to come back to the course when you drift away. Do not drift from full-time ministry. There are many things to drift into. Business, education, relief work, social work, etc., are common roads that full-time ministers drift into.

12. Become happy in full-time ministry.

...walk in a manner worthy...joyously

Colossians 1:10-11, NASB

Full-time ministry is a joyful time. You must have a joyful attitude in ministry. Working in the ministry is better than working in the bank. Full-time ministry is better than working in the hospital. People who have tasted working for the Lord will not want to go back to the world.

13. Be thankful that you are in full-time ministry.

...walk in a manner worthy...giving thanks...

Colossians 1:10,12 NASB

Your heart must be full of thanks everyday for the great opportunity that God has given you to work for Him. If you are not thankful, you are probably in the wrong place. The more time you spend working in the ministry, the more thankful you should become.

14. Do not lose heart in full-time ministry.

...since we have this ministry...we do not lose heart

2 Corinthians 4:1-2, NASB

Ministry is not easy. There are many things that can discourage you. Much of what you do is hard work, with no one appreciating your efforts. You are working for the Lord and not for any man. It is when you look to people for appreciation that you become discouraged.

15. Renounce hidden things of dishonesty.

...since we have this ministry...we have renounced the things hidden because of shame...

2 Corinthians 4:1-2, NASB

Dishonest people cannot flourish in ministry. The reason is that the boss (God) has His eyes everywhere. Unlike other jobs where you can get away with stealing and other dishonest practices, you cannot steal from God. There are people who think they have duped the Lord but no one can hoodwink the King of Kings.

16. Do not be crafty.

Since we have this ministry…not walking in craftiness

2 Corinthians 4:1-2, NASB

Craftiness speaks of being cleverly able to cut corners and get away with poor work. Unfortunately, this is not possible with Jehovah. Leave your crooked ways behind and let us work for the Lord without craftiness.

17. Do not adulterate the Word of God.

...since we have this ministry…not…adulterating the word of God...

2 Corinthians 4:1-2, NASB

The Word of God cannot be tampered with. Many people have tried to water down His precious Gospel. They have sought to re-present the Gospel as some kind of good advice for successful living. We cannot do anything that will destroy the truth of God's work. Do not change His Word; just preach it as it is.

18. Commend yourself to the conscience of men.

...since we have this ministry...commending ourselves to every man's conscience...

2 Corinthians 4:1-2, NASB

It is important to commend yourself to men's consciences. Often they will criticize you but in their hearts they respect what you are doing.

19. Commend yourself to men in God's sight.

...since we have this ministry…commending ourselves to every man's conscience in the sight of God.

2 Corinthians 4:1-2, NASB

All that we do must have approval in the sight of God. No human being or human institution can declare our work approved or disapproved. It is time to think only of what God says.

20. Make sure the Gospel is not hidden because of us.

And even if our gospel is veiled, it is veiled to those who are perishing, in whose case the god of this world has blinded the minds of the unbelieving so that they might not see the light of the gospel of the glory of Christ, who is the image of God.

2 Corinthians 4:3-4, NASB

Finally, the aim of full-time ministry is to ensure that the Gospel is known and heard in every corner of the world. How unfortunate it is that many people do not hear the Gospel.

All the efforts and money of the modern church must be directed to ensure that the Gospel is not hidden even from the remotest village. The Gospel must not be hidden from the poor. The way we operate the ministry must ensure that the Gospel is not hidden from anyone.

Chapter

21

Ten Types of Workers

CHAPTER SUMMARY

21. 1 Workers who are sons and daughters

21. 2 Workers who have the same spirit as the leader

21. 3 Workers who work for you because they owe their whole life to you

21. 4 Workers who are prone to abandoning you

21. 5 Workers who refresh you

21. 6 Workers who are servants of the church.

21. 7 Couples who are in full-time ministry together

21. 8 Hard-working workers

21. 9 Workers who are women and cannot stop quarrelling

21. 10 Full-time apostles

1. Workers who are sons and daughters

> **But ye know the proof of him, that, AS A SON WITH THE FATHER, he hath served with me in the gospel.**
>
> **Philippians 2:22**

There are people who work in the ministry as sons and daughters of the ministry. Such people live and work as though they are in a family business. They do not have the usual employee attitude. They are more of family members. Also, such people do not have the usual "I am here for what I can get" attitude.

I find that many difficulties are eliminated by working with sons and daughters. You will probably enjoy working with your father more than with your boss!

In reality, not all workers in full-time ministry are sons or daughters of the ministry. Some are simply good people who want to work for God.

2. Workers who have the same spirit as the leader

> **I desired Titus, and with him I sent a brother. Did Titus make a gain of you? walked we not in THE SAME SPIRIT? walked we not in the same steps?**
>
> **2 Corinthians 12:18**

There are people who work in the ministry but have a different spirit from their leader. It is a blessing to find people who work with you with "the same spirit".

Paul was not in the ministry for financial gain and he found in Titus someone with the same spirit. You do not need to stay long in the ministry to find out that people work in the ministry for different reasons. What a blessing it is to find someone who will work with you in the ministry with the same spirit!

3. Workers who work for you because they owe their whole life to you

> **I Paul have written it with mine own hand, I will repay it: albeit I do not say to thee how thou OWEST UNTO ME EVEN THINE OWN SELF besides.**
>
> **Philemon 1:19**

There are people who work in the ministry out of a sense of gratitude and indebtedness to God. Such people are often grateful for their salvation and feel that they owe their lives to you.

If people really understood what their salvation was, they would spend the rest of their days in full-time service to God. Seventy years of working for God would not be able to pay for the blessing of salvation.

4. Workers who are prone to abandoning you

> **For DEMAS HATH FORSAKEN me, having loved this present world, and is departed unto Thessalonica; Crescens to Galatia, Titus unto Dalmatia.**
>
> **2 Timothy 4:10**

Every ministry has a "Demas". Demas is the minister or employee who abandons ship in the midst of the journey. Do not become the Demas of your church and ministry.

There are people who are given to you for life. God has called some of us to live and work together for the rest of our lives. There is a feeling of peace as you work with this permanent family.

Sadly, there is a type of full-time minister who will abandon you midstream. After being in the ministry for some time, I can often see the type of person who will suddenly resign from the ministry.

5. Workers who refresh you

> **The Lord give mercy unto the house of Onesiphorus; for HE OFT REFRESHED ME, and was not ashamed of my chain:**
>
> **2 Timothy 1:16**

The most refreshing people are those who are not ashamed of you. They love everything about you, including the unattractive parts. It is only the deepest kind of love that embraces everything; the good, the bad and the ugly.

Such people are not serving you for money. They are there because of a very personal love for the leader. I always sense when people have a personal love for me. I also sense when they know I am not perfect but they still love me.

Every minister has a shameful chain around him. Not everyone who works in the ministry has this personal and permanent love. May you have the spirit of Onesiphorus. May you bring refreshing to the man God has called you to.

6. Workers who are servants of the church.

> **I commend unto you Phebe our sister, which is A SERVANT OF THE CHURCH which is at Cenchrea:**
>
> **Romans 16:1**

There are people who bestow much service on the church in general. They are a blessing to many people. The impact of the servants of the church is seen best when they die. I have never forgotten the different people who have served me through the years.

Some have made themselves into errand boys and girls. They have served and helped in almost every imaginable capacity. I know that God will bless them on the Day of Judgement.

Although most church members' deaths would go unnoticed, the whole church feels the loss of the Phebes of the ministry. Phebe, without using the pulpit, touched the lives of many people.

7. Couples who are in full-time ministry together

> **Greet Priscilla and Aquila my helpers in Christ Jesus:**
>
> **Romans 16:3**

It is a special privilege for a man of God to have both husband and wife working together to help him. What a blessing it is for the whole family to work together in full-time ministry. It is a special blessing for couples to both find a place in the house of God. Couples in ministry have a more synchronized lifestyle that may enhance their relationship.

Many full-time ministers take Mondays as their day off. However, in the secular world, Monday is the first and most important day of the week. This difference in schedules can separate couples who do not work together in the ministry.

In addition, a spouse who does not work in the ministry often despises the one in full-time ministry. They think their spouses are wasting their time by working for a church. They do not respect the ministry and therefore they do not respect people who work full-time in it.

These people also do not understand what could make someone busy in the church. Because the secular spouse despises full-time ministry he often sends the full-time spouse on domestic errands. Sadly, such people see the spouse in full-time ministry as unemployed.

There are also disadvantages of couples working in the same place, but the advantages outweigh the disadvantages.

8. Hard-working workers

> **Greet Mary, who bestowed MUCH LABOUR on us.**
>
> **Romans 16:6**

There are always the workhorses of ministry. Ministry involves a lot of hard work and there are always people who take on the burden of the work. They bestow much labour and exert much effort to accomplish ministry tasks.

This is what Paul meant when he spoke of Mary who worked so hard when he visited. God sees all the hard work that everyone puts into the ministry and He will reward it.

In His letter to the Ephesian church, the Lord made special mention of the labours and the hard work of the church. God notices hard work!

> **I know thy works, and thy labour, and thy patience, and how thou canst not bear them which are evil… And hast borne, and hast patience, and for my name's sake hast laboured, and hast not fainted.**
>
> **Revelation 2:2-3**

9. Workers who are women and cannot stop quarrelling

> **I beseech Euodias, and beseech Syntyche, that they be of the same mind in the Lord**
>
> **Philippians 4:2**

Women are most precious workers who love the Lord with all their heart and with all their feelings. One of the side effects of ladies working together is female bickering and quarrelling.

Paul found himself in the middle of female quarrelling and had to dedicate part of his church letter to solving a problem between two ladies.

Some of these quarrels and cold wars may be inevitable when women work together. God wants women to work for Him and they have a valuable contribution to make!

As we mature in the love of God, the Euodias-Syntyche syndrome will surely manifest! But the love of God will smoothen out all these things.

10. Full-time apostles

> **Salute Andronicus and Junia, my kinsmen, and my fellow prisoners, who are of note among the apostles, who also were in Christ before me.**
>
> **Romans 16:7**

The work of the apostle is to create something that did not exist. There are some workers who can make something out of nothing. You can send them on a mission and they will bulldoze their way through all obstacles, accomplishing and creating as they go along.

In every ministry, there are people whose contribution is of special note. After the apostle has built the church, every other ministry has something to do. Truly, the apostles are noteworthy among the team of full-time workers.

Beginning a ministry is very difficult. It takes determination, faith and resilience to pull through with a pioneering work. We must respect the grace of God that is upon apostles amongst us who are able to begin things that stand the test of time.

Chapter

22

The Ten Laws of Your Mission

CHAPTER SUMMARY

22. 1 The law of knowing your calling

22. 2 The law of concentration and perfection

22. 3 The law of trusting God for finances

22. 4 The law of flexibility

22. 5 The law of "absolute disconnection" from those who do not receive us nor believe in us

22. 6 The law of "snake wisdom"

22. 7 The law of wariness of men

22. 8 The law of the free Gospel

22. 9 The law of avoiding internal fighting

22. 10 The law of rewards

Working in the ministry is working for Christ Jesus. He has given us guidelines for the accomplishment of His mission. When He commissioned His apostles, He said many things which were intended to guide them in full-time ministry. These instructions can be called the "Laws of the Mission" since they serve as a guide on how to behave during the mission. I want us to go through several of these Laws of the Mission.

1. The law of knowing your calling

> **For ye see your calling, brethren, how that not many wise men after the flesh, not many mighty, not many noble, are called:**
>
> **1 Corinthians 1:26**

It is important to know your particular calling. Most people do not know what their calling is. As you serve the Lord, you will see things which help reveal your particular call. The Bible teaches that you see and know things about your calling.

> **For ye see your calling, brethren, how that...**
>
> **1 Corinthians 1:26**

It is important to discover a lot about your calling and to know what it actually involves.

> **But go rather to the lost sheep of the house of Israel.**
>
> **Matthew 10:6**

The disciples were called specifically to the house of Israel. Their call was to Israel and not to the Gentiles. If Jesus had not specifically told them to go to the lost sheep of Israel, with time the apostles would have noticed that their calling was to Israel.

For instance, they could have recognized a stronger anointing and more success when they ministered to the lost sheep of Israel. Perhaps they would have recognized how nothing worked when they tried ministering to Gentiles and Samaritans! They would soon have seen their calling; how that not many Gentiles or Samaritans were included in their ministry.

That is how you discover your calling. You watch what works. You observe what the Lord does with you and with your life. Then you begin to see and understand your calling. If you think you will have explicit details about your calling in a voice thundering from Heaven, you will probably wait forever. You have to watch your calling and flow with what God is doing.

2. The law of concentration and perfection

> **These twelve Jesus sent forth, and commanded them, saying, Go not into the way of the Gentiles, and into any city of the Samaritans enter ye not:**
>
> **Matthew 10:5**

In this law, Jesus teaches us to concentrate on our particular area of calling. In full-time ministry, we will only find true fruitfulness when we stay within the domain assigned to us.

Jesus told the Apostles to avoid Gentiles and Samaritans and concentrate on the lost sheep of Israel. When you know your calling, it is your duty to concentrate your efforts on your area of calling. As you do this you will become a better minister. People will recognize your gift in that area. This so-called gift is actually the fruit of you concentrating to perfect your calling.

3. The law of trusting God for finances

> **Provide neither gold, nor silver, nor brass in your purses, Nor scrip for your journey, neither two coats, neither shoes, nor yet staves: for the workman is worthy of his meat.**
>
> **Matthew 10:9-10**

Full-time ministry is all about trusting God for finances. Full-time ministry is not an alternative to your secular employment. Neither is it a place to achieve your financial aspirations.

It is all about trusting God for everything. God will take care of you as you work for Him. I cannot overemphasize this reality of ministry. Ministry is not for money. Ministry is for the service of God.

Anyone who does this sacred work with the intention of using the ministry as a source of riches is likely to end up in trouble. As old-fashioned as it may sound, you are going to have to trust God to provide everything for you.

4. The law of flexibility

> **And if the house be worthy, let your peace come upon it: but if it be not worthy, let your peace return to you. And whosoever shall not receive you, nor hear your words, when ye depart out of that house or city, shake off the dust of your feet.**
>
> **Matthew 10:13-14**

In ministry, you must be flexible and allow God to lead you in several different directions. It is good to start out trusting Him, but you must continue to be pliable in His hands. You must not be fixated to any particular role.

Sometimes, when something is not working, it is a sign that you must change direction. The Lord sent the disciples into the different cities. Some of these missions were doomed to fail but Jesus still asked them to go. However, He also told them to pack and leave immediately if the mission did not work.

Be ready to change course. Leave all options open. Be flexible and flow until you find your life's work!

5. The law of "absolute disconnection" from those who do not receive us nor believe in us

> **And whosoever shall not receive you, nor hear your words, when ye depart out of that house or city, shake off the dust of your feet.**
>
> **Matthew 10:14**

Not everybody is going to believe in your calling. There is no need to struggle with people who have reservations about what you are doing. Make new friends and stay with like-minded people. Avoid people who mock you. Blessed is the man that does not hang around mockers and scoffers.

There are people who consider full-time ministry to be madness of the highest order. There are born-again, Spirit-filled Christians who think that working in a church is for the elderly or emotionally unstable. Becoming a missionary is seen as something for people without a successful career.

6. The law of "snake wisdom"

> **Behold, I send you forth as sheep in the midst of wolves: be ye therefore wise as serpents, and harmless as doves.**
>
> **Matthew 10:16**

This law speaks of the importance and wisdom of privacy, confidentiality, and secrecy in ministry. It is fatally deficient wisdom to expose all that you are and all that you have to everyone. Once you are in the ministry, never believe that the world loves or accepts you. Assume that you are disliked, disbelieved, disregarded and disrespected by the world, its journalists and its politicians. We have been sent forth as sheep in the midst of wolves.

7. The law of wariness of men

> **But beware of men: for they will deliver you up to the councils, and they will scourge you in their synagogues;**
>
> **Matthew 10:17**

"Beware of men" are the words of Jesus to His disciples. He did not even say we should beware of devils. More harm can come to a minister through men than you imagine. A minister who makes close friends of worldly politicians and journalists may be setting himself up for an unpleasant experience.

Pastors are simply not respected by worldly business people and bank managers. Many of these businessmen see ministers as crooks. They just humour us and put up with us because they have to and because we sometimes give them good business. Beware of people who do not love you! Beware of men!

8. The law of the free Gospel

> **...freely ye have received, freely give.**
>
> **Matthew 10:8**

The Gospel was brought to us at no charge. We must endeavour to give it back freely. In order to give freely there are many things full-time workers must be conscious of.

We must reduce the cost of running the ministry. The cost of equipment, electricity, buildings, etc. must be brought to a minimum if we are to make the Gospel free. Our salaries also must be as low as possible. Does the ministry take care of our needs or does the ministry spend its money supporting our lifestyles?

9. The law of avoiding internal fighting

> **And he called them unto him, and said unto them in parables, How can Satan cast out Satan?**
>
> **Mark 3:23**

We stand no chance if we fight each other internally. There are some common but secret fights that go on in many churches and ministries. In the secret places of ministry, pastors often fight against other pastors.

Another internal but secret fight that goes on in the ministry is the fight between husbands and wives.

Yet another internal battle goes on amongst women who are jealous of each other. These battles are real and sometimes very bloody. Do not be surprised if you find yourself embroiled in one of these fights. But the warning is stern. We stand no chance against the real enemy if we exert our energies against one another!

10. The law of rewards

There is a reward for the smallest job in full-time ministry. Do not be discouraged if the work you do looks insignificant. In Heaven, you will be rewarded for your faithfulness to what you were given! I do not know what job you do, but I am sure it is more noteworthy than serving a glass of water. Is it not encouraging to know that even serving a glass of water will be rewarded in Heaven?

> **And whosoever shall give to drink unto one of these little ones a cup of cold water only in the name of a disciple, verily I say unto you, he shall in no wise lose his reward.**
>
> **Matthew 10:42**

Chapter

23

How to be a Good Personal Assistant

CHAPTER SUMMARY

23. 1 Accept the personal choices of the man of God

23. 2 Accept the values of the man of God

23. 3 Accept the man of God's need for genuine friends

23. 4 Accept the humble duties of a personal assistant

23. 5 Accept the spiritual opportunities that come with personal service

23. 6 Understand the dangers of familiarity in personal service

23. 7 Avoid the dangers of being unspiritual around a spiritual person

23. 8 Accept the opportunity to become part of a new family

> **...who had ability for serving in the king's court...**
>
> **Daniel 1:4, NASB**

As you set out to serve God in the ministry you may find yourself serving a man of God. Actually, the ministry is not about working in an institution but about serving an anointed man of God. Serving in the ministry is very different from working in the bank.

Not everyone will have the opportunity to work directly for the anointed man of God. Maybe, one day, you will have a chance to minister to God's servant personally. There are some things that are important for every full-time worker to know about becoming a personal servant to the man of God.

1. Accept the personal choices of the man of God.

> **And he goeth up into a mountain, and calleth unto him WHOM HE WOULD: and they came unto him.**
>
> **Mark 3:13**

Jesus chose whom He would. It was His personal decision. It was His preference. No one could choose His disciples for Him. Every leader has a right to choose those he wants to be with him.

God has designed us to make choices. Obviously, the leader cannot have everyone close to him.

Do not be angry if you are not chosen. Some people will be privileged and chosen to serve in the "king's court". This is a special calling. Do not fight the leader's choices. The leader will like you if you like his choice and will reject you if you reject his choice.

2. Accept the values of the man of God.

Every leader has personal needs. It is sometimes difficult to understand the needs and idiosyncrasies of some leaders. Depending on the needs a leader has, certain things will be important to him. The ability of someone to satisfy any of the special needs of the leader makes a person very valuable. Sometimes the value a leader places on the helper who meets his special needs may seem disproportionate to the importance ascribed to the person. You may not understand why the leader fusses over someone until you find yourself in his shoes.

Hiring a special singer or an organist may not seem important to some. For instance, a good singer may be worth millions to a ministering prophet.

Similarly, things that do not look valuable to us may be very valuable to God. You may be the most valuable person to God because you do something that your heavenly Father really loves.

3. Accept the man of God's need for genuine friends.

Every king needs friends, every king wants friends and every king has friends! If you can be the friend of the leader, you will be valuable to him.

King David's friend was Hushai the Archite (2 Samuel 15:37) and King Solomon's friend was Zabud (1 Kings 4:5). Jesus' friends were Lazarus, Martha and Mary, her sister.

> **Now Jesus loved Martha, and her sister, and Lazarus.**
>
> **John 11:5**

Every leader is still a human being and as such needs people to talk to. He needs people he can be relaxed with.

You can't be serious all the time; saying the right things, always behaving like the United Nations Secretary General on a diplomatic mission!

You need people with whom you can be relaxed and who are at ease around you. Somehow, not everyone can be relaxed in the presence of a king.

Also, most people cannot comprehend that they can have a down-to-earth friendship and relationship with the king. More and more, I realize that not everyone can serve in the king's court!

Shadrach, Meshach and Abednego were people who had, amongst other things, the ability to serve in the king's court. They had the special grace to hang around the king's environs and to relate with all that went on there.

> **Youths in whom was no defect, who were good-looking, showing intelligence in every branch of wisdom, endowed with understanding and discerning knowledge, and who had ABILITY FOR SERVING IN THE KING'S COURT...**
>
> **Daniel 1:4, NASB**

A wise king knows that he is often surrounded by liars, thieves, treacherous people, wicked men, accusers, fault- finders and many poor and hungry-eyed men, looking for what they can get!

Oh, how he wishes for a few moments of respite, where he can be relaxed without fear. Perhaps it is in this that the friend finds his highest value! Someone with whom the leader can be at ease!

4. Accept the humble duties of a personal assistant.

There are servants who meet the personal needs of the leader. These personal servants may be demeaned in the eyes of onlookers.

Joshua was a personal servant of Moses but he became the leader of Israel. Elisha was the personal servant of Elijah and he received a double portion of the anointing.

Becoming a personal servant may be your door to the anointing! Indeed it is a privilege to pour water on the hands of the man of God, because very few people will ever have the opportunity to do that.

> **Verily, verily, I say unto you, He that receiveth whomsoever I send receiveth me; and he that receiveth me receiveth him that sent me.**
>
> **John 13:20**

5. Accept the spiritual opportunities that come with personal service.

> **And he ordained twelve, that they should BE WITH HIM, and that he might send them forth to preach,**
>
> **Mark 3:14**

The Lord did not take on the disciples for any particular job. He took them on so that they would be with Him.

There are many people that I employ just so that they will be near me. After being around the anointing for some time, people are ready to be sent.

Personal servants thus go through two phases of ministry. The first phase is the *"be with me"* phase. The second phase is the *"sending out"* phase.

6. Understand the dangers of familiarity in personal service.

> **For neither did his brethren believe in him.**
>
> **John 7:5**

Personal servants can easily become familiar. Through familiarity, Jesus' own family did not believe in him.

When you see the human side of God's servant, you can be tempted to think you are not dealing with the power of God. Perhaps this is what happened to Judas. All personal servants must be careful of becoming another Judas. Beware of familiarity.

7. Avoid the dangers of being unspiritual around a spiritual person.

> **...Martha, Martha, thou art careful and troubled about many things: But one thing is needful: and MARY HATH CHOSEN THAT GOOD PART, which shall not be taken away from her.**
>
> **Luke 10:41-42**

When you are involved in personal service, make sure you get the "good part". The *good part* of personal ministry is not the physical advantage, but the spiritual treasure. Unfortunately, many people who work closely and personally with a man of God miss the spiritual treasures of close fellowship.

The book of John reveals the treasures experienced when Jesus interacted personally and privately with His disciples.

The things He said were not for public consumption. They would never be heard by the crowds but they would be heard by the few around Him.

Martha was very close to Jesus but Jesus was not happy with her spirituality. He would have preferred it if she was more interested in the Word of God. *Every personal servant must be careful of being unspiritual around a spiritual person.*

Jesus knew that the job of serving food would be taken away from Martha. But the spiritual treasures that Mary was receiving were eternal. It is interesting to note that Jesus was still friendly to Martha even though she was not interested in the Word. Jesus still liked her very much and He enjoyed her food.

The fact that the spiritual leader likes you does not mean that you will do well on the Day of Judgement.

This is a common delusion for those in the personal company of spiritual leaders. They have the greatest privilege to be close but are in great danger of being unaffected by the anointing and the Word.

8. Accept the opportunity to become part of a new family.

Christ's disciples were one big family. This family spirit often develops as several people work in the personal service of the apostle.

Jesus called the people who worked with Him, His "mother" and His "brothers". This must be the pattern for all followers of Christ. Create a family out of your full-time staff! Let them be your brothers, mothers and sisters.

> **And he answered them, saying, WHO IS MY MOTHER, OR MY BRETHREN? And he looked round about on them which sat about him, and said, Behold my mother and my brethren!**
>
> **For whosoever shall do the will of God, the same is my brother, and my sister, and mother.**
>
> **Mark 3:33-35**

A family spirit can be nurtured in every workplace. This family spirit is even more important for growth in the ministry.

Chapter

24

The Laws of Placement

CHAPTER SUMMARY

24. 1 The law of "those who came first"

24. 2 The law of personal preference

24. 3 The law of militarized work

24. 4 The law of spiritual intimacy in ministry

24. 5 The law of the candlestick position

24. 6 The law of increasing goods

Everybody wants to be at the top and everybody wants to have the best possible job. Somehow, everybody must be placed in the most suitable position. So how do we get to the best places and what is the reason for being put in certain positions?

There are spiritual laws that govern where you must be placed in the ministry. In this chapter I want you to look at some of these laws so that you will have the understanding and the humility that is necessary to function effectively.

1. The law of "those who came first"

> **...After me comes a Man who has a higher rank than I, for He existed before me.**
>
> **John 1:30, NASB**

This law teaches that those who come first are senior to those who come later. John the Baptist indicated that he had a senior in the ministry - Jesus Christ. He explained that Jesus was there before he was. In a spiritual sense, Jesus existed before John the Baptist. That is why Jesus was greater than he was.

2. The law of personal preference

This is another law that determines where you will be placed in the ministry. The "law of personal preference" can override the law of "those who came first". Generally speaking, the law of "who came first" usually applies.

Sometimes, someone who is a late entrant may be given a higher rank. This is because there may be other factors that necessitate a newcomer having a higher rank.

John came onto the ministry scene before Jesus. Yet Jesus was given a higher rank than him.

> **After me comes a Man who has a higher rank than I, for He existed before me.**
>
> **John 1:30, NASB**

Other Scriptures testify to the reality that God has a personal choice and He exercises it as He wills. God's election can override the law of "who came first".

> **For the children being not yet born, neither having done any good or evil, that the purpose of God according to election might stand, not of works, but of him that calleth. It was said unto her, The elder shall serve the younger. As it is written, Jacob have I loved, but Esau have I hated. What shall we say then? Is there unrighteousness with God? God forbid. For he saith to Moses, I will have mercy on whom I will have mercy, and I will have compassion on whom I will have compassion. So then it is not of him that willeth, nor of him that runneth, but of God that sheweth mercy.**
>
> **Romans 9:11-16**

3. The law of militarized work

> **No man that warreth entangleth himself with the affairs of this life...**
>
> **2 Timothy 2:4**

In full-time ministry, you cannot determine where you will be placed or where you will live. This is the reason why there are no guarantees and no securities in full-time ministry. The law of militarized work tells us that you can be sent anywhere at any time.

When you work in a militarized environment expect changes at any time. When you are in the army, you can be sent to your death at any time. Militarized work has no working hours. Militarized work is hard and full of risks. Many people die doing militarized work. You must have a militarized attitude in the ministry. Be ready to be sent anywhere or to be placed anywhere. Be ready to die for the cause when you are called upon.

4. The law of spiritual intimacy in ministry

> **Seemeth it but a small thing unto you, that the God of Israel hath separated you from the congregation of Israel, to bring you near to himself to do the service of the tabernacle of the LORD, and to stand before the congregation to minister unto them?**
>
> **Numbers 16:9**

The most important place for you is to be close to the Lord. Instead of seeking to be placed in seemingly prestigious positions, seek to be placed close to the Lord. Whether you are on the top floor or underground, aim to be close to the Lord.

Get this! Full-time ministry is intended to bring you close to the Lord; to make you an intimate friend of Jesus! God's intention for you in full-time ministry is to bring you close to Himself.

Notice what Moses told Korah. He pointed out that Korah had been brought near to do the service.

Spirituality and intimacy are choices you must make for yourself in full-time ministry.

5. The law of the candlestick position

This law teaches that love and intimacy will guarantee your position in the presence of the Lord. Everyone has a candlestick and your candlestick will be moved from where it is if you depart from love and intimacy with the Lord!

Hard work is no substitute for love and intimacy. God wants people to come close to Him. If we seek Him, we will find Him. In the book of Revelation, there was a church that worked harder than any other did. However, the Lord was not pleased with them. Hard work is not a substitute for a loving and intimate relationship. On two different occasions the Lord said to the church,

I know your labor." He knew they were a hard-working group.

He said to them:

> **I know thy works, and thy labour, and thy patience, and how thou canst not bear them which are evil: and thou hast tried them which say they are apostles, and are not, and hast found them liars:**
>
> **And hast borne, and hast patience, and for my name's sake hast laboured, and hast not fainted. Nevertheless I have somewhat against thee, because thou hast left thy first love.**
>
> **Revelation 2:2-4**

They were indeed a labouring and toiling church but they were not intimate with the Lord. Because of this, they were in danger of being removed from their position. He warned them, "I will come and remove your candlestick out of its place."

6. The law of increasing goods

> **When goods increase, they are increased that eat them: and what good is there to the owners thereof, saving the beholding of them with their eyes?**
>
> **Ecclesiastes 5:11**

This law teaches that no matter where you are placed or what you earn, there will be things to swallow up your earnings.

Many workers are deluded into thinking that if they had a better position and earned more money they would be better off. But this is simply not the case.

As money increases, there are more things to do with the money. It is this delusion that drives people to attain certain positions. It is this delusion that makes workers dissatisfied with where they are placed.

Discover the secret of contentment. Believe that God rules in your affairs. You can be blessed in every position and in every circumstance.

Chapter

25

How Your Value Is Determined

CHAPTER SUMMARY

When you work for the Lord, you must seek to increase your value! You must understand what makes you valuable and do those things. You must understand what valuable thing God has placed in you and develop it.

■ How to Increase Your Value

25. 1 **Your value increases when you can be sent**

25. 2 **Your value increases when you can bring projects to a close**

25. 3 **Your value increases when you can accomplish tasks with speed**

25. 4 **Your value increases with your ability to solve diverse problems**

25. 5 **Your value is greater if you are involved in building a foundation**

25. 6 **Your value increases with your ability to keep secrets**

25. 7 **Your value increases when you are "good" company**

25. 8 **Your value increases when you can relate well with outsiders**

25. 9 **Having a specialized ability increases your value**

25. 10 You are valuable when you save the organization money

25. 11 Your value greatly increases when you can work without supervision

25. 12 Loyalty makes a person valuable

25. 13 Good organizers and managers are valuable

25. 14 You are valuable when you are a contented person

25. 15 Your value increases when you can learn anything required

25. 16 Long-standing workers are valuable

25. 17 Spirituality makes you valuable

25. 18 Anointed people are valuable

25. 19 Experienced people are valuable

25. 20 Morality makes you valuable

25. 21 Working with excellence increases your value

25.22 Your choleric personality makes you valuable

25.23 Your phlegmatic personality makes you valuable

25.24 Your melancholic personality makes you valuable

25.25 Your sanguine personality makes you valuable

Determining the value of anything is not easy. People go to the university for years to study "valuation". What is the value of a house? What is the value of a car? What is the value of a person? What is the value of a person to God? Obviously, the values of things change from person to person. Someone may value a diamond whilst another may kick it away as a worthless stone.

Several things determine your value. Different people value different things. It is important to know some of the different things that increase or decrease your *personal* value.

■ How to Increase Your Value

1. Your value increases when you can be sent.

> **...Here am I; send me.**
>
> **Isaiah 6:8**

Not everyone is sendable. A person being sent on a mission must have the special ability to be faithful without varying the message. Most people who are sent on a mission become sympathetic to the people they are sent to and modify their mission and their message!

If you look closely at the church today, you will find a modified message with a modified mission. I once sent somebody on a very simple mission. After a while, I realized that the person had become sympathetic to the group I had sent him to. This individual fell in love with the group and wanted me to support them financially. He constantly referred to the needs of the group rather than the message I had sent him with.

Once, without my knowledge, this person pledged my financial support to things I had not intended to do. After a while, I realized that I was sending the wrong person. My messenger had become sympathetic to the people he had been sent to. O how valuable it is to have someone you can send!

Someone who will not change the message! Someone whose heart will not change with time! Someone who will stay with the mission. Thank God for those who can stay with the message no matter how hard or ridiculous it sounds.

2. Your value increases when you can bring projects to a close.

To the inexperienced, this point may seem even frivolous. But I have employed different people, assigned them to various projects, and found them unable to conclude just the final little part.

Some people are able to start projects and carry them for a good distance. Amazingly, they are not able to conclude on their project even though they have come ninety per cent of the way. The last ten per cent of every project is a crucial final piece.

Hope deferred makes the heart sick; when the hope of accomplished tasks is dashed repeatedly, the heart of the leader is sickened.

A beautiful car, without one of its tyres, is the same as not having a car because a car with three tyres cannot be driven. Many people do not realize that one little uncompleted segment neutralizes everything else. Jesus is the author and finisher of our faith. Some people are authors of things but not finishers. Your value greatly multiplies when you can finish what you have begun.

Every task has a whole lot of problems that will prevent its conclusion. Some people who are sent are unable to find solutions to these problems. They simply report back with their list of insurmountable problems.

However, the finisher will break through the barriers and overcome every obstacle. Such people are truly valuable. They just come home with a list of victories. They tell you how they overcame the different obstacles they encountered.

3. Your value increases when you can accomplish tasks with speed.

It is a pleasure to have a fast and reliable worker. I have had workers who accomplish tasks at different speeds. I prefer to work with people who bring projects to a close quickly. In fact, the value of someone who can rapidly conclude projects is very high.

I place a high premium on speed because delays are expensive and often lead to the cancellation of the original vision.

4. Your value increases with your ability to solve diverse problems.

There are people who can solve diverse problems and bulldoze their way through obstacles. I have people on my staff like that. They can deal with all kinds of people and solve all kinds of problems.

Whether the issues are private or public, they are able to sort them out. They can deal with difficult people, manage crises, help with personal matters and defeat the enemy. Such people are very valuable because life is full of diverse problems. Problems do not come in departments or under any particular headings. You need people who can solve problems no matter the category they fall into.

5. Your value is greater if you are involved in building a foundation.

> **You are those who have stood by Me in My trials; and just as My Father has granted Me a kingdom, I grant you that you may eat and drink at My table in My kingdom, and you will sit on thrones judging the twelve tribes of Israel.**
>
> **Luke 22:28-30, NASB**

The foundation of a building is the most difficult part to build. There are always some people who help to set things up. The contribution of such people is priceless. These people must never be forgotten. They are to be treasured and valued above those who come later. Anyone who wishes to set them aside does not understand what he is doing.

Jesus Himself promised His disciples that He would remember them especially because they had been with Him during the most trying times of His ministry.

Foundation builders suffer things that future workers will never experience. They experience the greatest pressures of the ministry. There are pastors who can build large churches but cannot actually begin one. Do not shy away from starting things. It may be your great opportunity to become valuable.

6. Your value increases with your ability to keep secrets.

No king would like to have a blabbermouth by his side. Many confidential things go on in the king's palace. Keeping things private and confidential may be one of the most important things to do. Anyone who works in the office of leadership must learn the importance of privacy and secrecy. Unfortunately, some people do not have the ability to work without talking about what they do.

Working in banks requires lots of secrecy because you deal with people's private wealth; one who cannot keep official information out of his domestic chatter will be unsuitable for such a job. Upon employment, banks will make you sign the oath of secrecy.

Working in a pastor's office may involve listening to private counselling sessions. Working in a doctor's office may also involve hearing and seeing people's personal problems. These private matters are nobody's business and should not be broadcast to the world. No one would like the whole world to know his personal problems.

Your value increases when you prove that you are capable of handling the responsibility of secrets. Some people will be employed simply because they do not have many friends! Some people will get certain jobs because they do not talk much with anyone about anything!

For this kind of job, you will have to avoid people who talk too much and have too many friends!

These "talkative" people will become valuable for the office party and other social gatherings where they will bring everything to life. Please understand what makes you valuable.

7. Your value increases when you are "good" company.

And he ordained twelve, THAT THEY SHOULD BE WITH HIM.
Mark 3:14

Jesus ordained twelve disciples simply so they would be with Him. He chose them to be in His company until He finished His ministry.

Not everybody can work comfortably with the boss. To work directly with the boss requires varied skills. The commander requires people who can engage in interesting and meaningful conversation. Some people just have nothing to say and therefore are not good company.

The Silent Hungry Look

Quiet people can be intolerable for a wise leader, as he has to constantly pry into their minds to find out what they are thinking.

His wisdom will cause him to search out hidden thoughts in case there are evolving plots against his life.

When I am with "quiet" people I always ask, "What do you think?" "How is your mind working? Is it a good idea?" I want to know what people around me are thinking.

Julius Caesar commented on Cassius, a worker in his court.

He said, "Yon Cassius has a lean and hungry look. He thinks too much: such men are dangerous."

Cassius was one of the conspirators who murdered Caesar. Long before the assassination, Caesar mistrusted Cassius because of the silent, hungry look on his face.

The Empty Look

Others only enjoy talking about light and frivolous matters, which may not interest the leader. Leaders are not light-hearted men of straw. They are serious people who have serious issues to deal with.

Rulers have many issues to juggle with and value people who are full of good counsel and wisdom. Leadership is a very lonely job with few who understand the real issues and challenges at hand. Many people simply see the leader as a superman who knows everything and who is always right. Such an attitude will not go well with a leader who wants the input of those around him. He therefore needs people who think and analyze issues in a certain way.

The Suspicious Look

A leader is someone who fights many battles. He does not need a cabinet member who is suspicious and opposed to all he does. This only transfers the battle from outside to within. Why should you employ someone to oppose and resist you?

Leaders also need people who think in a certain way. Paul said of Timothy,

> **...I have no man likeminded, who will naturally care for your state.**
>
> **Philippians 2:20**

King David had Hushai as his friend and King Solomon had Zabud as a friend. These friends were good company, good fellowship and gave good counsel.

The Creative Look

Creativity is the nature of God. People who are innovative and come up with good ideas when they are needed are also very valuable company.

Another important and valuable trait is the ability to meet the personal needs of the leader. Not everyone can work comfortably in the personal service of the king. Daniel and his three friends had the ability to serve in the king's court. This, too, is an important skill.

> **...bring in some of the sons of Israel...who had ability for serving in the king's court...they were to enter the king's personal service.**
>
> **Daniel 1:3-5, NASB**

8. Your value increases when you can relate well with outsiders.

There are people who can relate easily with the outside world. However, not all workers are up to this role.

To effectively relate with outsiders, you need to develop the art of diplomacy. You must understand protocol. Not everyone is skilled in diplomacy. Some people are simply unrefined and unrefinable!

Your dressing may have to be modified if you are to appear in public. Your speech will have to be appropriate and polished for the occasion. Some people simply do not have the background that enables them to function in this role.

Some people are unable to communicate with the public without offending people. Some simply do not have the patience or the ability to be a public relations person. A person who knows how to serve in the public eye is therefore valuable.

9. Having a specialized ability increases your value.

When you have some unusual talent, you become valuable. For instance, your ability to speak an unusual language can increase your value greatly. You must find a place where your particular ability is valued. There are people whose ability to sing has earned them special jobs in special places.

Not everyone has the ability to be a world-class singer. Some people have the ability to type with speed and accuracy. Such things give unusual value to a person. When I began to write books, I discovered how few people really know how to type with speed and accuracy.

The ability to host people and cater for them is also a special skill. Not every woman cares for people in a way that makes them feel at home. Some women actually drive people away with their unfriendly and expressionless faces. Some people do not even bother to learn what to do to make a particular person comfortable. Such motherly hosts are specially endowed and are of great value to churches that host guests frequently.

The ability to be a good public speaker or presenter is a special skill that can increase your value. Such a person may be invaluable for public relations and improving the corporate image of the organization.

Special computer skills and technical abilities can also make a person valuable. Discover what special ability you have and exploit it to the fullest. Let your gift make room for you and take you to the highest place!

10. You are valuable when you save the organization money.

There are people who have the ability to help save money. They negotiate on behalf of the organization as though they were negotiating for their own lives. Such people save lots of money for the ministry through their bargaining skills. People who make purchases and payments for the ministry are often not concerned about how much everything costs. But there are some who care and try to get the best deal every time. Such people are priceless treasures to an organization!

Other people view the opportunity to make a purchase on behalf of the organization as a chance to make some money for themselves. These are dangerous people who slowly undermine the ministry.

Paul said,

> **For I have no man likeminded, who will naturally care for your state.**
>
> **Philippians 2:20**

11. Your value greatly increases when you can work without supervision.

Supervising people can be one of the most tiresome jobs. Having to constantly monitor what someone is doing is wearisome, to say the least. What a joy it is to have someone who can work with little or no supervision. Just give him the job and he will come back with the results. When you have to chase a person, giving a hundred reminders and promptings about the same thing, you may just want to do the job yourself!

Unfortunately, most people need supervision and cannot be trusted to work on their own. Become someone who works without supervision!

12. Loyalty makes a person valuable.

Loyalty is more important than any qualification or skill I know. Any leader who does not value loyalty will live to discover the pain of treachery. A loyal person is far more valuable than an educated but disloyal person. When an employer does not know the value of loyalty, he often chooses people who are impressive but intrinsically disloyal.

After a while, these impressive people turn out to be painful choices. I have watched as ministers set aside faithful people and choose exciting people who have no loyalty. These people have not learnt about the great value of loyalty.

With the passage of time, most people will prefer a loyal person to any other. Every worker has to choose between his loyalty to the boss and his loyalty to the rest of the workers.

I once told a new employee, "You will either be liked by me or by the people. It's your choice." His value to me would rise greatly if he was loyal to me rather than to the rest of the staff.

13. Good organizers and managers are valuable.

Some people are able to gather people around and make them do their jobs. Others are simply unable to control anyone. I once found out that one of my newly appointed managers was unable to control the janitor. I realized that I had chosen the wrong person to be a manager.

Someone who is incapable of controlling drivers, cleaners and housemaids will not be able to control more educated and confident people. Your value goes up when you are able to control difficult people.

14. You are valuable when you are a contented person.

Satisfied people are a joy to have around.

> **Better is an handful with quietness...**
>
> **Ecclesiastes 4:6**

Moses had the difficulty of leading a discontented and grumbling crowd. Such people cannot be satisfied by anything. Good relationships are not built on money. No amount of money can make a person happy. Discontented people want more and more but they are never satisfied!

A worker who is happy with the little you can give is truly a valuable person. One discontented person can poison the entire workforce. Such people love to be part of unions, strikes and disruptions of work.

Such things are not needed in the church! Get rid of discontented people. Send them off to get a better job where they will be happier. It is not worth having them around.

15. Your value increases when you can learn anything required.

You may be required to produce television programs. If you are rigid and unprepared to learn completely new things, you will be limited in your value.

People who are prepared to learn new things are valuable! You may be required to run an orphanage or a radio station. Are you prepared to learn a completely new skill? I have watched as lawyers have learnt the art of construction and doctors have learnt how to run bookshops and schools. Their value increased because they were prepared to acquire new skills.

16. Long-standing workers are valuable.

Time speaks! Someone who has been around for years has a value that "Johnny-just-come" does not have! Years of stability and faithful service definitely confer value on every employee. Time tells whether a person is faithful or not!

Time tells whether a person is a liar or not. Time tells whether a person is a thief or not. Time tells whether a person is morally upright or not. The long years spent together assure us that we can depend on you.

17. Spirituality makes you valuable.

Spiritual people are valuable. Every church should endeavour to employ spiritual people. Sometimes spiritual people do not have certain qualities or abilities but their spirituality gives them great value in the ministry setting.

Unfortunately, some churches end up employing all sorts of unspiritual people; even unbelievers. They do this in order to fill some vacancies.

But it is often better not to have anyone, than to have a carnal person working in the church. Someone who has not been spiritual is not likely to become spiritual when he is in full-time ministry.

Gradually, a little leaven leavens the whole lump. Unspiritual and unsaved people gradually dilute the intensity of the zeal and anointing of any ministry. Soon you may have a full-time ministry staff of pseudo-Christians.

Wrong decisions will soon be taken because of the influence of carnal people. Full-time ministry is a place for zealous people who are on fire for Jesus. The Lord said to the Laodecian church, "I wish you were hot." God wants us to be hot and not lukewarm. Lukewarmness is a deadly enemy that destroys every true church.

18. Anointed people are valuable.

An anointed person is a special person with the grace of God operating in his life. Such people have great value because the grace and wisdom of God makes them operate above human ability. It is a joy to watch anointed people as they operate in the gift of God. They are special, they are different and they are wise!

> **The Spirit of the LORD will rest on Him, the spirit of wisdom and understanding, the spirit of counsel and strength, the spirit of knowledge and the fear of the LORD.**
>
> **And He will delight in the fear of the LORD, and He will not judge by what His eyes see, Nor make a decision by what His ears hear;**
>
> **Isaiah 11:2-3, NASB**

This is the wisdom that comes through the anointing. May you be an anointed worker!

19. Experienced people are valuable.

Experienced people have an uncanny knowledge of the future. Most things actually work out the way experienced people envisage.

Many things do not happen the way you would expect. There is some special knowledge that comes only through experience. People with experience often turn the tide in a battle. A person's value increases greatly because he is experienced. Do not shy away from things that make you experienced. The more experience you have, the more valuable you become.

20. Morality makes you valuable.

Moral and upright people are especially valuable as you can count on them to do the right thing behind closed doors. Joseph had the opportunity to sleep with his boss' wife but he did not. He could be trusted in very tempting circumstances. Such people are truly valuable. The presence of one lecherous person (someone who is unduly interested in sex) can spoil the work of many years and end the employment of everyone else.

The higher you go in ministry the deeper your safety pegs must be. When you get to the eighth floor and you lean on the balcony, you would not want to discover that it is made of cardboard! The higher you go, the more the need for stronger character.

21. Working with excellence increases your value.

Sloppy workers who deliver shoddy work are a pain to most employers. They need extra supervision and are stressful to have around. What a joy it is to have someone who delivers a quality job every time! Such people are valuable and it is worth paying the price to have their services.

22. Your choleric personality makes you valuable.

Your choleric personality will make you valuable in difficult projects that need a driving force. This is the personality that will make you valuable in building up something from scratch. Choleric people are usually the best leaders but not very good assistants.

23. Your phlegmatic personality makes you valuable.

If God made you a phlegmatic, you will have special abilities, which no one else has. Phlegmatic people are stable workers and able to carry out monotonous jobs. There are many important jobs, which must go on in spite of their repetitiveness.

Where would we be without teachers and lecturers who stick to their jobs for years? These precious and steady trainers produce the high achievers and skilled workers of tomorrow. Phlegmatic workers are usually valuable because they are good assistants.

24. Your melancholic personality makes you valuable.

Melancholic people are usually very gifted and very organized. They are usually thoughtful, contented and deeply sacrificial. Melancholic people became the great missionaries of the past. These people are often quiet and can work where privacy and secrecy is required.

If God has made you a melancholic, you will be useful for many things in the office environment. You will keep things organized and private. You will have the ability to bring order and good management into places which are often disorganized.

25. Your sanguine personality makes you valuable.

If you are a sanguine, you will not be useful for things which require much organization. The scatter-brained and disorganized sanguine is of no use with sensitive documents. However, without a sanguine, your office will be a sad place! It will be lifeless because the life and excitement of the team is often created by the valuable sanguine. This is where a sanguine is most helpful.

If you put a melancholic in an office which a sanguine should occupy, people will leave because of the silent, stern and unfriendly melancholic.

I value the sanguine people in my office. They have no replacement. All the melancholics and cholerics put together cannot make the contribution of one sanguine.

Chapter

26

How to Enjoy Your Work

CHAPTER SUMMARY

■ Wisdom for Enjoying Your Work

26. 1 Enjoy your work by eating and drinking while you work

26. 2 Be happy and joyful at work

26. 3 Accept your lot

26. 4 Enjoy work by living joyfully with your spouse

26. 5 Eat of your wealth and take your portion as you work

26. 6 Remember that people are envious of hard-working people

26. 7 Be content as you work for God

26. 8 Patience will make you go further

26. 9 Wisdom will make you work better

26. 10 Working in twos is always more fruitful and enjoyable

It is important to enjoy your work since that is what you will spend most of your time doing - working. Most people do not enjoy work and look forward to the slightest chance to escape.

It is therefore one of the greatest blessings to be given the kind of work that makes use of your God-given qualities.

Work then becomes like play, leisure and pleasure! No longer will you spend your working days longing for a vacation. No longer will you spend your working hours glancing at the clock and wondering why closing time is so far away.

It takes the God-kind of wisdom to enjoy work. You need to apply heavenly wisdom to what you are doing, otherwise you will end up depressed and wondering what life is about.

Even king Solomon, the richest and wisest man that ever lived, found life to be a vexation of spirit. He condemned his working experience on the earth and called it vanity. He spoke of the toil he had undertaken and the uselessness of it all. He considered the future and wondered what would happen to all the things he had built.

He thought to himself, "What if the person who comes after me destroys everything?"

> **Yea, I hated all my labour which I had taken under the sun: because I should leave it unto the man that shall be after me. And who knoweth whether he shall be a wise man or a fool? yet shall he have rule over all my labour wherein I have laboured, and wherein I have shewed myself wise under the sun. This is also vanity.**
>
> **Ecclesiastes 2:18-19**

As his melancholic thoughts deepened, he could only utter the words, "Vanity of vanities. All is vanity." Indeed, the one who succeeded him was a fool.

The son of the wisest man who ever lived (Rehoboam), indeed demonstrated great folly at his very first cabinet meeting. His very first decision split the kingdom up. The son of the wise man was now left with one tribe out of twelve to govern.

What a drastic reduction of the kingdom that his father had ruled! To make matters worse, he was unable to keep all the gold vessels that King Solomon had heaped up in the temple. Rehoboam replaced the golden vessels with brass - a poor substitute indeed! Solomon's son was a pale reflection of his father.

Such is the futility of all our life's work. It is vanity. Perhaps most working people have not reflected on these realities. If they do they would not find much meaning in what they are doing. This is the difference between secular work and full-time ministry.

When a Christian works for the Lord in full-time ministry, it is still important to apply a certain kind of wisdom.

This wisdom will make you enjoy your work and live joyfully under the sun. The term "under the sun" is used frequently in the book of Ecclesiastes. This phrase speaks of the life we live "under the sun" or the life we live on this earth. Solomon gave us words of wisdom that can dramatically improve life "under the sun". However, most of the wisdom for life "under the sun" does not give guidance for the life hereafter.

If you fail to apply this wisdom "under the sun" you will probably hate your life in the end. You will find life and work a futile experience. Why would the Queen of Scotland say as she died, "Shame on life"? She sounded just like Solomon.

> **Therefore I hated life; because the work that is wrought under the sun is grievous unto me: for all is vanity and vexation of spirit.**
>
> **Ecclesiastes 2:17**

■ Wisdom for Enjoying Your Work

1. Enjoy your work by eating and drinking while you work.

The phrase "eat and drink" refers to having your basic needs met as you work. Eating good food and living well is wisdom that will make you enjoy working.

Some people save up for a good retirement but never reach that age.

> **Then I commended mirth, because a man hath no better thing under the sun, than to eat, and to drink, and to be merry: for that shall abide with him of his labour the days of his life, which God giveth him under the sun.**
>
> **Ecclesiastes 8:15**

It is time to enjoy your food and drink. Eat what you actually enjoy and drink to your fill. Bring out the best plates in the house and use the nicest glasses. Don't save them up for visitors any more. You are as good as any visitor!

> **Behold that which I have seen: it is good and comely for one to eat and to drink, and to enjoy the good of all his labour that he taketh under the sun all the days of his life, which God giveth him: for it is his portion.**
>
> **Ecclesiastes 5:18**

2. Be happy and joyful at work.

It is important to be joyful and happy whilst working. You will spend most of your lifetime working. You must enjoy the company of those you work with. You must be able to laugh, holler, and have a good time. If you do this, you will love going to work. You will actually miss being at work because you will miss the good company and the good fun of it all. Home may even seem boring to you when you are joyful at work.

> **Then I commended mirth, because a man hath no better thing under the sun, than to eat, and to drink, and to be merry: for that shall abide with him of his labour the days of his life, which God giveth him under the sun.**
>
> **Ecclesiastes 8:15**

Fight till you work in the right environment and with the right people.

3. Accept your lot.

> **Then I realised that it is good and proper for a man to eat and drink, and to find satisfaction in his toilsome labour under the sun during the few days of life God has given him-- for THIS IS HIS LOT.**
>
> **Moreover, when God gives any man wealth and possessions, and enables him to enjoy them, TO ACCEPT HIS LOT and be happy in his work-- this is a gift of God.**
>
> **Ecclesiastes 5:18-19, NIV**

Accept what God has given you. God has not given you everything. There are things we all wish we had but everyone must accept his lot. If you do not have a husband and spend all your life fighting to get one, you will probably become bitter and frustrated. If you do not have a child and spend the better part of your adult life trying to have one, you are likely to experience many disappointments.

As long as you do not accept your lot, you will have a life of unwinnable battles and humiliating defeats. "Accept your lot" is the wisdom of God for a happy life under the sun.

4. Enjoy work by living joyfully with your spouse.

> **LIVE JOYFULLY WITH THE WIFE whom thou lovest all the days of the life of thy vanity, which he hath given thee under the sun, all the days of thy vanity: FOR THAT IS THY PORTION IN THIS LIFE, and in thy labour which thou takest under the sun.**
>
> **Ecclesiastes 9:9**

One of the ways to enjoy your work is to live happily with your spouse. Anyone who has been married knows that marital conflict is a painful and discomfitting experience. It discolours everything and releases shadows of depression into your entire life. Indeed marital harmony is one of the rewards and blessings a person could have.

Many millionaires live alone and estranged from their wives. Their homes are filled with empty rooms and unused swimming pools. There are no shouts of joy and no peals of laughter from these homes.

Do these millionaires really have the blessings of life "under the sun"? Life is more than a pay package. There are many other things that God teaches us to consider.

It is time for you and your spouse to laugh at each other and enjoy a few moments "under the sun" together.

Do not be fixated on the negatives. There are many things to talk about. Have dinner together! Make tea for each other. Have fun! Enjoy and accept each other's friendship! Do not accuse each other! Play with each other and make light of all the ugliness in your spouse. This world is not our home. We are just passing through and under the sun for a season! Pass your tests of this life under the sun!

5. Eat of your wealth and take your portion as you work.

> **There is an evil which I have seen under the sun, and it is common among men: A man to whom God hath given riches, wealth, and honour, so that he wanteth nothing for his soul of all that he desireth, yet God giveth him not power to eat thereof, but a stranger eateth it: this is vanity, and it is an evil disease.**
>
> **Ecclesiastes 6:1-2**

Spend money on yourself. Use some of the wealth you have earned on yourself. That is part of enjoying your working life. Invest in your surroundings. If you spend most of your time in your bedroom, make it the nicest bedroom in the world. Have fun with the goodies God has given you. It is an evil thing to be unable to use the wealth you have earned. Failure to eat your portion will make you hate life and hate work.

> **And I gave my heart to know wisdom, and to know madness and folly: I perceived that this also is vexation of spirit. For in much wisdom is much grief: and he that increaseth knowledge increaseth sorrow.**
>
> **Ecclesiastes 1:17-18**

6. Remember that people are envious of hard-working people.

> **Again, I considered all travail, and every right work, that for this a man is envied of his neighbour. This is also vanity and vexation of spirit.**
>
> **Ecclesiastes 4:4**

This world has six billion selfish, greedy and lazy people. When a hard-working person comes along, he tills the ground, prospers and creates wealth. Unfortunately, his wealth and success only stir up the jealousy of his brothers.

Abel did not do anything to hurt his brother Cain. Cain was jealous of Abel's success and eventually killed him.

Under the sun, hard-working and successful people will always be surrounded by envious people. Successful men all over the world live under the teeming threat of envious people.

Jesus Christ was crucified because of envy. "For he knew that the chief priests had delivered him for envy" (Mark 15:10).

7. Be content as you work for God.

> **Better is an handful with quietness, than both the hands full with travail and vexation of spirit.**
>
> **Ecclesiastes 4:6**

This may be one of the most important strengths that you will ever develop. The ability to be content is so important for full-time ministers and their families. It is this ability that keeps your mind and heart on eternity.

In this all-important spiritual state, you will be content with food, clothes and somewhere to live. This truly is the biblical prescription for all spiritual pilgrims.

8. Patience will make you go further.

> **Better is the end of a thing than the beginning thereof: and the patient in spirit is better than the proud in spirit.**
>
> **Ecclesiastes 7:8**

Impatience is the brother of discontentment. Impatient people cannot wait for the seeds they have sown to germinate. They must have all the money now. They must have cars, houses, gold and other rewards now and in this life. It is this spirit of impatience that cuts us off many a minister from realizing their full potential.

9. Wisdom will make you work better.

> **This wisdom have I seen also under the sun, and it seemed great unto me:**
>
> **Ecclesiastes 9:13**

Every job can be made easier and faster through wisdom. Farming, carpentry, fishing and even the practice of medicine are much easier today because wisdom has made everything a little easier. Use wisdom to make whatever work you do faster and more fruitful.

10. Working in twos is always more fruitful and enjoyable.

> **Two are better than one; because they have a good reward for their labour.**
>
> **Ecclesiastes 4:9**

An eternal law of fruitful work is the law of working in teams of twos. I have tried sending out people alone and I have discovered that two are always better than one. Believe and practise the principle of "two are better than one". It will make your life's work much easier.

Chapter

27

How to Find Your Life's Work

CHAPTER SUMMARY

- **Eight Ways to Identify Your Life's Work**

27.1 Your life's work will give a new meaning to your life

27.2 Your life's work is something God has called you to

27.3 Your life's work is something that you will not hate

27.4 In your life's work, you will enjoy the rewards of your labour

27.5 In your life's work, money will no longer drive you

27.6 In your life's work you will not labour in vain

27.7 Your life's work makes you become a blessing to others

27.8 In your life's work your talents will be revealed

Your life's work is a gift from God. Many people would be surprised to find out that work is actually a gift from God. Without the gift of work, many would be listless, lacking the energy and vitality of life.

It is the work God has given us to do that energizes us. As soon as you sense that the work you are doing is worthless, it is difficult to continue working. This revelation of how futile secular work is, is what spurs many into full-time ministry.

It is difficult to spend all your energy doing something that you know is a waste of time.

Seven Things You Must Know about Work

1. Know that work is better than rest, because God worked six days and rested one day **(Exodus 20:11).**
2. Understand why too much rest is a negative thing. **(Proverbs 6:10-11)**
3. Know that happiness at work is one of the gifts of God. **(Ecclesiastes 5:19)**
4. Know the things that take away the joy of work. **(Songs 2:15)**
5. It is possible to work without craving for leave. **(John 9:4)**
6. Keep searching till you find your life's work. **(Esther 4:14)**
7. Decide to work rather than to play or to rest. **(Nehemiah 4:6)**

Eight Ways to Identify Your Life's Work

1. Your life's work will give a new meaning to your life.

When you find your life's work, it will give you something more than money. There is more to life than the amount of money you have. King Solomon had all the money in the world yet he said, "Vanity of vanities; all is vanity."

2. Your life's work is something God has called you to.

> **Jesus saith unto them, My meat is to do the will of him that sent me, and to finish his work.**
>
> **John 4:34**

When I followed the call of God on my life, I found my life's work. Many people live and die without beginning their life's work.

3. Your life's work is something that you will not hate.

Solomon hated his work and his life. This is the futility of those whose work is related only to life on this earth. Solomon was depressed and miserable at the end of his life.

Therefore I hated life; because the work that is wrought under the sun is grievous unto me: for all is vanity and vexation of spirit.

> **Yea I hated all my labour which I had taken under the sun: because I should leave it unto the man that shall be after me.**
>
> **Ecclesiastes 2:17-18**

Solomon's wisdom was the wisdom *under the sun* - the wisdom for life on this earth. As far as earthly achievements were concerned, Solomon accomplished very much. But as he approached the gates of eternity, his earthly accomplishments paled into insignificance. Work that focuses on eternity will not leave you depressed.

Queen Margaret of Scotland at the end of her life said, "Shame on life!"

However, the missionary, dying on his ship in the midst of the sea said, "I go with the gladness of a boy bounding from school. I feel so strong in Christ."

Since I entered into full-time ministry, I have not hated my work or my life. When I worked in the secular world, I hated work and I found my life useless. A little analysis of those ahead of me showed me the futility of all my labour. O what a blessing it is for me to have found my life's work!

4. In your life's work, you will enjoy the rewards of your labour.

Many people do not enjoy the fruits of their hard work. They work all day and all night but never sit down to enjoy the simple benefits of life.

> **...every man should eat and drink, and enjoy the good of all his labour, it is the gift of God.**
>
> **Ecclesiastes 3:13**

The gift of God enables you to be happy, enjoy the little pleasures, and rest from your labours. When you find your life's work you will experience all these.

5. In your life's work, money will no longer drive you.

When you find your life's work, money will not matter so much anymore. You will work for the joy of fulfilling God's will.

Like Jesus, you will say, "My meat (satisfaction) is to do the will of Him that sent me."

You will also know that a man's life does not consist in the abundance of things that he possesses (Luke 12:15). You will know that money is elusive and no one ever has enough.

> **He that loveth silver shall not be satisfied with silver; nor he that loveth abundance with increase: this is also vanity.**
>
> **Ecclesiastes 5:10**

6. In your life's work you will not labour in vain.

Working in the world is vanity. Solomon told us that repeatedly. It is working in the Lord that is not vanity. Paul described his work differently. Solomon called his work vanity but Paul said his work was not in vain.

> **Therefore, my beloved brethren, be ye stedfast, unmoveable, always abounding in the work of the Lord, forasmuch as ye know that your labour is not in vain in the Lord.**
>
> **1 Corinthians 15:58**

7. Your life's work makes you become a blessing to others.

As you fulfil God's calling, you will become a blessing to others. God will bless you abundantly and you will help many people.

> **I have shewed you all things, how that so labouring ye ought to support the weak, and to remember the words of the Lord Jesus, how he said, It is more blessed to give than to receive.**
>
> **Acts 20:35**

8. In your life's work your talents will be revealed.

When I worked in the secular world, most of the gifts God had given me were submerged. I was never a leader, I was never appointed to any special position and I did not shine.

In full-time ministry, my abilities and talents have been utilized to the full. I have found a job that taxes my mind and my strength to the uttermost. Working in full-time ministry makes my sleep enjoyable.

> **The sleep of a labouring man is sweet, whether he eat little or much: but the abundance of the rich will not suffer him to sleep.**
>
> **Ecclesiastes 5:12**

Chapter

28

Why Some People Do Not Prosper at Work

CHAPTER SUMMARY

28. 1 You cannot prosper without a calling

28. 2 You cannot prosper with the wrong temperament

28. 3 You cannot prosper in the wrong company

28. 4 You cannot prosper in a meaningless job

28. 5 You cannot prosper working for someone you dislike

28. 6 You cannot prosper without a proper preparation

Some people do not prosper because they are in the wrong job. Even when you are diligent and hardworking, being in a job you are not suited for will destroy you. You will not shine and you will not excel because you are not born for the kind of job you have chosen.

1. You cannot prosper without a calling.

When you are not called to something, you get into all sorts of difficulties. A train is not designed to fly. No matter how it is positioned on the runway, flying is impossible! It was designed to stay on the ground and to move along rail tracks.

It is important that you find your calling because you are designed to do specific things. Many difficulties come from doing jobs that you are not suited for. Functioning in a call which is not your own is like taking an honour which is not yours.

> **And no man taketh this honour unto himself, but he that is called of God…**
>
> **Hebrews 5:4**

2. You cannot prosper with the wrong temperament.

Perhaps this is one of the most important points in this book. In a previous chapter we discussed how each temperament is suited for certain jobs. Make sure that you are doing a job suited to your particular temperament. If you are a choleric person, find a leadership job that is suitable for choleric people. If you are phlegmatic, ask to be excused from jobs that require a driving, leadership personality!

It is in your interest that you work according to your particular temperament. If you do not, you will repeatedly be regarded as a failure.

3. You cannot prosper in the wrong company.

If you do not have to sit with sinners all day long, you are truly blessed. Pray that God will give you people whose company you enjoy.

> **Blessed is the man that walketh not in the counsel of the ungodly, nor standeth in the way of sinners, nor sitteth in the seat of the scornful.**
>
> **Psalms 1:1**

4. You cannot prosper in a meaningless job.

> **Then I looked on all the works that my hands had wrought, and on the labour that I had laboured to do: and, behold, all was vanity and vexation of spirit, and there was no profit under the sun.**
>
> **Ecclesiastes 2:11**

It is unfortunate to have to do a meaningless job. During the Second World War, one of the punishments given to intelligent professors and scientists was the carrying of rocks from one end of a prison yard to the other.

From morning until evening, they carried these rocks to and fro, creating a heap and then taking it apart when it reached a certain height. It was indeed a sore vexation to these honourable men. Some of them went crazy as they did years and years of this meaningless work. Perhaps that is why you are going crazy at your current job.

5. You cannot prosper working for someone you dislike.

> **Surely oppression maketh a wise man mad; and a gift destroyeth the heart.**
>
> **Ecclesiastes 7:7**

It is a painful experience to work for someone you dislike. It is truly a joy to work for someone whose company and leadership you enjoy. I pray that you will find an opportunity to work for someone who does not oppress you.

6. You cannot prosper without a proper preparation.

> **Prepare thy work without, and make it fit for thyself in the field; and afterwards build thine house.**
>
> **Proverbs 24:27**

The lack of preparation makes work a very difficult thing. Preparation is necessary for every job. Sometimes you have not read your notes or prepared adequately. A lack of preparation makes you incapable of your tasks.

This lack of preparation makes work a difficult experience everyday. It is important to prepare yourself adequately so that you will find yourself enjoying the work God has given you.

Chapter

29

How to Have Favour with Your Boss

CHAPTER SUMMARY

29. 1 See him as one who is placed there by God

29. 2 Recognize and relate to him as you would relate with God Himself

29. 3 Be humble towards your boss.

29. 4 Learn all you can about your job

29. 5 Listen to instructions carefully

29. 6 Understand the spirit of the instruction

29. 7 Discover what your boss likes and wants, then do it!

29. 8 Learn what displeases your boss and avoid those things like the plague

29. 9 Learn to anticipate your boss's next move

29. 10 Repeat his instructions to be sure you understand them

29. 11 Start writing when your boss starts speaking

29. 12 Do not be jumbled up and confused in his presence

29. 13 Be dressed properly and decently whenever he is present

29. 14 Do what you are asked to do immediately

29. 15 Never stop routine jobs until instructed

29. 16 Carry out all instructions to their logical conclusion

29. 17 Become your boss's no.1 problem solver

29. 18 Never criticize your boss publicly or privately

29. 19 At all costs, avoid the job of the "office complainer"

29. 20 Never be angry or irritated at new instructions

29. 21 Humbly receive all corrections no matter how long you have been around

29. 22 Be spiritual, be restful and be wise

1. See him as one who is placed there by God.

> **...For there is no authority except from God, and those which exist are established by God.**
>
> **Romans 13:1**

2. Recognize and relate to him as you would relate with God Himself.

Do your work as though you are doing it for the Lord.

> **...with good will doing service, as to the Lord, and not to men:**
>
> **Ephesians 6:7**

3. Be humble towards your boss.

Humility is the only way to promotion in God's house.

> **And whosoever will be chief among you, let him be your servant:**
>
> **Matthew 20:27**

4. Learn all you can about your job.

> **A wise man will hear, and will increase learning; and a man of understanding shall attain unto wise counsels**
>
> **Proverbs 1:5**

There is a lot to learn every day. We will never stop learning until we die. Open your heart and discover all there is to know about your job.

5. Listen to instructions carefully.

Recognize that the person in authority over you knows something that you don't. That is why he is in that position.

> **Hear, ye children, the instruction of a father, and attend to know understanding.**
>
> **Proverbs 4:1**

6. Understand the spirit of the instruction.

Long-winded meetings and lengthy discussions are intended to make you understand your instructions. When you understand the spirit of the instruction, you are able to carry out your orders better.

7. Discover what your boss likes and wants, then do it!

There are certain things that please every important person. They often do not care about many things. Often they look out for just one thing and if you can get that right, you will always be in their good books.

Surprisingly, people do a hundred different things that have not been asked for and leave out the one thing that means everything to the boss.

8. Learn what displeases your boss and avoid those things like the plague.

Notice what angers your boss and learn to avoid them. Understand why he is upset by certain things and discover what to do to avoid them. Like I said, it takes very little to please important people. They do not have time for many things. There are just a few things they notice.

9. Learn to anticipate your boss's next move.

How refreshing it is to have a servant who knows what you will do next. It is like a cool drink on a very hot and sunny day. Anticipating your boss's next move is to think the way he thinks and to plan with him in mind. This ability to anticipate things shows a good level of intelligence and is also a sign of partnership.

10. Repeat his instructions to be sure you understand them.

When you receive instructions, develop a habit of repeating what you have heard to make sure you got it right. Sometimes, a slight variation in understanding the instruction can lead to a disaster.

11. Start writing when your boss starts speaking.

This shows you are smart, intelligent and ready for action., Always have a book ready when he calls. There may be nothing to write, but you must be ready. It is discouraging to give a lot of instructions only to find that nothing has been written by a scatter-brained employee.

12. Do not be jumbled up and confused in his presence.

It is important to be composed and ready for every task. Have your note book and pen at hand at all times so that you do not look silly and disorganized.

13. Be dressed properly and decently whenever he is present.

Throw away clothes that are unacceptable and inappropriate so that even in your most casual moments you will be professional and ready for action.

14. Do what you are asked to do immediately.

There is no better time to start carrying out an instruction than right now. Start immediately! Carry out new instructions first and do routine things later. Your boss's heart will warm up to you when you deal with his urgent requests.

15. Never stop routine jobs until instructed.

Some routine activities will never be checked unless there is some problem or other. Often, it is in a time of crisis that the negligence of routine work is discovered. This is the point at which many people lose their jobs.

16. Carry out all instructions to their logical conclusion.

Every boss wants to hear that the mission is accomplished. No supervisor wants to be told about unsolved problems.

He wants to hear about solutions. He wants to hear how you overcame the obstacles you met. Within one command lies a host of challenges that must be overcome. Every boss is looking for problem solvers. Everyone can narrate a string of unsolved problems but who can solve them?

Solve any problems that come up in the course of doing your job. Just make sure you bring your instructions to a thorough conclusion.

17. Become your boss's no.1 problem solver.

Every boss is attracted to solution-bringers, bridge-builders, problem solvers and accomplishers. Never leave unsolved a problem that you could have solved. The one thing that will devalue you in your boss' eyes is when you do not solve problems. Most bosses know that there are a host of problems to be overcome. That is the very reason why he gave you the job.

18. Never criticize your boss publicly or privately.

It will erode your spiritual relationship with him and open the door for demons. Ask the Israelites what happened to them when they began complaining about Moses. A grumbling employee is a liability and I would advise any leader to dismiss all the grumblers.

19. At all costs, avoid the job of the "office complainer".

There are always people who are not happy about something. They have a chronic spirit of murmuring. Make sure you never become the "office complainer".

20. Never be angry or irritated at new instructions.

Do not be upset when instructions are changed. Do not be angry when instructions are repeated. Your job is to be humble and do what you are told. If you get irritated at a change of instructions, you are probably too big for your job.

21. Humbly receive all corrections no matter how long you have been around.

The longer you stay in a job, the more likely you are to think that you know everything. Humble yourself and receive correction. You may have been around for ten years but there are still things to learn.

22. Be spiritual, be restful and be wise.

When you do not use your time wisely, you never have time to pray. It is important to be prayerful and restful. It makes you wiser and more effective. When you are not restful, you become incomplete, inconclusive and untidy. Watch out! Redeem the time because the days are evil.

Redeeming the time, because the days are evil.

Ephesians 5:16

Spiritual leaders always know those around them who are not spiritual.

Chapter

30

How to Choose between Part-Time and Full-Time Ministry

CHAPTER SUMMARY

Failure or success in the ministry often hinges on whether to be a full-time minister or to be a lay person. There are many people who should be unpaid church workers but are full-time ministers. There are also part-time ministers who should be in full-time ministry.

■ Are You Called to Full-Time Ministry?

30. 1 If you are not called into full-time ministry, God will not give you the anointing for it

30. 2 If God has not called you into full-time ministry, He will not give you the financial support for it

30. 3 If you are not called into full-time ministry, God will not protect you in it

30. 4 You will make a fool of yourself in full-time ministry if you are not called to it

Failure or success in the ministry often hinges on whether to be a full-time minister or to be a lay person. There are many people who should be unpaid church workers but are full-time ministers. There are also part-time ministers who should be in full-time ministry.

When someone called into part-time ministry goes into full-time ministry, he becomes a misfit. He lacks the grace for what he is doing and often misrepresents true ministry. Unfortunately, the church is replete with examples of these errors.

Does the ministry really have to be done on a full-time basis? If it is to be done on a full-time basis, what are the reasons for such a decision? Who should be a full-time minister and who should be a part-time (lay) minister? These are some of the questions this book seeks to address.

Three Ducks in a Vision

Years ago, I was an executive member of a Christian fellowship. Seven people formed the leadership committee.

One day, I had a vision in which I saw three waddling ducks wearing top hats. It was indeed a strange sight. You must know that a top hat is much bigger than the head of a duck.

Obviously, these three ducks were a strange sight to behold. Something was wrong, and something was in the wrong place. Ducks are not supposed to wear hats! Somebody was wearing something he was not supposed to wear.

Somebody in the executive was holding a position he was not supposed to hold. That is what God showed me through this vision.

I began to find out more and to seek God's will concerning this vision. After a while, we discovered that one member of the executive was completely out of place. He did not qualify in the least for the position he held. I do not know how he came to be among us.

By the time we had finished delving into this fellow's issues we had no choice but to ask him to leave the group. It was a painful and embarrassing experience for us all.

I do not wish to go into details, but believe me, the description of a duck wearing a top hat should be enough to explain how inappropriate it was for him to be in the executive.

That is how it is when people are wrongly placed. It is time to move into what God has called you to. You will be rewarded for faithfulness.

If God has called you to full-time ministry, you will be rewarded for doing it faithfully. If He has called you to be a layperson, remain in lay ministry and be faithful.

■ Are You Called to Full-Time Ministry?

1. If you are not called into full-time ministry, God will not give you the anointing for it.

There will be no oil on your head as you attempt to function in a full-time capacity. It will be just like frying an egg without oil. Let thy head lack no ointment (Ecclesiastes 9:8).

2. If God has not called you into full-time ministry, He will not give you the financial support for it.

Such people often lack the financial support that is necessary. God does not support things that he has not ordained. Because these people do not have God's financial support, they wrongly portray the ministry as a place of great lack. Such people make ministry look like the most unfortunate vocation a person could ever have. Such people also cause the priesthood to be despised and relegated to school dropouts and people without a future.

3. If you are not called into full-time ministry, God will not protect you in it.

There are many evils in the ministry. Many temptations and trials await full-time ministers. Lay ministry is like walking on the sandy part of the beach but full-time ministry is like walking on rocks.

God is the only one who can protect you in ministry. People do not survive temptations because they are clever! People do not survive attacks of the enemy because they are morally strong! It is the grace of God that carries us through. You will need God's protection. You cannot make it without God's grace.

4. You will make a fool of yourself in full-time ministry if you are not called to it.

You will incur the wrath of God for not staying in your calling. It is important not to force yourself into areas that you have not been called to.

Saul Forced Himself

Saul was a king and not a priest but he forced himself to do priestly work. Samuel told him that he had been a fool.

> **Therefore I said, "Now the Philistines will come down against me at Gilgal, and I have not asked the favor of the LORD.' SO I FORCED MYSELF and offered the burnt offering."**
>
> **Samuel said to Saul, "YOU HAVE ACTED FOOLISHLY; you have not kept the commandment of the LORD your God, which He commanded you, for now the LORD would have established your kingdom over Israel forever."**
>
> **1 Samuel 13:12-13, NASB**

Uzziah Forced Himself

Another example of someone who forced himself into ministry without invitation was Uzziah, the king. The priests warned that "IT APPERTAINETH NOT ONTO THEE". Azariah the priest told Uzziah that it was a sin for him to operate in the office of a priest. He warned, "You will have no honour from the LORD God" (2 Chronicles 26:18).

> **But when he was strong, his heart was lifted up to his destruction: for he transgressed against the LORD his God, and went into the temple of the LORD to burn incense upon the altar of incense.**

> **And Azariah the priest went in after him, and with him fourscore priests of the LORD, that were valiant men:**
>
> **And they withstood Uzziah the king, and said unto him, It appertaineth not unto thee, Uzziah, to burn incense unto the LORD, but to the priests the sons of Aaron, that are consecrated to burn incense: go out of the sanctuary; for thou hast trespassed; neither shall it be for thine honour from the LORD God.**
>
> **Then Uzziah was wroth, and had a censer in his hand to burn incense: and while he was wroth with the priests, the leprosy even rose up in his forehead before the priests in the house of the LORD, from beside the incense altar.**
>
> **And Azariah the chief priest, and all the priests, looked upon him, and, behold, he was leprous in his forehead, and they thrust him out from thence; yea, himself hasted also to go out, because the LORD had smitten him.**
>
> **And Uzziah the king was a leper unto the day of his death, and dwelt in a several house, being a leper; for he was cut off from the house of the LORD: and Jotham his son was over the king's house, judging the people of the land.**
>
> **2 Chronicles 26:16-21**

This is a somber warning for those who have not been called into such things. The Bible says that "many" are called but it does not say that "all" are called.

Mistakenly in Lay Ministry

On the other hand, lay people who are supposed to be in full-time ministry are equally out of place. Full-time ministry involves abandoning yourself to God's grace. You can no longer trust in your own strength for your life. You now have to depend on God's supernatural supply of finances. God's call cannot be ignored. You ignore what the Lord has asked you to do at your own peril.

Jesus Was in Full-Time Ministry

Our Lord Jesus was a carpenter. At a point, he laid aside carpentry, and branched into preaching, teaching and healing. What would have happened to us if he had continued to build his carpentry career?

> **Have this attitude in yourselves which was also in Christ Jesus…**
>
> **Philippians 2:5, NASB**

Peter Was In Full-Time Ministry

Peter was a fisherman. But a time came when he had to stop fishing and follow the Lord. That was full-time ministry. Peter said,

> **...Behold, we have left everything and followed You.**
>
> **Mark 10:28, NASB**

Paul Was in Full-Time Ministry

Paul was a tent maker. A time came when he gave himself wholly to the Lord and the benefits were seen by all.

> **More than that, I count all things to be loss in view of the surpassing value of knowing Christ Jesus my Lord, for whom I have suffered the loss of all things, and count them but rubbish so that I may gain Christ.**
>
> **Philippians 3:8, NASB**

Paul explained that he had suffered the loss of everything in order to do the work of God. A lay person does not suffer the loss of all things.

A lay person does not suffer the loss of his job, his profession, his prestige, etc. When you come into full-time ministry you will suffer the loss of many things.

You just have to imagine what it would be like if Peter and Paul had continued in their secular professions. It would truly have been the mother of all sins.

We would not have been saved if Jesus had insisted on being a carpenter. The foundations of the church would not have been laid if Peter had insisted on continuing with his fishing business.

I Despised Full-Time Ministry

When God called me into full-time ministry, I knew that it was of paramount importance that I obey. I had been a very successful lay minister. As a lay minister, I had built a church and had a sizeable congregation. I had won many souls without being in full-time ministry.

I actually prided myself in working for God without being paid. I remember one occasion when I stood by the gate of my house talking to my friend Uncle James. I told him how I had won so many souls that week. I also told him how I did not think there was a need to do the ministry on a full-time basis.

However, at the end of 1990 the Lord directed me differently. He said very clearly, "Give thyself wholly to me and to the ministry." At that time I was a doctor turned businessman but I knew then that the Lord wanted me to go all out in the Ministry.

I love obeying the Lord and I find His commands quite exciting. It was a new challenge for me and an exciting one at that. I began what I call full-time ministry from January 1991. I have been serving the Lord full-time ever since. I have never looked back and I have never regretted that decision. I am blessed to be a full-time minister.

You must seek God in full-time ministry so that all His plans will come to pass.

Chapter

31

Accept The Season of Full-Time Ministry

CHAPTER SUMMARY

God sometimes gives very contrasting instructions. "I know both how to be ABASED, and I know how to ABOUND: every where and in all things I am instructed both to be FULL and to be HUNGRY, both to ABOUND and to SUFFER NEED" (Philippians 4:12) Paul explains that he had received instructions from the Lord. Once he was asked to be full, at another time he was asked to be hungry. Sometimes he was asked to be abased and at other times he was asked to abound. Questioning God will not help you. Learning to bend, to flow, to yield and to give in will help you in your walk with God.

> **To every thing there is a season, and a time to every purpose under the heaven:**
>
> **Ecclesiastes 3:1**

The Moving Pillar

The children of Israel had to learn to follow the moving pillar of God. There were times the cloud would stay in a place and all the Israelites would camp there. There were times the cloud would move on.

> **The LORD was going before them in a pillar of cloud by day to lead them on the way, and in a pillar of fire by night to give them light, that they might travel by day and by night.**
>
> **Exodus 13:21, NASB**

Why did it stay sometimes and why did it move on other days? Somebody would have said, "Can't God make up His mind? Does He want us to stay or go? Are we little children to be tossed to and fro? God! Make up Your mind! Are we travelling by day or by night?"

Questioning God will not help you. Learning to bend, to flow, to yield and to give in will help you in your walk with God.

In my walk with God, I have found that there is no fixed method by which God operates. You simply need to put your ear to Heaven and to receive daily guidance from the Holy Spirit. In your ministry, there may be a season for lay people to do a substantial portion of the pastoral work. However, there may be another season for full-time workers to take up the mantle.

Some years ago, there were hardly any full-time workers in my ministry. Most of the work was done by lay people. The lay people were fantastic champions who built churches in many countries of the world.

But a time came when the Lord began to lead me to increase the number of full-time workers. On one occasion, he asked me to employ twenty more people. I did not know what work these twenty people would do. I resisted the Lord but He repeated the instruction until I obeyed Him. Mysteriously, we needed far more than twenty new employees.

The Cloud Moves

As the years have gone by, the emphasis of my ministry has shifted from lay people to full-time people. Large sections of the outreaches and new missions are run by full-time ministers.

The Lord told me about how He had shifted the mantle from the lay ministry to full-time ministry.

I Called for Full-Time Workers

As led by the Spirit, I began to encourage people to come into full-time ministry. For a season, God gave me messages that centred on coming into full-time ministry.

I preached powerful messages about being set free from working for Pharaoh (a type of Satan and the world system).

I preached about sacrifice and the need to take up the cross.

I taught a series on "proton" in which I encouraged them to choose God first.

I taught on another Greek word "Bebelos" (which means, to despise sacred things) and admonished them not to despise working for God in the ministry.

I taught on the parables of Jesus and how the kingdom was a treasure for which everything must be sacrificed. There was a frantic call for all-out commitment.

Sadly, large sections of the lay fraternity rejected this call. I tried so hard to personally recruit people to join the sacred group of full-time priests. I shared visions and dreams. I read poems to the pastors and the church. I wept over some of them asking what greater honour they wanted from the Lord?

Amazingly, I had very little response from the oldest and most faithful lay pastors. Most of them could not make the transition to full-time ministry.

Enter the Outsiders

In the end, a completely new group of people came from nowhere in response to my frantic calls. They were mostly new and unfamiliar faces. They were young, unknown and untested people.

Many of them were women with little or no pastoral capabilities. Naturally, many of them were not welcomed by the old guard. They steadily filled the places that I thought belonged to my older, faithful lay pastors.

The season had changed, but many could not see what was happening. God was moving on! The same God who had instructed us to do the lay ministry was instructing us to launch into full-time ministry. The God who had anointed me to write a book on lay people and the ministry was leading me to recruit full-time ministers.

The same God who instructed Paul to abase, was now instructing him to abound.

Lamb or Lion

Jesus Christ is both a lamb and a lion. In the book of Revelation, He is called "the Lamb of God that taketh away the sins of the world". However, He is also called "the Lion of the tribe of Judah". Dear friend, a lion is very different from a lamb. Can the same person that appeared as a lion, also appear as a lamb?

It is so important to understand this principle. It is amazing to find these completely contrasting descriptions in the same passage.

And one of the elders said to me, "Stop weeping; behold, THE LION that is from the tribe of Judah, the Root of David, has overcome so as to open the book and its seven seals."

And I saw between the throne (with the four living creatures) and the elders A LAMB standing, as if slain, having seven horns and seven eyes, which are the seven Spirits of God, sent out into all the earth.

Revelation 5:5-6, NASB

If you told people to expect a lamb and then a lion showed up, there would be chaos! The kind of preparations you need to handle the visit of a lion are different from what you need to handle a lamb. Preaching about the lion will sound very different from preaching about a lamb.

When you are used to "lamb sermons" and your pastor comes up with a "lion sermon", you are likely to say he has changed or backslidden. But perhaps you are the one who does not have the heart to flow and yield to the Spirit.

Killing the Messiah

The children of Israel prayed for the Messiah for years and years but when He appeared, they put Him to death. They could not recognize the answer to their own prayer. Jesus walked with the two disciples on the road to Emmaus but they could not recognize Him because He appeared in a different form. Notice the Scripture:

> **After that HE APPEARED IN ANOTHER FORM unto two of them, as they walked, and went into the country.**
>
> **Mark 16:12**

If Jesus appeared in another form, would you recognize Him? Perhaps you can only recognize Jesus in a particular form. It is time to be flexible and see when God is working in different ways. Perhaps you only recognize the lay ministry. Perhaps you only recognize full-time ministry. It is time to recognize Jesus in whichever form He appears.

Chapter

32

Seven Wrong Perceptions About Full-Time Ministry

CHAPTER SUMMARY

32. 1	Wrong perception #1:	There is nothing important to do in ministry
32. 2	Wrong perception #2:	The ministry is not actually work
32. 3	Wrong perception #3:	Full-time ministry is a step downwards
32. 4	Wrong perception #4:	Full-time workers have a lot of time on their hands
32. 5	Wrong perception #5:	Ministry can be done after retirement
32. 6	Wrong perception #6:	Ministry does not require educated people
32. 7	Wrong perception #7:	Full-time ministry makes you an insignificant member of society

To many outsiders, the concept of being in full-time ministry is absurd. "What is there to do?" they ask. "Can't I come at the weekend to help the church? Do I really have to leave my job? Is it necessary to go to such extremes? We must be cautious! We must be careful! We must not take drastic and emotional decisions!"

1. Wrong perception #1: There is nothing important to do in ministry.

To many lay people, full-time ministry is unnecessary. They do not see why such a move is necessary. This is why I teach about the mysterious purposes of full-time ministry.

I call it mysterious because it is not easy to see what there is to be done in the house of God.

A Lazy Priest?

After all, the church looks like a place where a lazy priest offers sleepy prayers to God all week. At the weekend, this priest will conduct one funeral service, one wedding and one christening. He will then read out his sermon on Sunday and return to his home to continue his long rest!

Why should a doctor, lawyer, or the treasurer of a bank leave their important careers only to work in such a place as a church?

I do not blame anyone who thinks it is not worth it. That is the picture you may have from the outside. The kingdom of Heaven is like a treasure hidden in a field. There are many hidden things about the kingdom of God. Even the work that has to be done is not obvious. The purpose for anyone being in full-time ministry is indeed mysterious.

Jesus said, if you do my will THEN you will know that it is good. Knowing the greatness of the will of God comes by doing it and not just by reading about it. Somehow, it was only after working in full-time ministry that I truly appreciated the work of a priest.

> **If anyone is willing to do His will, he will know of the teaching, whether it is of God or whether I speak from Myself.**
>
> **John 7:17, NASB**

It is only when you actually enter full-time ministry that you will discover what it is. That is when you will know God's mysterious purpose for full-time ministry.

2. Wrong perception #2: The ministry is not actually work.

When I started full-time ministry, my wife was often asked, "So your husband doesn't work anymore?" There is a perception that ministry is not work.

That is why people want to be counselled on the pastor's day-off. They do not understand that to counsel someone is actually work.

I Will Come in the Afternoon

Some years ago, a lady applied for a job in the ministry. We finally agreed that she should work with us and even gave her a letter of appointment. A few days before she was to start work, she received a job offer from some other organization. To my surprise, she accepted the other job and asked whether she could do the church's work on some afternoons and weekends. I was taken aback.

I realized that this lady did not appreciate the amount of work she would have to do in the ministry. I told her, "I do not think you are ready for full-time ministry."

Somehow, this lady did not even understand why I rejected her proposal to work in the church in the afternoons. I realized that she did not appreciate what full-time ministry was.

3. Wrong perception #3: Full-time ministry is a step downwards.

Moving from secular work into full-time ministry is a step upwards. It is not a step downwards! The Apostle Paul said that he counted all things as dung for the excellency of the knowledge of Christ.

This means that to set aside your medical, legal or engineering profession is the same as flushing away your faeces. No one cries when he flushes away his faeces (unless he is suffering from coprophilia).

To set aside your job as the treasurer of a bank and to take up ministry is like dumping a bag of faeces and taking up a bag of diamonds!

4. Wrong perception #4: Full-time workers have a lot of time on their hands.

That is why full-time workers are sometimes treated as though they are not employed. Relatives and friends of full-time workers love to send them on different errands. Some full-time ministers are made to baby-sit and do house chores by their spouses. These spouses despise ministry and that is why they assign an array of odd jobs to their partners.

5. Wrong perception #5: Ministry can be done after retirement.

Many people would like to work for God but they want to do it after they have accomplished something else. They give their best years to their lofty secular goals and ambitions. They hope that God's work will be waiting for them when they finally retire!

After all God's work can wait! It is not that important. Do you think God can wait for you? I am sorry, God cannot wait for anyone! Souls are dying. Thousands of souls would have died and gone to Hell by the time you finish fulfilling your dreams.

By the time you are older, you will be less active, less energetic, slower, more easily tired, full of the sicknesses of middle age, less able to learn new things, unable to do a full day's work, heavily in debt, and GENERALLY LESS USEFUL TO GOD!

Why do you want to give God an expired and worn out vessel? Give that to the bank!! Give that to the corporate world!! It is time to give your best to God!

It may shock you to know that God has his own retirement package. He also wants young, fresh, able-bodied people to serve in His temple.

GOD DOES NOT WANT THE LEFTOVERS AND REJECTS OF THE WORLD TO BE HIS PRINCIPAL WORKERS.

He defined the age bracket of His workers and asked Moses to retire priests after a certain age. Amazingly, the prime period for doing God's work is between the ages of twenty-five and fifty.

Shockingly, the retirement age for priests is even lower than the world's retirement age.

> **Then the LORD spoke to Moses, saying, "This is what pertains to the Levites: From twenty-five years old and above one may enter to perform service in the work of the tabernacle of meeting; And at the age of fifty years they must cease performing this work, and shall work no more. They may minister with their brethren in the tabernacle of meeting, to attend to needs, but they themselves shall do no work. Thus you shall do to the Levites regarding their duties.**
>
> **Numbers 8:23-26, NKJV**

Yet another Scripture gives the age of doing God's work as between the ages of thirty and fifty.

> **Take a census of the descendants of Kohath from among the sons of Levi, by their families, by their fathers' households, FROM THIRTY YEARS AND UPWARD, EVEN TO FIFTY YEARS OLD, all who enter the service to do the work in the tent of meeting.**
>
> **Numbers 4:2-3, NASB**

God wants the best for His church. The grey-haired men and women of wisdom have a role in the church. The retirees of this world also have their place in God's house. But the prime work of ministry is to be done by able-bodied people between the ages of twenty-five and fifty. For-... for-... for-... forgive!

6. Wrong perception #6: Ministry does not require educated people.

Many people think that ministry does not require educated or intelligent people. Ministry is considered a job for dropouts and a haven for the intellectually less endowed. Why should God's work have such educated people?

God gave us the dearest and the best. He gave us Jesus Christ. Jesus was nailed on the tree for you and for me. If the dearest and the best gave Himself, should we not give our best to Him? I believe that the dearest and the best kind of people must be given to the service of God.

7. Wrong perception #7: Full-time ministry makes you an insignificant member of society.

When a person says, "I am the Managing Director of such and such a company" he sounds important.

When he says, "I am the Treasurer of Barclays Bank" he sounds very important.

But when he says, "I work in a church" he seems to have lost his lustre.

Most of the time there is little glamour associated with the work of the ministry. But in reality, ministry is the most important job in society.

Where Millionaires Kneel

Someone said to his son who was entering full-time ministry, "You are doing the right thing."

He continued, "It is only in the church that a millionaire can be asked to kneel down and have hands laid on him."

No millionaire will kneel down before his bank manager, he explained. But in the church the millionaire will kneel down before his pastor for prayer.

Chapter

33

Why You Must Choose Full-Time Ministry

CHAPTER SUMMARY

God will show us what is good and what is required of us. We cannot do His work in our own way. It is His work and it must be done His way, using His methods. Full-time ministry is God's ordained method of administering His church. No one is wiser than God is.

> **He hath shewed thee, O man, what is good; and what doth the LORD require of thee...**
>
> **Micah 6:8**

I believe there was a time I thought I knew better than God on this matter. Mercy! Forgive!

I was a successful lay pastor and had started a church that was growing. I was called Reverend and even had assistant pastors. I was winning souls on a weekly basis through dawn broadcasts, crusades and other programmes.

I prided myself in the fact that I was not a financial burden to the church. Our church was not under any kind of financial pressure and the wisdom of lay ministry was working well.

Did I Know Better than God?

One day, I travelled to Geneva and had a discussion with an American Pastor who had a ministry there. At a point, I told him that I was not paid by my church.

I proudly explained how I supported myself in the ministry. He listened to me and seemed to be impressed.

I told him, "We don't receive tithes and sometimes we don't even take offerings. We do not burden our church financially in any way."

However, at a point, he said, "You are not wiser than God. God has ordained His church to run in a certain way."

He continued, "There is a blessing that comes on a congregation when they pay tithes." He explained how there is a blessing in accepting God's method of running His own church.

Somehow, this conversation stayed with me and I began to study and to seek for God's ordained method of running his church.

Lay Ministry Is Not God's Ordained Way

> **Even so hath the Lord ORDAINED that they which preach the gospel should live of the gospel.**
>
> **1 Corinthians 9:14**

When something is ordained to be a certain way, it means it is intended, predestined and designed to be that way. God intended and designed that preachers should be paid for preaching the Gospel.

Preaching without being paid is a special arrangement that God allows and blesses at certain times. The Apostle Paul practised this unpaid style of lay ministry better than anyone else. But he is the one who also taught that God's intended method of running the ministry was for pastors to be paid from the work they do.

Lay ministry cleverly removes the burden of looking after priests. It is a wise and helpful method of building a church. I have actually written a book about Lay Ministry. I believe in the lay ministry and have not changed my doctrine. However, God's Word contains many different things, which sometimes look contradictory to the unlearned.

Lay ministry and full-time ministry do not contradict each other. Actually, they complement each other.

The wisdom of lay ministry does not cancel out the need for full-time ministry. Full-time ministry is a ministry of "priests" and "helpers of priests" who work in the temple.

These priests are supported by the offerings and gifts brought to the Lord by the people. The full-time *priests* and *helpers* of priests are to live off the gifts and sacrifices in the temple.

■ Living off the Gospel

> **Do ye not know that they which minister about holy things live of the things of the temple? and they which wait at the altar are partakers with the altar?**
>
> **Even so hath THE LORD ORDAINED THAT THEY WHICH PREACH THE GOSPEL SHOULD LIVE OF THE GOSPEL.**
>
> **1 Corinthians 9:13-14**

God has ordained priests to live off their jobs as preachers. "So also the Lord directed those who proclaim the gospel to get their living from the Gospel" (1 Corinthians 9:14, NASB). This is a very humbling thing for people who could have had other jobs.

It sounds nicer to say, "I earn money from my secular job and I work for God without charge." It sounds very sacrificial indeed!

But it is better to accept God's method of running His church than to do anything else. Don't forget that obedience is better than sacrifice.

■ Is a Salary from the Church Stolen Money?

Living off a church salary is a little different from living off a salary from the bank. Living a life that depends on offerings and gifts can be even more unsettling.

It seems more acceptable to drive a car you bought whilst working in the bank. Sometimes living in a nice home that was acquired through church money does not seem right. It is almost as though you are using pilfered goods.

But it is important to accept God's ordained method of administering His church and looking after His priests. Are you called of God? Does God want you to be in full-time ministry? Then get ready to live a different kind of life.

■ Why Preachers Earn Money

1. Every true minister is worthy of his pay.

> **Do not acquire gold, or silver, or copper for your money belts, or a bag for your journey, or even two tunics, or sandals, or a staff; for the worker is WORTHY of his support.**
>
> **Matthew 10:9-10, NASB**

This verse means that a preacher *ought to have* support. He has *earned* an income. It means he is *justified to receive* money and he truly merits it.

2. Ordained preachers are to live off their jobs as preachers.

God wants His preachers to live in a particular way. He wants to provide for them and pay them Himself for preaching His Word.

3. God has changed the way preachers earn money.

Jesus called His disciples and changed their professions. They lived by fishing. He offered them a new way of making money - winning souls.

> **As He was going along by the Sea of Galilee, He saw Simon and Andrew, the brother of Simon, casting a net in the sea; for they were fishermen.**
>
> **And Jesus said to them, "Follow Me, and I will make you become fishers of men..."**
>
> **Mark 1:16-17, NASB**

4. Anyone who refuses God's ordained method is choosing his own way.

Every true minister must desire to walk in what God has prescribed for His priests.

> **There is a way which seemeth right unto a man, but the end thereof are the ways of death.**
>
> **Proverbs 14:12**

5. Living a life dependent on income from preaching is one of the signs that you are a priest.

The true priests of God lived in this way. Your method of acquiring possessions such as a home, a car, etc, shows where you work.

> **But I have used none of these things: neither have I written these things, that it should be so done unto me: for it were better for me to die, than that any man should make my glorying void.**
>
> **1 Corinthians 9:15**

Paul declared that though he could have benefited materially from his work as a priest he did not. He did not want anyone to speak evil of his ministry.

6. Preachers deserve the benefits they receive.

> **And remain in the same house, eating and drinking what they provide, for the laborer deserves his wages...**
>
> **Luke 10:7, RSV**

The eating and the drinking of a true preacher must be at the expense of those preached to. Those are the instructions of our Saviour.

Jesus explains why pastors should eat and drink at the expense of their hosts. He said, "You deserve it."

After ministering, you deserve to be paid. Jesus said preachers deserve salaries!

I deserve to be paid for preaching, teaching, writing, ministering, counselling, encouraging people, talking to people, praying for people, and the list goes on!

Preachers deserve cars, houses, servants and food!

All these are products of wages!

Do not let anyone deceive you with false humility and self-righteousness!

7. Full-time ministers are supposed to collect money from the people.

> **And those indeed of the sons of Levi who receive the priest's office have commandment in the Law TO COLLECT a tenth from the people, that is, from their brethren, although these are descended from Abraham.**
>
> **Hebrews 7:5, NASB**

The King James Version says priests are COMMANDED TO TAKE TITHES from the people.

Taking and collecting tithes is actually a direct command from God. That means that it is a sin not to collect these tithes. Do not let any worldly person move you away from God's ordained and prescribed method.

8. It is better to obey than to sacrifice your wages.

Samuel replied,

> **Has the Lord as much pleasure in your burnt offerings and sacrifices as in your obedience? OBEDIENCE IS FAR BETTER THAN SACRIFICE. He is much more interested in your listening to him than in your offering the fat of rams to him.**
>
> **1 Samuel 15:22, TLB**

You will be more pleasing to God if you humbly receive your wages than if you make any unwanted sacrifices. Not all commands of God involve suffering and pain. Do not be wiser than God!

Chapter

34

How God Called Me to "Give Myself Wholly"

CHAPTER SUMMARY

At the end of 1990 the Lord spoke to me. He said, "From now on, I want you to give yourself wholly to my work." I knew what that meant. He explained that if I gave myself completely to the work of God my "profiting" would appear to all. That meant that people would see my progress in ministry.

> **...GIVE THYSELF WHOLLY to them; that thy profiting may appear to all.**
>
> **1 Timothy 4:15**
>
> **...throw yourself into your tasks so that EVERYONE MAY NOTICE YOUR IMPROVEMENT AND PROGRESS.**
>
> **1 Timothy 4:15, TLB**

Armed with this Scripture, I launched into full-time ministry in January of 1991. I have been in full-time ministry, totally dedicated to kingdom business since then. I can say that my little progress and improvement has become evident to some people. The fact that you are reading this book attests to this fact.

Unfortunately, many give themselves half-heartedly to the ministry. That is why they do not make significant strides in it. If you suggested to your boss that you would come to work twice a week in the evenings, do you think he would accept you? Certainly not! The inputs you can make by giving a couple of evenings is different from what you can do when you spend the whole day working. Suggest to your boss that you will work for him only on Sunday afternoons and see if he will keep you. Your value to him would drop sharply.

By this same logic, your value to God is reduced if you are available to Him only on Sunday afternoons. God wants to have people who work for Him during the day and not only in the evenings. Why do you want to be a night officer for Christ?

To give yourself wholly to the Lord means to give everything you are and everything you possess to Jesus. How do you give everything to God? What does it mean to give yourself wholly to the Lord?

1. "Give thyself wholly" means to give your heart.

Many people who work in the secular world have not given their hearts to what they are doing. To give yourself wholly means you must first of all give your heart. Whilst working in the government hospital, I noticed that many of the doctors did not give their hearts to what they were doing. Most of them were looking for an opportunity to leave the country.

Prostitutes give their bodies to their clients but they do not give their hearts. One of the rules of prostitutes is to never kiss a client. Doing something physically does not mean that your heart is in it. Full-time ministry is not something you can do without giving your heart.

This is why full-time ministry is not the same as taking up another secular job. It is the giving of your heart to God. It is the pouring out of your soul into God's work and leaving nothing behind!

People who work in the bank are not pouring out their souls. They are merely looking for more money and higher positions. When you give your heart to the Lord's work, you will see the difference.

2. "Give thyself wholly" means to give your mind, intelligence and ideas.

Full-time ministry involves bringing your intelligence to bear on God's work. Intelligence is not only required in banks, hospitals, science laboratories, political parties, factories, law firms, farms and consultancies. Intelligence is required to do God's work. God's work is not the lowest calling. It is the highest calling! It is the greatest job! Maybe you have despised God's work and given your intelligence and ideas to the building of earthly institutions.

Instead of God's kingdom benefiting from your clever suggestions, it is political parties and banks that do. They make more money and accomplish more of their goals by using your ideas. God could equally use your intelligence and creativity.

I did very well in school. In 1982, there were hundreds of applicants for the only accredited medical school in Ghana. In order of merit, I was the fifth person in the whole country to be interviewed for entry into the medical school.

Whilst in medical school, I earned a distinction and won a prize, which was given to the two best students in the fifth year. God had truly blessed me with intelligence through which I became a medical doctor.

After seven years of medical training and a year of housemanship, God called me to apply the intelligence He had given me to ministry. After all, it was the Lord who had given me everything I had. It was the Lord who had made me excel in school. As the Scripture says,

> **For who maketh thee to differ from another? and what hast thou that thou didst not receive? now if thou didst receive it, why dost thou glory, as if thou hadst not received it?**
>
> **1 Corinthians 4:7**

The kingdom needs intelligent, educated people who can make a difference. To be successful in ministry you will need more than the anointing and miracles. You will need intelligence, good ideas and creativity. I believe that throwing in the numerous good ideas and thinking abilities God has given me has made a difference to the ministry.

God has blessed me with a number of highly educated and intelligent professionals who make a lot of difference to the ministry. Actually, these clever people are gifts given to me by the Lord. They make such a difference to all that happens in our church. They have humbly acknowledged that what they are is just a gift from God.

Indeed, it is a privilege to be called upon to serve the Master with the intellect He has given you.

3. "Give thyself wholly" means to give your education and training.

After being educated and trained by Pharaoh, Moses launched out into God's will and built Israel into a nation. Obviously, he was trained in Pharaoh's palace to rule and to govern nations. Your education and training will be useful to God.

When I entered full-time ministry, people were aghast, saying, "How could you abandon your medical profession and become a pastor?" They said this only because they despised God's work.

Sadly, the kingdom of God is despised and is esteemed to be worthy of only emotionally unstable and uneducated people.

Five Doctors Become Presidents

As I write this book, I know of five medical doctors who have launched campaigns to become the president of Ghana. One of them is an obstetrician/gynaecologist who used to live and work in America. Another is a cardio-thoracic surgeon who used to live and work in Germany. The third one is a pathologist who used to live and work in England. The fourth is practising medicine in the U.S.A. The fifth of these has his own medical practice in one of the cities of Ghana.

It is interesting that these highly trained specialists are not criticized for leaving their field of training to jump into politics. Even though politics is what we know it to be, no one seems to think that it is a waste of their education and training. The ministry is an even higher calling. It is a demanding job, which requires intelligent, well-trained people to give of themselves. Currently, I work with some twelve medical doctors who have set aside medicine for the ministry.

Their training in medicine makes them more capable to do the tasks set before them. I am proud of them and blessed to have such noble people join me in this great calling.

I also have at least eight lawyers who have set aside their law practice to take up ministry.

The list goes on and I could tell you of pharmacists, architects, engineers, IT consultants, bankers and accountants who work full-time in the ministry. They are fully engaged in building God's kingdom by applying their education and training to their new tasks.

4. "Give thyself wholly" means to give your personality and temperament.

God has made us all differently. Some people are choleric, others are melancholic, others sanguine and yet others phlegmatic. A choleric is good at work involving leadership. A melancholic person is good at work involving details and administration. A sanguine is good at work that involves human relations and the phlegmatic is the best at steady and monotonous jobs. All these features are God-given and are important for the progress of any venture.

Businesses, banks and corporations employ people based on these natural abilities. Temperament tests are done routinely by Human Resource Departments.

To give yourself wholly is to take whatever temperament you have and apply it to the church. There are several areas of work, which require your particular temperament. I place people mainly according to their temperaments.

Why do you want to give your God-given temperament to the world? Is it not the greatest opportunity to give something back to God? Do you feel that giving it to the world is more worthwhile? It is time to stop despising the church. Let's give ourselves wholly to the Lord.

God made me choleric and melancholic. When I was in school, I was not seen as anything special. I was never chosen to be a prefect or a leader. But God who created me and put within me my temperament, chose me to be a leader for His people. I could have used my God-given ability to build a bank or a nightclub.

He Built Nightclubs

I recently met a young man who had great leadership abilities. He had built a well-known computer firm and was doing very well. One day, I needed to see him and we set up an appointment in his office.

When we got there, I asked him, "What goes on here? I thought this was your office."

He answered, "Actually, this is a night club as well. Daytime for certain things and night-time for the night club."

"Wow," I said. "I did not know you were into night clubs. Does your wife come here sometimes?"

"Not really, she does not enjoy night life much," he answered.

Some weeks later, I happened to be in another town ministering in one of our churches. When I looked out of the window, I saw a building with a familiar sign and I asked. "What is that building and what do they do there?"

"Oh, it's a night club belonging to so and so."

To my amazement it belonged to the same person. I realized that this man had built a chain of night clubs.

The question is, what will you use your God-given temperaments and abilities for? You can use your gifts to build nightclubs, banks or businesses. I choose to use my abilities to build churches!

Melancholism at Work

God made me melancholic. I often find myself analyzing things and thinking deeply about issues. This ability helped me to analyze loyal and disloyal behaviour, even when it was not obvious.

It has contributed to the things that I have taught over the years. A conversation, which means nothing to someone, becomes a revelation to me because of this analytic gift.

I also find myself arranging and reorganizing what needs to be reorganized. This melancholic nature has helped me to administer and manage churches in different countries of the world.

I have been able to organize many things at the same time because of this "grace" of melancholism. To give yourself wholly is to pour everything you are into God's work until the benefits are seen.

5. "Give thyself wholly" means to give your family.

To give yourself wholly also means to give your family to the Lord. Sadly, there are many ministers who do not want their children to be in the ministry. The Levites served the Lord with their entire families. Their wives and children belonged to the service of God's tabernacle. Give your husband, wife and children to God! Some ministers withhold their wives and use them as a business outreach to make money on the side. They fulfil their secular and business dreams through their wives.

It is important that we examine our hearts and see whether we have given ourselves wholly to God's will. Ask yourself: "If ministry is a good thing, why do I not want my child to be a minister?"

Why do you want him to be a pilot or a lawyer rather than a minister of the Gospel? Do you not believe in your own profession?

6. "Give thyself wholly" means to give your background.

Everybody has a family. We all come from somewhere. This fact was seen even in the life of Jesus. The genealogy of Christ goes to great lengths to describe his origins and heritage. He was the lion of the tribe of Judah and not the lion of the tribe of Benjamin. Christ came from Judah and not from Reuben. Where do you come from? It affects you and your calling!

To give yourself wholly means to allow all that is in your background to help the ministry advance. Your background is one of God's gifts to you. It will enable you to do things that no one else can.

The Half-Caste

I am half-caste. Because of this background, there are certain things I cannot do. In my home, Ghanaian languages were not spoken. English was the language my father spoke to my mother. This limited my ministry's entry into certain areas of the country. It was difficult to establish churches where English was not spoken. It took us years to make a headway in these places.

However, the English-speaking nature of our ministry gave me great access to international fields. I found myself easily establishing churches in other countries. After a while, I realized that my background had played a role in what I could accomplish.

7. "Give thyself wholly" means to give your time.

Many people who work in the secular world do not give themselves wholly to their work. They look forward to the end of the working day and yearn for holidays. When I worked in the hospital, I longed for the end of the day.

I longed to get away from the wards and the clinics. I dreamed of holidays where I would not have to come to this dreary hospital. I counted the available holidays in the year and complained about the brevity of the leave period.

Giving God a daily ten-minute prayer time and a weekly two-hour Sunday morning service is not full-time ministry. Full-time ministry is much more than that. It is to give all of your time to the Lord.

One brother who had worked in a gold mine for years remarked, "I had never worked so hard till I came to work in the ministry. When I worked for the gold mine we would close at five o'clock and I would drop everything and leave. I never thought about the office until I got back the next day."

He continued, "Now, I take work home with me and the work never ends. It's day and night and it goes on and on."

That is how full-time ministry is. All of your time is given to God.

My ministry does not end when I walk out of church. My mind is always on God and His work. There is nothing like a closing time for me. Every moment and everyday belongs to Him now. I do not think of going on leave anymore, neither do I think of retirement.

8. "Give thyself wholly" means to give your money and your assets.

When I began in the ministry, my car was the church bus. My personal stereo became the church's public address system. You have to put everything into the ministry if it is to work. There is a certain throwing in of everything that is necessary for success in ministry. What are you withholding from the Lord?

Looking back at my life, I realize how much I have thrown into the ministry. I threw in office equipment that I owned. I used my father's office as the church's office. I made all my money and everything I owned available for God's work. I believe that all this is part of *giving thyself wholly.*

9. "Give thyself wholly" means to give your energy.

You will experience tiredness in ministry. But I call it sweet exhaustion. You are tired but there is joy bubbling in your heart. It is said that the world is run by tired men. I can assure you that real ministry involves much hard work.

> *One day, a friend of mine visited Sierra Leone. He told me how he found several of the peacekeeping soldiers involved in different businesses. Some of them had become taxi drivers and others were involved in diamond mining. So I asked, "How do soldiers who are supposed to be fighting and keeping the peace become taxi drivers and diamond miners?"*
>
> *He answered, "They don't want to die a foolish death."*
>
> *I asked, "What is a foolish death?"*
>
> *He explained, "They are frustrated with a hopeless war and see no reason why they should die for a worthless cause."*

You see, these soldiers sensed the inconsequential nature of the battle they were involved in. They knew that if they were to die they would have sacrificed themselves for nothing.

In the ministry, that feeling of chasing worthless goals goes away. The emptiness that comes with heaping up unusable treasures is gone. There is a great motivation to pour out your energy and your very life for an eternal cause.

10. "Give thyself wholly" means to give your life.

Many people have died on their jobs. Some of them died at work and in the course of duty. Soldiers die at work! Police officers on duty are killed all the time! Numerous doctors are infected with viruses and germs from their patients!

Businessmen and politicians die of stress and heart attacks. Pilots die in plane crashes and the list goes on. All these deaths are related to their jobs.

To give yourself wholly means to work for God even if you lose your life. It means to be ready to die doing His will.

When you give yourself wholly, you will be prepared to be a missionary in dangerous countries. There are many things in the ministry that will expose you to danger but in full-time ministry you can give yourself wholly to dangerous things.

The Airline Steward

Some time ago, I offered a job to an airline steward. He accepted the ministry opportunity but said he would have to speak to his father. His father was not happy that his son would work in a church and indicated that he would like to talk with me about it.

This man wanted to talk me out of his son's employment. But I refused to speak to the young man's father.

I made it clear that I would be prepared to speak to the father if it was about salvation, the Holy Spirit or any spiritual problem.

But if the discussion was about his son's employment then I would not to speak to him. My reasoning was simple.

When this steward applied to work for the airline his father did not ask to see the Managing Director of the airline.

Apart from being almost bankrupt, this airline was known to be dangerous and poorly maintained.

Was it not more dangerous for his son to work for this airline than for him to work in the church? Why did this father want to speak to me to prevent his son from working for the Lord? People simply have no respect for the church!s

People risk their children's lives everyday and take no thought of it. Many do jobs which are dangerous and life-threatening. They do these heartily and without a second thought. However, when it comes to the work of God, the risks seem to be too high! Giving yourself wholly to God includes giving your life to the Master even if you lose it.

Chapter

35

The Mysterious Purposes of Full-Time Ministry

CHAPTER SUMMARY

It is important to magnify the ministry. Full-time ministry is important. It is the priesthood. It is the fulfilling of the call of God. Full-time ministers are the New Testament Levites. Full-time ministry is mysterious in that it is not easy to perceive or even faintly quantify what a priest does to occupy himself all day long and everyday of the year. Yet, it is the highest calling and the most important work that a person could be involved in. I can confirm this to be a reality.

This section of the book will help you to understand some of the hidden purposes, which are accomplished through full-time ministry.

It is time to magnify full-time ministry. I have magnified the lay ministry for years and many have taken that road. As Paul said,

> **But I am speaking to you who are Gentiles. Inasmuch then as I am an apostle of Gentiles, I magnify my ministry**
>
> **Romans 11:13**

Paul made his ministry important by stressing on it and teaching about it.

> **As you know, God has appointed me as a special messenger to you Gentiles. I lay great stress on this and remind the Jews about it as often as I can,**
>
> **Romans 11:13, TLB**

Because of the mystique surrounding the work of a priest, little is known about it. That is why I am writing this book.

1. Enter full-time ministry to avoid the neglect of your gift.

> **NEGLECT NOT the gift that is in thee...**
>
> **1 Timothy 4:14**

Many gifts will be neglected until you give yourself wholly to them! Because these gifts are spiritual, it is not easy to see that they are being neglected. This is one of the reasons why God is calling you to full-time ministry. He wants you to have time to attend to the spiritual gifts and callings on your life.

The first thing I noticed when I entered full-time ministry was how free I was to travel to plant churches and to do the work of God. Without being in full-time ministry, I would not have been able to attend to the work of planting churches. There is no secular job that would accommodate my absence from work for such long periods. It may not be apparent to you, but many things are neglected because people do not give themselves wholly to the ministry.

So Busy in Ministry

One of the mysterious things about my full-time staff is that they are so busy and have hardly any time for anything else. It makes you wonder about what was happening to the issues they attend to now. Obviously, those things were being neglected until they came along to attend to them fully.

> *One medical doctor now in full-time ministry remarked, "I am so busy now and I have no time for anything else."*
>
> *He continued, "Yet, a year ago I was equally busy running my hospital."*
>
> *He said, "It's amazing. There is so much work to be done and I was busy elsewhere."*

You see, God's work lies largely undone and neglected. God is calling many to come into His service and do His work and nothing else.

Is There Anything to Do?

When you are a layperson, the largeness of the work to be done is not apparent. Somehow, it is not obvious from the layman's point of view. That is why newcomers to full-time ministry, who have laboured in banks, hospitals, companies, etc., are genuinely surprised to find themselves inundated with work, which they cannot finish. They are simply amazed at how they are continually exhausted with work which never ends.

I smiled to myself when a lay brother said to me, "Of course I will come to work in the ministry if there is something to do." There is something to do indeed! The whole world is waiting for us to come to them.

God has sent us to tell six billion people about Jesus. Do you think that that is a lot of work? I do, and I think there is a lot of work for as many as are willing.

A song I love says,

There are so many jobs in God's vineyard for all of us to do.
The harvest is plentiful but the labourers are few
There are so many jobs in God's vineyard for all of us to do
We must work while it is day spreading the Word of God
As we walk along the way
We live to do His will, spreading the Word of God
Till it reaches to every hill.
We must witness to everyone we meet in every song we sing
We must tell them of the soon coming King
We must witness to everyone we meet in every song we sing
We must tell them of the soon coming King.

God called me to be a pastor and a teacher. I could have neglected that gift and spent my days doing something else. For the last several years, I have given attention to my calling. Indeed, it has been several years of growing in the anointing and gifting of the Lord.

2. Full-time ministry is for meditation, reading, exhortation.

Till I come, give attendance to reading, to exhortation, to doctrine.
1 Timothy 4:13

Many people do not even understand the purpose for which they are in full-time ministry. One of the principal reasons for full-time ministry is meditation, reading and exhortation. Each of these activities is different and has a unique place.

Reading

When you work in the secular world there is little time for reading. A minister is someone who must be "given" to reading. Reading is one of the most important activities of someone called to full-time ministry.

Reading the Bible and reading other books takes a lot of time and has no substitute. Unfortunately, many who are in full-time ministry do not do the very thing for which they became full-time ministers. Forgive!

Reading is not regarded as work. It is generally seen as something to be done in one's leisure. Sadly, many pastors do not understand that reading is their God-given work. As you read, you go deeper into the things of God. Your depth determines the height you can climb to.

I have found reading to be even more important than praying. Reading has opened doors for me and lifted me to new heights in ministry.

Meditation

The church is filled with ministers who glance briefly at Scriptures and read over large portions rapidly. That is why there is a lack of personal revelation. Sermons are empty and there is no depth in what is being said. Instead of spending hours meditating, ministers love to repeat and relay the revelations of others who have sought God and meditated on His Word.

Meditation is thinking deeply about God's Word. Indeed, the lack of meditation is the cause of a lack of personal conviction.

Both Kenneth Hagin and Rick Joyner have had powerful visions. I love reading their visions and benefiting spiritually from them. I long for visions from the Lord that will teach me precious hidden truths. However, I cannot spend my whole life waiting for a vision, I have to do what all ministers are supposed to do - meditation.

Sometimes people have visions that are deep revelations about the Word. God gives these supernatural blessings. However, most of us will not have these special revelations. We will have to depend on meditation. I can always tell when I speak to someone who meditates on the Word of God. He is full of wisdom and understanding. It is dangerous to relay the messages of others without taking the time to meditate for yourself. You could easily become a false prophet reading out dead sermons whose relevance have expired.

Exhortation

Exhortation is all about sharing the Word with one another. I love to share the Word with anybody who loves the Word. It is sweet like honey and tasty like spicy, grilled pork chops. It is such a delight for me to share wonderful truths with small groups and individuals.

What people do not realize is that, as you share, you become more grounded in the truth. You understand and remember the Word better. Exhortation helps you to preach better. That is why exhortation is important for full-time ministers. Just like reading and meditation, it grooms you for your ministry.

3. Full-time ministry is to ensure salvation.

> **...for in doing this thou shalt both SAVE THYSELF, and them that hear thee.**
>
> **1 Timothy 4:16**

> **Take pains with these things; be absorbed in them, so that your progress will be evident to all. Pay close attention to yourself and to your teaching; persevere in these things, for as you do this you will ENSURE SALVATION both for yourself and for those who hear you.**
>
> **1 Timothy 4:15-16, NASB**

One of the mysterious purposes of full-time ministry is to ensure salvation and to save yourself. How can that be? If God has called you to ministry, it would be dangerous to do anything else. Paul said, "Woe is me if I preach not the gospel". He also said, "necessity is laid upon me". In other words, it is very necessary that I preach the Word.

If your boss sent for you, wouldn't you go? If you did not go when you were called what would happen? He is likely to dismiss you for refusing to come when called. That is why servants are quick to respond and ready to do anything. Servants want to keep their jobs and their lives.

There are people who have died prematurely because they refused to give themselves wholly to God's calling.

Years ago, a young man said to me, "God has called me to ministry. I want to be in full-time ministry."

But I told him, "There is no opportunity for you to work in the ministry at this time."

But he insisted, "If I don't work for the Lord in full-time ministry, I feel that I will die."

"Wow," I said. "I know that feeling."

I allowed him to be in full-time ministry and today he has a great church and ministry.

"Woe is me" simply means something terrible will happen to me. You see, the genuine call of God leaves you with no options. Who are you to refuse God's outstretched hand?

Do you know the One who has called you? He is El Shaddai, the Almighty God.

Do You Dare Disobey This Call?

Jonah experienced the terror of rejecting the call of God. Rejecting the call to full-time ministry will only provoke the storms of life and prepare the whales in the sea to receive you.

By rejecting the call of God, Jonah walked right into the storms of life. He fell into the hands of wicked men who heartlessly threw him overboard.

As if that was not enough, he was swallowed by a big fish and stayed in the belly of the fish for some days.

Finally, he was vomited out and given a second chance to obey the call of God.

> **Now the word of the LORD came to Jonah the SECOND TIME, saying, "Arise, go to Nineveh the great city and proclaim to it the proclamation which I am going to tell you.**
>
> **Jonah 3:1-2, NASB**

Expect storms and expect wicked people to take over your life if you disobey the Master. God controls everything.

When Jonah had a bad attitude, the Lord appointed a plant to cover him and then sent a worm to eat the plant. God also sent the wind to Jonah. This illustrates the almighty power of the One who calls us.

> **So the LORD God appointed a plant and it grew up over Jonah to be a shade over his head to deliver him from his discomfort. And Jonah was extremely happy about the plant.**
>
> **But God appointed a worm when dawn came the next day and it attacked the plant and it withered.**
>
> **When the sun came up God appointed a scorching east wind, and the sun beat down on Jonah's head so that he became faint and begged with all his soul to die, saying, "Death is better to me than life."**
>
> **Jonah 4:6-8, NASB**

Even the growing of a plant and the movement of a worm are determined by God. I believe there are many people whose lives are ruined because they failed to come into full-time ministry. Their lives are ruined because they could not trust and obey God. Sadly, some people even lose their salvation by running away from full-time ministry. This is why Paul said giving yourself wholly would ensure salvation. Our very lives depend on obeying God. You can make light of God's call, but you may pay dearly for it.

4. Full-time ministry sets a good example.

> **...that thy profiting may APPEAR TO ALL.**
>
> **1 Timothy 4:15**

Several good examples are set when you enter full-time ministry. You set an example of faith and of trusting in God. Full-time ministry sets an example of loving God and obeying Him. Full-time ministry demonstrates that you believe in the sacrifice of the cross. You have taken up your cross and are following the Saviour.

Full-time ministry sets a good example of implementing the Scriptures practically. It makes you a doer of the Word.

Interestingly, we cannot relate with large sections of the Scriptures unless the model of full-time ministry is practised.

Many of the truths relating to the tabernacle, the Levites and the priests have no relevance to people who do not practise the complete dedication that full-time ministry requires.

Many things that Paul said about the ministry relate to people who are completely immersed in ministry.

Many of his struggles and teachings are from the perspective of someone completely dedicated to the service of God. Even the often-quoted Scripture, "My God shall supply all your needs" had to do with him receiving support in full-time ministry.

The famous verse in Galatians 6:7 about reaping what you sow is also related to him receiving financial support for full-time ministry.

5. Full-time ministry permits the continuation of your ministry.

> **Take heed unto thyself, and unto the doctrine; CONTINUE IN THEM...**
>
> **1 Timothy 4:16**

Many people practise a part-time ministry, giving God some weekends and some evenings of their lives. This is all well and good and sometimes is a necessary phase of ministry.

However, full-time ministry is a logical continuation of the lay ministry. What you have done for years on a part-time basis can be continued and upgraded in full-time ministry. It is indeed a privilege to have the opportunity to continue to fulfil your call at a higher level. If God has called you to the ministry, pray for the opportunity to go all the way. I have experienced both lay ministry and full-time ministry. I can tell you, it is the greatest blessing to give yourself wholly to the Lord.

6. Full-time ministry is for the protection of yourself and your message.

> **TAKE HEED unto THYSELF, and UNTO THE DOCTRINE; continue in them...**
>
> **1 Timothy 4:16**

An ambassador is a special envoy with a special message. Every minister is an ambassador.

> **Now then we are ambassadors for Christ, as though God did beseech you by us: we pray you in Christ's stead, be ye reconciled to God.**
>
> **2 Corinthians 5:20**

It is important that a messenger does not change the message he was given. The messenger himself must not be corrupted or swayed by the people. He must be faithful to the one who sent him.

Recently, I needed to send a message to someone. The message was a very hard message of judgment. I did not want to do it myself so I looked for a messenger. Somehow, I knew that each of the people I was thinking of would modify the message.

They would say things differently and tone the message down.

Then I got discouraged and gave up the idea of delivering that message. I understood why God had said, "Who will go for me?" I began to identify with God's problem of finding a faithful, reliable messenger who would deliver the truth without compromise. Unfortunately, the very sight of the recipients of the message frightens the messengers and they come up with amazing variants of the original.

In full-time ministry, spending more time with the Lord ensures that you protect the doctrine and the message given to you. It is easy to deliver a mutant of the original message.

I believe that much of what is preached currently is a mutation of God's Word. Because Scriptures and Bibles are used in the pulpit, innocent and ignorant people swallow the modified messages of the modern church.

Listening to present-day preaching would leave any genuine student of the Bible wondering. Rick Joyner, in his vision of the *Final Quest* described how he met the apostle Paul. He asked Paul for any comments he had about the church. Paul had one comment. He said he could not recognize the message nor the ministry of the present-day church. Paul said the message of the first church was the message of the cross and that message had been quickly lost by the church. How sad!

I am not surprised that Paul cannot recognize what we are preaching. Many messages centre on the felt needs of people. These felt needs in Christian parlance are called blessings - things that people feel, need and want. Things like money, cars, houses, children, visas, jobs, wives, husbands and how to acquire them, take centre stage of most teachings.

In addition, many messages sound like good advice for successful living. Most of the preaching has very little divine and mystical content.

Where are the sermons on salvation and the blood of Jesus? What about the cross, Heaven and Hell? Can we even preach about sacrifice in this lukewarm Laodecian church? What about eternity and the power of God?

Full-time ministry is intended to give you time for attending to God and His Word. A full-time ministry of meditation, Bible study, waiting on God and praying, will help us to protect the message and the doctrine of the church.

Chapter

36

The Principles behind Full-Time Microsoft

CHAPTER SUMMARY

- **TEN GUILT REMOVING PRINCIPLES**

36. 1 The principle of fighting a war whilst someone else pays the bills

36. 2 The principle of being the first to drink the wine of your vineyard

36. 3 The principle of not muzzling the ox that treads out the corn

36. 4 The principle of feeding a flock and being the first to drink the milk

36. 5 The principle of having a farm and eating of the produce

36. 6 The principle of sowing spiritual seeds and reaping material things

36. 7 The principle of ministering holy things and living off these holy things

36. 8 The principle of waiting at the altar and partaking of the altar

36. 9 The principle of eating and drinking as you work

36.10 The principle of taking a break from work

One of the barriers to full-time ministry is the guilt that comes from earning money from a church. Acquiring any kind of benefit for working in a church seems almost sinful to many traditional Christians. A guilty feeling that you are living off the gifts that people bring to God can be overwhelming.

Many well-meaning Christians find it virtually impossible to cross this barrier and to work for the Lord in full-time ministry. This guilty feeling is not unfounded. Even though a bank is a heartless, money-grabbing institution, earning or getting some of that money for yourself by working there is seen as legitimate.

Somehow, earning money through the church seems immoral. It is therefore a struggle for professionals to subject themselves to earning money from a charity, which they once contributed to.

Generally, coming into full-time ministry is a humbling experience. It must be embraced by all who love the Lord. The apostle Paul throws much light on what happens when you earn money through the ministry.

He teaches powerful principles which every full-time minister must understand. Even lay people must understand these principles. They help put everything in context.

These principles are fulfilled by being in full-time ministry, that is, a ministry which pays you or from which you benefit financially. These principles are not fulfilled by lay ministry.

You must not feel guilty about receiving pay or benefits through ministry work. All these ten principles are in favour of you receiving money and other benefits from your work.

■ Ten Guilt Removing Principles

1. The principle of fighting a war whilst someone else pays the bills.

> **Who at any time serves as a soldier at his own expense?**
>
> **1 Corinthians 9:7, NASB**

Paul likens ministry to going to war. Indeed, it is a battle on many fronts. After being in full-time ministry for more than ten years, I would describe ministry as a series of battles, struggles and fights.

If I am at war through the ministry, who is going to pay for the war? Certainly not the soldiers who are fighting on the battle front!

If you are in full-time ministry, you can expect to be paid for going to war. Actually, you should expect to be paid well! You are in a danger zone and have taken many risks.

2. The principle of being the first to drink the wine of your vineyard.

> **...Who plants a vineyard and does not eat the fruit of it?**
>
> **1 Corinthians 9:7, NASB**

In this verse, the work of the ministry is likened to the planting and tilling of a vineyard. This principle gives the planter of the vineyard the right to enjoy the wine that comes from his vineyard. The next time you are offered a cup of wine from the ministry vineyard, do not feel guilty to drink it. Drink deeply, brother. You deserve the wine from the vineyard.

3. The principle of not muzzling the ox that treads out the corn.

> **For it is written in the Law of Moses, "You shall not muzzle the ox while he is threshing..."**
>
> **1 Corinthians 9:9, NASB**

In this principle, the mouth of the ox, which is treading the corn, must not be gagged! The ox spends the whole day mashing the corn for its master. The mouth of this ox must not be tied. The ox must be allowed to eat some of the corn he is stamping on. How much corn can this poor animal eat in a day?

Now, God does not use this principle because He cares about oxen! He cares about His full-time priests.

A full-time pastor is an ox who spends all day crushing the corn for the farmer. He is entitled to a few mouthfuls to give him enough energy to continue happily in his work.

Dear Minister, you are also entitled to enjoy a few mouthfuls personally. Don't feel bad because you have to eat. It is God's blessing for you.

4. The principle of feeding a flock and being the first to drink the milk.

> **...Or who tends a flock and does not use the milk of the flock?**
>
> **1 Corinthians 9:7, NASB**

Once again, a full-time minister feeds the flock as he ministers the Word of God. These sheep are definitely going to get fatter. They will be blessed and increased in size and number. Soon milk will start coming out of those teats.

Who should be the first to drink this milk? You are abnormal when you do not drink the milk from your sheep.

Feel free from today and enjoy the milk! Put it in the fridge if you want. Have a cup of tea with this God-given milk. You may turn the milk into cheese, butter, yoghurt, ice cream and all the other nice things. I know you never thought that God would bless you so much in full-time ministry.

5. The principle of having a farm and eating of the produce.

> **Yes, for our sake it was written, because the plowman ought to plow in hope, and the thresher to thresh in hope of sharing the crops.**
>
> **1 Corinthians 9:10, NASB**

Pastoring a church is like owning a farm. Think of all the cows, pigs, goats, chickens, wheat, barley, maize, potatoes, oranges, bananas, tomatoes, pepper and onions that are grown on your farm. Being in full-time ministry is the same as having all these at your disposal.

Is it wrong to taste spicy, grilled pork chops once a week? Is there anything wrong if you use some of the tomatoes, pepper and onions to make chicken stew for your family? What about some steak or beef with onions? How do you want your potatoes? As french fries, parsley potatoes or baked potatoes?

These are God's blessings for his full-time ministers. It is a small compensation for the humility and service of a servant of God. No one is wiser than God. Accept God's provision and flow fully in full-time ministry. Enjoy the fried rice that comes from the farm.

6. The principle of sowing spiritual seeds and reaping material things.

> **If we sowed spiritual things in you, is it too much if we reap material things from you?**
>
> **If others share the right over you, do we not more? Nevertheless, we did not use this right, but we endure all things so that we will cause no hindrance to the gospel of Christ.**
>
> **1 Corinthians 9:11-12, NASB**

The ministry is all about sowing spiritual seeds. I would have thought that the harvest would be equally spiritual. However, God's Word reveals this surprise of carnal blessings as well. What are carnal blessings? They are physical things that you receive only on this earth. There is nothing carnal in Heaven. Eternal rewards await you in Heaven but carnal harvests may be reaped here and now. People should not be surprised when God blesses full-time ministers with cars, houses, clothes, food and other little carnal pleasures.

Unfortunately, there are many who want us to sow and never reap. There are lay people who cannot understand why they should pay the bills for the war which we are fighting. Well, that is God's ordained way.

7. The principle of ministering holy things and living off these holy things.

> **Do you not know that those who perform sacred services eat the food of the temple...**
>
> **1 Corinthians 9:13, NASB**

Full-time ministry is based on the levitical priesthood. All the tribes of Israel were given land but the tribe of Levi was given nothing. Their portion was the Lord. They were to trust God for everything.

> **The priests the Levites, and all the tribe of Levi, shall have no part nor inheritance with Israel: THEY SHALL EAT THE OFFERINGS of the LORD made by fire, and his inheritance.**
>
> **Therefore shall they have no inheritance among their brethren: the LORD is their inheritance, as he hath said unto them. And THIS SHALL BE THE PRIEST'S DUE FROM THE PEOPLE, from them that offer a sacrifice, whether it be ox or sheep; and they shall give unto the priest the shoulder, and the two cheeks, and the maw.**

> **THE FIRSTFRUIT also of thy corn, of thy wine, and of thine oil, and the first of the fleece of thy sheep, SHALT THOU GIVE HIM. For the LORD thy God hath chosen him out of all thy tribes, to stand to minister in the name of the LORD, him and his sons for ever.**
>
> **Deuteronomy 18:1-5**

So practically, they were to receive the tithes, offerings, and gifts on behalf of the Lord. After presenting these gifts to the Lord with a wave, they were to take them home and enjoy them.

It might seem like sacrilege to you, for me to eat people's offerings! How can someone eat and drink holy gifts that have been presented to God? How could I use money that was placed in the Sunday offering bowl? Nevertheless, it is a principle that those who minister with holy things are to eat and to drink these very holy things. Because I am in full-time ministry, I use holy money, I drink holy milk with my tea and I eat holy beef stew.

Why do I call it holy? Because I eat the offerings and tithes that people have brought. I use these offerings and tithes to buy food and drink.

Next time you see a full-time minister spending a dollar, remember that it is a holy dollar that he is spending.

All full-time ministers spend holy money and eat holy food. They drive holy cars and live in holy houses because all these were acquired with holy offerings! I am sorry I cannot change what God has ordained.

8. The principle of waiting at the altar and partaking of the altar.

> **...those who attend regularly to the altar have their share from the altar?**
>
> **1 Corinthians 9:13, NASB**

The principle of partaking of things brought to the altar is similar to the one above. God's people bring tithes, offerings and gifts to His house. In the Old Testament, these altar sacrifices were sheep, oxen, chicken, etc. After receiving the gifts, the priests presented them on the altar.

After church, we take these gifts to our homes and share them. Sometimes there are larger portions of beef and this is good for khebab! Sometimes there are many chickens and that can be used for chicken soup, grilled chicken and other delicacies that the Levitical children love!

Things presented on the altar are sacred and belong to God. We do not eat these sacrifices with presumption. We see it as an honour from the Lord. It is His way of looking after His priests.

It is truly humbling to own nothing except that which comes from people's gifts. Everyone can point to your house and say that it is not earned by "honest work".

But God sees His priests as hard-working men and women who deserve to be rewarded. The work they do is more than "honest work". It is God's work!!

9. The principle of eating and drinking as you work.

> **Do we not have a right to eat and drink?**
>
> **1 Corinthians 9:4, NASB**

It is important to eat and drink as you work. When people do not eat and drink as they work, they grow weary and give up. Can you imagine having to fast every day of your life just because you work at a particular place? Why should full-time ministers not eat whilst they work?

10. The principle of taking a break from work.

> **Or do only Barnabas and I not have a right to refrain from working?**
>
> **1 Corinthians 9:6, NASB**

How can someone work without ever resting? Rest is part of God's plan for His cherished ministers. God wants full-time ministers to have vacations, days off and times of rest. It is their right. Please do not feel bad to have a day off. In my church we have Mondays off. It is our resting day and it is our little time of leisure and family respite from our work.

Shouldn't I Play Golf?

One Monday, I was on the golf course with some other pastors. A gentleman who did not know that my associate pastor was tying his shoe laces behind him, began to criticize me.

He said, "If that guy was working as a doctor, would he be playing golf here today?"

My pastor reacted to his comments and challenged him about what he was saying.

He told him, "We are all gentlemen on the course. What do you mean by what you are saying? Respect yourself!"

"You are a grown up!" he was told sharply.

We asked the man whether he was paying for us to play golf. The man sputtered out a lame response, claiming to enjoy my radio programs. Quite irritated, we decided to ignore this fellow and to carry on with our game.

But this is the question Paul was asking. "Or I only and Barnabas, have not we power to forbear working?" (1 Corinthians 9:6).

People feel that they have the right "to forbear working" and to have days off, vacations, and times of relaxation. But they see no reason why a priest should have the same privileges.

The Response of Apostle Paul

> **This is my answer to those who question my rights.**
>
> **Or don't I have any rights at all? Can't I claim the same privilege the other apostles have of being a guest in your homes?**

If I had a wife, and if she were a believer, couldn't I bring her along on these trips just as the other disciples do, and as the Lord's brothers do, and as Peter does?

And must Barnabas and I alone keep working for our living while you supply these others?

What soldier in the army has to pay his own expenses? And have you ever heard of a farmer who harvests his crop and doesn't have the right to eat some of it? What shepherd takes care of a flock of sheep and goats and isn't allowed to drink some of the milk?

And I'm not merely quoting the opinions of men as to what is right. I'm telling you what God's law says.

For in the law God gave to Moses he said that you must not put a muzzle on an ox to keep it from eating when it is treading out the wheat. Do you suppose God was thinking only about oxen when he said this?

Wasn't he also thinking about us? Of course he was. He said this to show us that Christian workers should be paid by those they help. Those who do the plowing and threshing should expect some share of the harvest.

We have planted good spiritual seed in your souls. Is it too much to ask, in return, for mere food and clothing?

You give them to others who preach to you, and you should. But shouldn't we have an even greater right to them? Yet we have never used this right but supply our own needs without your help. We have never demanded payment of any kind for fear that, if we did, you might be less interested in our message to you from Christ.

Don't you realize that God told those working in his temple to take for their own needs some of the food brought there as gifts to him? And those who work at the altar of God get a share of the food that is brought by those offering it to the Lord.

In the same way the Lord has given orders that those who preach the Gospel should be supported by those who accept it.

1 Corinthians 9:3-14, TLB

Chapter

37

Wrong Reasons for Full-Time Ministry

CHAPTER SUMMARY

It is important that you have right motives. God looks at the heart. You are dealing with someone who does not care what you say or what impressions you make. He looks straight at your heart. There are many possible reasons for doing the same thing. If you are genuine, you will always question your heart. You will search and check constantly to see if any corruption has seeped in.

> **...the LORD looks at the heart.**
>
> **1 Samuel 16:7, NASB**

Almost every aspect of the ministry has a list of wrong reasons that motivate ministers. For instance, there are many wrong reasons for wanting to have a big church. You may desire power and fame. You may love the praises of men.

You may do evangelism and feed the poor but your motive may again be fame. You may be motivated by your own human compassion for poverty and disease and not by the inspiration of the Holy Spirit.

You may preach powerful messages on the financial harvest. You will say it is because you want the people to prosper. You may say Jesus spoke more about money than anything else. You may say, "God told me to speak these words." But the real reason may be that you simply want a good offering for that service! Mercy!

As I grow in the Lord, I have noticed an increasing uncertainty in me about everything I do. Every genuine minister will suffer some amount of confusion because of a constant searching of his heart.

Why are you doing what you are doing? Has God called you? What is in your heart? What is the real reason for what you are saying? We are rapidly approaching Heaven and the throne of judgement. Nothing about us will be hidden.

Everything will be laid bare before the King of Kings. Our evil motives will be even uglier when exposed to the glory of God. It is time to search our hearts and judge ourselves so that God will not have to do it. As the psalmist said,

> **Search me, O God, and know my heart: try me, and know my thoughts: And see if there be any wicked way in me, and lead me in the way everlasting.**
>
> **Psalm 139:23**

Can there be wrong reasons for entering into full-time ministry? Certainly! Many wrong reasons and motives hide in the hearts of priests. It is important to know these and make sure you have the right motive for ministry.

Wrong Reasons for Entering Full-Time Ministry

1. I could desire to be in full-time ministry because I did not do well in school and I am not qualified for any other profession.

2. My desire to be in full-time ministry could be because people in full-time ministry look prosperous.

3. My desire to be in full-time ministry could be because those in full-time ministry travel abroad often.

4. I could desire to be in full-time ministry because I am currently unemployed.

5. I could desire to be in full-time ministry because it is a better paying job than my current one.

6. I could desire to be in full-time ministry because I need a stepping stone to that which I really want to do.

7. I could be in full-time ministry because my spouse pressured me into it.

8. I could be in full-time ministry because I need to work in a family-oriented organization during my childbearing years.

9. I could desire to be in full-time ministry because I am too lazy to look for another job.

10. I could be in full-time ministry because I have earned all the money and acquired everything I will ever need so I now feel secure enough to work for God.

11. I could be in full-time ministry because I do not want to look unspiritual and uncommitted.

12. I could be in full-time ministry because I think I will have a job with a lighter schedule.

These are just a few of the wrong reasons why someone could desire to be in full-time ministry. Please check your heart and make sure that you are in full-time ministry for the right reason.

Chapter

38

Right Reasons for Full-Time Ministry

CHAPTER SUMMARY

38. 1 Enter full-time ministry because you love God

38. 2 Enter full-time ministry because you fear God

38. 3 Enter full-time ministry to fulfil your calling

38. 4 Enter full-time ministry to finish your work

38. 5 Enter full-time ministry to be able to travel

38. 6 Enter full-time ministry to be able to be sent

38. 7 Enter full-time ministry to be able to live at certain places

38. 8 Enter full-time ministry because you despise earthly things

38. 9 Enter full-time ministry to be able to fight a good war

38. 10 Enter full-time ministry because of the rewards in Heaven

1. Enter full-time ministry because you love God.

> **...the greatest of these is love.**
>
> **1 Corinthians 13:13, NASB**

There are many good reasons for someone to be in full-time ministry, but the greatest of these is love.

Believing and obeying a command from God is a very good motive for doing something. However, the greatest of motives is love. Going into full-time ministry with hope for eternal or earthly rewards is also a good thing. After all, you must believe that God is a rewarder of them that diligently seek Him. However, an even greater motive is the motivation of love.

I realize that my reason for serving God has gradually shifted from doing things because I need to obey His calling to doing things because I love Him. And that is a major shift!

Choosing the Best of Three

If I had to choose between three employees: one who was very qualified, one who was very experienced and one who simply loved and believed in me, I would choose the one who loved me.

Peter Worked for Love

Peter loved Jesus. That was the basis of all the work that he did. The ministry of the apostles was not for money or fame. The money lover (Judas) was kicked out at the beginning of the ministry. Jesus capitalized on Peter's love and urged him on in the ministry.

> **So when they had finished breakfast, Jesus said to Simon Peter, "Simon, son of John, do you love Me more than these?" He said to Him, "Yes, Lord; You know that I love You." He said to him, "Tend My lambs."**
>
> **He said to him again a second time, "Simon, son of John, do you love Me?" He said to Him, "Yes, Lord; You know that I love You." He said to him, "Shepherd My sheep."**
>
> **He said to him the third time, "Simon, son of John, do you love Me?" Peter was grieved because He said to him the third time, "Do you love Me?" And he said to Him, "Lord, You know all things; You know that I love You." Jesus said to him, "Tend My sheep."**
>
> **John 21:15-17, NASB**

Paul Worked for Love

Paul was constrained by his love for Christ. He was not just a hard worker trying to achieve many things at the same time. He loved the Saviour!

> **For the love of Christ constraineth us...**
>
> **2 Corinthians 5:14**

2. Enter full-time ministry because you fear God.

> **For if I preach the gospel, I have nothing to boast of, for necessity is laid upon me; yes, woe is me if I do not preach the gospel!**
>
> **1 Corinthians 9:16, NKJV**

Elijah said to Elisha, "What have I done to you?" He knew that by throwing the mantle on him he had changed the young man's life forever. He had no options. He had to go. If he did not obey the call, there would be plenty of trouble. Jonah found out first-hand what it meant to run away from the call of God. His troubles never ended until he obeyed the call.

Come into full-time ministry now because you have no other options! One of the great problems of modern Christians is a lack of the fear of God. You can detect that there is little fear of God by the way Christians treat God's representatives. When Miriam criticized Moses, the Lord asked her, "Were you not afraid to speak against my servant?

> **Why then were you not afraid to speak against My servant, against Moses?"**
>
> **Numbers 12:8**

3. Enter full-time ministry to fulfil your calling.

> **...make full proof of thy ministry**
>
> **2 Timothy 4:5**

Do not die without discharging all your duties. Do not leave anything undone! Many ministries cannot be fulfilled until you do it on a full-time basis! You will not live for long. That is not a curse. It is the truth! Your days are numbered and so are mine.

We have a very short time in which to finish our work. How sad it will be if you get to Heaven and find out that you could have done much more with your ministry.

As with everything, if you give yourself wholly to it, it will blossom. Another version says "...Leave nothing undone that you ought to do" (2 Timothy 4:5, TLB). Yet another version puts it this way, "...discharge all the duties of your ministry" (2 Timothy 4:5, NIV).

4. Enter full-time ministry to finish your work.

> **I have fought the good fight, I HAVE FINISHED THE COURSE, I have kept the faith;**
>
> **2 Timothy 4:7**

A Visit from the Dead

I had a vision in which I found myself sitting at a dining table with two dead pastors who had come back to life for a short period. The men, who were brothers, had died years ago and had been brought back to life and given a chance to revisit the earth.

Whilst on this short visit they had gone around some churches that they had established in their lifetime and tried to minister to them.

We Talked

I was privileged, in the vision, to have a meal with them before they returned to be with the Lord. Actually, my home was the last place they were visiting on earth. As we ate and shared fellowship, I asked them a few questions.

"How was your stay on earth and how did you find the churches?"

They shook their heads and said, "Our messages did not work. They seemed irrelevant to the people. No one wanted to listen to us."

He continued, "Our songs also did not work. No one wanted to sing them. They had new songs and were not interested in our old songs."

They seemed discouraged and disappointed that they had made no impact at all.

They Warned Me

I asked, "Is there anything you would like to share with me before you leave?"

One of them answered, "There are some things that we would like to tell you. First of all, we were very surprised to die when we died! We never expected to have died when we did. You see, we were very fruitful and active in the ministry. Of course, we thought that this was a good reason for us to live much longer. Why would God remove someone who was doing so well in ministry?"

He continued, "The second thing is that even though we tried to influence people during this visit, the people were not impressed by our ministry at all. We had no impact at all."

Then he turned, pointed to me and said, "You have the best chance now. This is your time to be fruitful. Our time is past. Our chance is gone. This is your best chance now."

The vision ended and I realized that God had spoken to me. It was clear that I could depart from this earth at any time in spite of what good works I was doing. God had told me that this was my chance to do His will and to finish His work.

Dear brother, this is our best chance. Soon you will be out of this world. You will not have a chance to work for God. Why do you want to serve Him in drips and drops? Throw fear and caution to the wind. Launch out into full-time ministry and give God your best. This is your best chance now. Make sure you finish your course.

5. Enter full-time ministry to be able to travel.

> **In journeyings often...**
>
> **2 Corinthians 11:26**

Ministry involves a lot of travelling. The souls Christ died for are not in one place. They are scattered all over the surface of the earth. They are found in cities, towns and villages dotted all over the world. We can never fulfil God's calling by staying in one place. We must go, we must travel, and we must spread out our wings and fly!

When you work for secular institutions, you will not be able to travel freely. Every normal job will restrict and restrain you from true ministry. Enter full-time ministry so that you can travel to where God sends you.

6. Enter full-time ministry to be able to be sent.

> **And Tychicus I have sent to Ephesus.**
>
> **2 Timothy 4:12, NKJV**

How can you be sent if you are tied down to a particular job? Your boss will dismiss you for absenteeism. This is the first thing that I realized when I entered full-time ministry. I was free to be sent. The Lord could send me anywhere, any day.

Here am I, send me! We sing it but it is not real. How can you be sent to the villages and towns when you have to report to the bank at 8.00am???

7. Enter full-time ministry to be able to live at certain places.

> **For this cause LEFT I THEE IN CRETE, that thou shouldest set in order the things that are wanting, and ordain elders in every city, as I had appointed thee:**
>
> **Titus 1:5**

I have left several young men in different towns of the world.

How could I leave them there to "set in order things that are wanting" if they had to be at work on Wednesday morning? The young men that I have left in different towns are called missionaries. Paul sent Titus as a missionary to Crete. How can you be a missionary when you have to go to work in the bank every morning?

8. Enter full-time ministry because you despise earthly things.

> **Yea doubtless, and I count all things but loss for the excellency of the knowledge of Christ Jesus my Lord: for whom I have suffered the loss of all things, and do count them but dung, that I may win Christ,**
>
> **Philippians 3:8**

It is sad to see Christians aspiring to join the ranks of the world's great. Pastors want to be numbered among society's elite. We love to take pictures with earthly presidents and to be associated with rich people. Forgive!

Somehow, rich worldly people are the best friends of many pastors! What do they talk about? That spirit of worldliness in ministers is transmitted to the church.

Our churches are filled with people who are in awe of this world! If they were heavenly-minded they would be despising the world.

How different we are from the Apostle Paul. Paul considered these things as dung and we consider them as glamorous treasures. Heaven cannot relate with our strange desires for things that fade so easily.

It is time to put everything in its right place. Every earthly achievement is dung in the light of the glory of God.

Spiritual men must despise the riches, the accomplishments and the prestige of this world.

> **For all flesh is as grass, and all the GLORY OF MAN AS THE FLOWER OF GRASS. The grass withereth, and the flower thereof falleth away...**
>
> **1 Peter 1:24**

It is time to set your affection on things above.

> **Set your affection on things above, not on things on the earth.**
>
> **Colossians 3:2**

Falling in love with full-time ministry is setting your affection on things above. The rewards of serving God can be found in Heaven where our hearts and minds should be.

9. Enter full-time ministry to be able to fight a good war.

> **No man that warreth entangleth himself with the affairs of this life; that he may please him who hath chosen him to be a soldier.**
>
> **2 Timothy 2:4**

Ministry is war! To fight a war well, you need soldiers that are committed to fighting. Soldiers cannot go shopping when they want to. The American soldiers in Iraq cannot go to their old jobs in Houston, Texas. They cannot go shopping in the beautiful shopping malls of America. They cannot go to McDonald's or watch films in the evenings with their girlfriends. They have to watch out for bombs. They cannot fight the Iraqis from their comfortable and safe positions in America. They have to go away from their comforts and luxuries and join the battle. They will risk their lives and everything they have ever known for the sake of their mission.

That is how full-time ministry is. You have to leave behind the old life with its routine and launch out into a completely different life. *Come into full-time ministry so that you can fight the war properly.*

10. Enter full-time ministry because of the rewards in Heaven.

There are many rewards for God's servants. I am looking forward to mine and I hope you have yours.

> **Peter began to say to Him, "Behold, we have left everything and followed You."**
>
> **Jesus said, "Truly I say to you, there is no one who has left house or brothers or sisters or mother or father or children or farms, for My sake and for the gospel's sake, but that he will receive a hundred times as much now in the present age, houses and brothers and sisters and mothers and children and farms, along with persecutions; and in the age to come, eternal life."**
>
> **Mark 10:28-30, NASB**

Chapter

39

How to Assess Your Readiness for Full-Time Ministry

CHAPTER SUMMARY

- **Ten Questions to Ask Yourself Before Full-Time Ministry**

39. 1 Are you ready to leave familiar things behind?

39. 2 Are you ready to leave your own country?

39. 3 Are you ready to break away from your father's influence and provision?

39. 4 Are you ready for uncertainty?

39. 5 Can you follow a mysterious mission, which has no details?

39. 6 Can you sojourn?

39. 7 Can you live in unsettled circumstances?

39. 8 Can you make your whole family follow you into this adventure?

39. 9 Can you look for a city with foundations?

39. 10 Can you give up your Isaac?

As you get ready for the challenge of full-time ministry, you must ask yourself some questions. You must go through some issues in your heart and settle them forever.

Full-time ministry is not about finding a new job. It is not a career move. There are many better-paying jobs elsewhere. Full-time ministry is all about following God into the unknown. It is a walk of faith and faith is all about "things not seen". I want to take you through a series of questions that you must ask yourself before you embark on something as challenging as full-time ministry.

■ Ten Questions to Ask Yourself Before Full-Time Ministry

1. Are you ready to leave familiar things behind?

Now the LORD said to Abram, Go forth from…your relatives

Genesis 12:1, NASB

Are you ready to leave your old friends and acquaintances behind? Do they mean so much to you that you cannot do without them? I assure you that being in full-time ministry separates you from many familiar things. In full-time ministry your day off is usually on Monday. Most secular workers are at work on Monday morning. This reality will separate you from lay people and their lives.

2. Are you ready to leave your own country?

Now the LORD said to Abram, Go forth from your country,

Genesis 12:1, NASB

It would appear that there is little need for full-time ministers. This seems to be the picture if we do not travel to other countries on Gospel missions. God's command is for us to go to the uttermost parts of the earth. Thousands of full-time ministers are needed for the great commission.

If we are ready to go to the nations, there will never be enough people for full-time ministry. Ask yourself therefore, if you are ready to leave your country, region or neighbourhood. Going away from your country is a real option for anyone coming into full-time ministry.

3. Are you ready to break away from your father's influence and provision?

Now the LORD said to Abram...Go forth from…your father's house,

Genesis 12:1, NASB

Are you ready to leave the influence of your home? Can you be free from your father's influence, control and money? One day a prophet told me about a revelation he had had. It was about one of our lay pastors who had declined to come into full-time ministry.

The Vision

In the vision, this pastor was seen depending on his father to give him certain things like money, houses, inheritance, etc. This pastor did not want to do anything that would upset his father and so he rejected the offer to come into full-time ministry. In the vision, the father died but did not give his son any of the things he was expecting. The brother was very disappointed. He had sacrificed full-time ministry for an earthly inheritance that never materialized! How sad!

You see, you must be ready to leave your father's house and all its good things. They are all "dung" compared to the riches and rewards that Christ has for you.

4. Are you ready for uncertainty?

> **Now the LORD said to Abram, Go forth from…to the land which I will show you;**
>
> **Genesis 12:1, NASB**

I get amused when people want to know details of what full-time ministry involves. They want to know what the offer is. Someone said his career progression in the ministry was not clear. Would he rise quickly from Zonal Pastor to Sub-District Pastor to District Pastor? How would he rise on the salary scale? By the way, is there a scale? Will I be in this office forever? Will I be transferred? Will I be able to do the work? Will I have a pension? Is there a retirement package? What about my children's future? Where will they go to school? Will I have enough money to pay their fees? What will be my income and is it guaranteed? Sorry, not many answers for the son of man who has nowhere to lay his head!

5. Can you follow a mysterious mission, which has no details?

> **By faith Abraham, when he was called to go out into a place which he should after receive for an inheritance, obeyed; and he went out, NOT KNOWING WHITHER HE WENT.**
>
> **Hebrews 11:8**

How would Abraham become a great nation? What kind of blessings should Abraham expect and what do they entail? Do they include a financial package? God's promises may sound vague. If you want details of what God has in store, you may not get them. When Paul was called to the ministry, the Lord told him very little. He could not know what to expect.

And he fell to the earth, and heard a voice saying unto him, Saul, Saul, why persecutest thou me?

> **And he said, Who art thou, Lord? And the Lord said, I am Jesus whom thou persecutest: it is hard for thee to kick against the pricks.**
>
> **And he trembling and astonished said, Lord, what wilt thou have me to do? And the Lord said unto him, Arise, and go into the city, and IT SHALL BE TOLD THEE WHAT THOU MUST DO.**
>
> **Acts 9:4-6**

On the day of his encounter with the Lord, there were no details! The details came much later. And when the details came, they were scary! It was a mission of suffering! Wow!

> **And there was a certain disciple at Damascus, named Ananias; and to him said the Lord in a vision, Ananias. And he said, Behold, I am here, Lord.**
>
> **And the Lord said unto him, Arise, and go into the street which is called Straight, and inquire in the house of Judas for one called Saul, of Tarsus: for, behold, he prayeth,**
>
> **And hath seen in a vision a man named Ananias coming in, and putting his hand on him, that he might receive his sight.**
>
> **Then Ananias answered, Lord, I have heard by many of this man, how much evil he hath done to thy saints at Jerusalem:**
>
> **And here he hath authority from the chief priests to bind all that call on thy name.**
>
> **But the Lord said unto him, Go thy way: for he is a chosen vessel unto me, to bear my name before the Gentiles, and kings, and the children of Israel:**
>
> **FOR I WILL SHEW HIM HOW GREAT THINGS HE MUST SUFFER FOR MY NAME'S SAKE.**
>
> **Acts 9:10-16**

Ananias was sent to tell Paul that he was being sent on a mission of suffering. Are you ready to follow something that has no detailed plan? Are you willing to follow something in which you will suffer?

6. Can you sojourn?

> **By faith HE SOJOURNED in the land of promise, as in a strange country...**
>
> **Hebrews 11:9**

There is a Greek word "paroikeo" translated "sojourn". This word means to reside as a foreigner and to be a stranger. It is a very difficult thing to be a foreigner in a strange land. Much of God's work today involves living as a stranger amongst people in order to save them.

Do not think that the era of mission work is past. It has just begun. The reason why many think there is nothing to do is because the concept of going into a strange land has been removed by our backslidden churches.

Most pastors would not want to lose their prized members to a foreign land. No one thinks of sending people away.

We want to build one big mega church and huddle together! It is time to sojourn in a strange land for the sake of the Gospel.

7. Can you live in unsettled circumstances?

...DWELLING IN TABERNACLES with Isaac and Jacob, the heirs with him of the same promise:

Hebrews 11:9

In the secular world, people love to establish themselves, build homes and settle down. The ministry is not like that. There is not much certainty about many things. You cannot settle down. You must be ready to dwell in tabernacles (tents) all your life.

Abraham dwelt in tents because his eye was fixed on something eternal. A twenty-five year mortgage will force you to remain in a particular city. Sometimes this kind of arrangement is not compatible with the uncertainty of full-time ministry. God may require you to move on at any time.

8. Can you make your whole family follow you into this adventure?

For I know him, that he will command his children and his household after him, and they shall keep the way of the LORD...

Genesis 18:19

It is important that you bring your family along this road. Some spouses totally reject the uncertainty of it all. I have seen wives who refused to go along with their husbands. A wise man will not marry someone who shows signs of allergy to uncertainty.

The Ordination Service

Many years ago, I attended an ordination service in my city. The pastor preached powerfully and then told the story of how his wife had deserted him.

He said, "One day I came back from a ministry trip and my wife said, 'I can't take this anymore'."

She declared, "I want a normal husband and a normal home. I am tired of this kind of life."

She went on, "I want a husband who comes home at five o'clock. I want to be like every other person. I can't stay here waiting for days for my husband to come home."

She warned him, "If you don't change I'm out of this marriage and you will have to find yourself another wife."

As he ministered, he began to cry and told us how his wife eventually left him. It was very sad, and we all felt like crying. But he ended by saying he was not prepared to sacrifice his ministry for his wife's desires.

Dear friend, such is the reality of ministry. Can you make your whole household follow you on this perilous and uncertain journey?

9. Can you look for a city with foundations?

For he looked for a city which hath foundations, whose builder and maker is God.

Hebrews 11:10

Full-time ministry is all about seeking spiritual realities. We are talking about a city with foundations.

Cities like Accra, New York City, Toronto, Paris, London, Lagos, Johannesburg and Nairobi are merely cities without foundations. Sadly, most Christians are in love with these cities that have no foundations!

Christians love to write their addresses and to say they live on Martin Luther Boulevard, in Los Angeles or in Birmingham.

They don't want to be associated with despised places. They would not want anyone to know that they go to church at Kpakpo Brown Road or Ama Badua Street in Korle-Gonno.

Dear friend, neither Martin Luther Boulevard nor Kpakpo Brown Road has a foundation. It is time to lift up your eyes and see the eternal cities that have foundations. Be prepared to go anywhere because all earthly cities have no foundation anyway.

10. Can you give up your Isaac?

And he said, Take now thy son, thine only son Isaac, whom thou lovest, and get thee into the land of Moriah; and offer him there for a burnt offering upon one of the mountains which I will tell thee of.

Genesis 22:2

Isaac is the precious thing in your life. What is precious to you? Is it your job? Is it your school? Is it your beloved? Is it your lifestyle? Is it your career? Is it your American citizenship? Is it your British citizenship? Is it living in South Africa? Is it living in London?

What do you love so much? Is it your child? Is it your status in this life? Is it your security?

Don't Let Him Get Close

One day, some ladies were chatting. They discussed a brother who had recently left his high-earning job to come into full-time ministry. They were amazed that he could take such a decision.

They said to each other, "As for me, I would not like my husband to get near the Bishop. Everybody who becomes his friend ends up in full-time ministry! His influence is too strong."

They continued discussing, "I don't know how the wife and family will cope with this full-time thing."

Their conclusion was simple, "I really don't want my husband to go near that man."

These women were worried for their own security. The jobs their husbands had and the luxuries they provided meant everything to them. Is it too precious to sacrifice? Full-time ministry means that you leave behind the most precious things of your life.

Before you come into full-time ministry, go through these ten questions. It is an important pre-departure checklist. They will help you to be ready for life in the ministry.

Chapter

40

What it Means to Choose Full-Time Ministry

CHAPTER SUMMARY

40. 1 Full-time ministry is to choose something sacred

40. 2 Full time ministry is a choice to reject greatness in the secular world

40. 3 Full-time ministry is a choice for affliction

40. 4 Full time ministry is to esteem, and treasure reproach

40. 5 Full time ministry is to choose to respect the rewards of Heaven

40. 6 Full time ministry is to choose to forsake the world system

40. 7 Full time ministry is to choose not to fear the king

40. 8 Full time ministry is to choose to follow invisible things

> **...choose you this day...**
>
> **Joshua 24:15**

Anyone contemplating full-time ministry is going to have to make some serious choices. Entering full-time ministry is a decision of a lifetime. You must count the cost. You must think it through. Never enter full-time ministry using lightness and frivolous reasoning.

I want you to think through six important realities that you are choosing from. Do not think that you will escape any of these realities. If Moses experienced these things, so will you.

> **By faith Moses, when he was come to years, refused to be called the son of Pharaoh's daughter;**
>
> **Choosing rather to suffer affliction with the people of God, than to enjoy the pleasures of sin for a season;**
>
> **Esteeming the reproach of Christ greater riches than the treasures in Egypt: for he had respect unto the recompence of the reward.**
>
> **By faith he forsook Egypt, not fearing the wrath of the king: for he endured, as seeing him who is invisible.**
>
> **Hebrews 11:24-27**

1. Full-time ministry is to choose something sacred.

People value different things. Some people value soccer. I hardly even know the names of famous footballers. They are not of much value to me. We who are full-time ministers value sacred things. Many people who are not into full-time ministry actually despise sacred things. The Bible teaches about Esau and describes him as a profane person.

> **Looking diligently lest any man fail of the grace of God; lest any root of bitterness springing up trouble you, and thereby many be defiled; Lest there be any fornicator, or profane person, as Esau, who for one morsel of meat sold his birthright.**
>
> **For ye know how that afterward, when he would have inherited the blessing, he was rejected: for he found no place of repentance, though he sought it carefully with tears.**
>
> **Hebrews 12:15-17**

The word "profane" is the Greek word "bebelos". It is a word used to describe Esau as an irreligious man and a despiser of sacred things. Esau despised sacred things because he was not a spiritual man. Spiritual people called to the ministry place a value on holy things.

The account in the Scripture above shows us that Esau had the opportunity to receive an inheritance, a blessing and a birthright. By simply accepting the gift and position he would have had an inheritance, a blessing and a birthright. This is what full-time ministry is about. It is all about handling sacred things.

Unfortunately, many people do not value sacred things. They actually despise them and look down on them. I believe in these sacred spiritual things. A word spoken over my life means everything to me. The unearned and undeserved position God has given me means everything to me. I cherish the presence of these unquantifiable sacred blessings.

Years ago, I took some brethren on a trip to attend a Benny Hinn meeting. It was an exciting time and we all looked forward to it. When we got to the meeting, I was ushered on stage whilst my friends were given very good seats in the first few rows. The auditorium was packed and thousands of people were turned away. We were truly privileged to have our special seats.

There was excitement in the air and the congregation buzzed with expectation. Suddenly the worship began and Benny Hinn walked onto the stage. I was so excited to be right there at the ringside. In a few minutes, Benny Hinn was ministering.

As the service progressed, I could not help thinking about how fortunate I was to be on stage and how blessed my other friends were to be about five rows from the very front. I looked across into the congregation to see if they were enjoying everything as much as I was. To my surprise, one of them was fast asleep with his head bent over and his mouth hanging open.

I thought I was not seeing aright! How could somebody sleep in such an atmosphere? Was it not a special occasion to be sitting live in a Benny Hinn miracle service? The service was not more than ten minutes old. How tired could anyone be at this time? I felt I was so blessed and it was a sacred moment for me. But somehow, it was such a boring moment to my friend that he had fallen asleep.

The point I am making is that people value different things. Perhaps if a politician or some non-Christian motivational speaker were on stage, he would have been wide awake. But the healing and miracle service of Benny Hinn was simply not interesting enough to him.

2. Full time ministry is a choice to reject greatness in the secular world.

> **By faith Moses…refused to be called the son of Pharaoh's daughter,**
>
> **Hebrews 11:24**

Incredibly, Moses refused to be called the king's son. It was a rejection of earthly honour and prestige. Are you ready for that? Are you ready to forsake every human title and acknowledgement?

When I chose to be in full-time ministry, it was a rejection of human greatness. I would never be called a cardio-thoracic surgeon. I would never be called a neurologist or a psychiatrist. The medical and academic fraternity would never honour me. Professors would now exclude me from their circles. I would be associated with priests, pastors and other religious weirdos. This was the choice I made when I chose full-time ministry.

3. Full-time ministry is a choice for affliction.

> **…Moses…Choosing rather to suffer affliction with the people of God, than to enjoy the pleasures of sin for a season;**
>
> **Hebrews 11:25**

There are certain sufferings that go along with full-time ministry. To choose full-time ministry is to choose affliction. I constantly tell people who are coming into full-time ministry to expect poverty.

There is no biblical basis for a life of luxury. All the Bible has to say are things to do with crosses, sacrifices, sufferings and afflictions.

We cannot say anything against the truth but for the truth. The affliction of full-time ministry for you may be different from the affliction that I experienced. Whatever the case, you will suffer some affliction. You must accept that you will never enjoy certain pleasures in this life. Are you ready for that?

I Will Never Forget

I always remember when I took the decision for full-time ministry. I knew I would never live in a home like the one I had known in my childhood; a large house in a prime area with many rooms, a big garden, a swimming pool, a summer hut and lots of space. I estimated that the highest kind of comfort I would ever have would be a tiny two-bedroom flat in a poor suburb of Accra, Ghana.

I also thought that I would never travel on an airplane again. I knew that my days of flying were over. I would never have enough money to buy a ticket for the rest of my life. I genuinely took that decision when I came into full-time ministry. Poverty and affliction is a definite choice that you make when you choose full-time ministry.

4. Full time ministry is to esteem, and treasure reproach.

> **Esteeming the reproach...**
>
> **Hebrews 11:26**

From the time I chose to be in full-time ministry, it became important for me to value reproach.

One day, I heard that someone had called me "Satan". Instead of getting angry, I knelt down and thanked God for the honour of being insulted with the same insults that my Saviour had received. Jesus was associated with Beelzebub by unbelieving critics.

> **But when the Pharisees heard it, they said, This fellow doth not cast out devils, but by Beelzebub the prince of the devils.**
>
> **Matthew 12:24**

You must value every insult and criticism. One professor asked his students whether I was mad for starting a church whilst in medical school. But I was grateful that somebody was enquiring whether I was mad because Paul had also been accused of madness. I am glad to be associated with the reproaches of people like Christ Jesus and Paul.

Festus, a ruler before whom Paul was arraigned asked Paul whether he was mad.

> **While Paul was saying this in his defense, Festus said in a loud voice, "Paul, you are out of your mind! Your great learning is driving you mad." But Paul said, "I am not out of my mind, most excellent Festus, but I utter words of sober truth."**
>
> **Acts 26:24-25, NASB**

Somebody said, "I can't stand insults. I do not like it when people talk about me."

Then I said, "Then you cannot be in the ministry."

Ministry work involves people having a field day discussing, analyzing and criticizing you!

5. Full time ministry is to choose to respect the rewards of Heaven.

> **...for he had respect unto the recompense of the reward.**
>
> **Hebrews 11:26**

To come into full-time ministry, you must have a great regard for heavenly rewards. You must respect the concept of receiving white gowns, crowns and white stones. If all you respect are earthly appointment letters with fat remuneration packages from the bank, you are not fit for full-time ministry and are unlikely to succeed in it.

There are no such appointment letters for full-time ministry. There is no promise of cars, houses or fat bonuses. Moses respected the thought of rewards in Heaven. "For he had respect unto the recompense of the reward" (Hebrews 11:26).

6. Full time ministry is to choose to forsake the world system.

> **By faith he forsook Egypt...**
>
> **Hebrews 11:27**

Coming into full-time ministry also involves forsaking the world. In the world salaries are guaranteed every month. Moses forsook the life in the Egyptian palace and opted for the wilderness. Can you imagine what it felt like as he walked away from the glorious city of Ramses into the dark frightening desert? That is what full-time ministry is all about.

It is to walk away from a glamorous job in a glassy bank building to a simple church building where even the mice are said to be poor.

7. Full time ministry is to choose not to fear the king.

> **...Not fearing the wrath of the king...**
>
> **Hebrews 11:27**

Who is the king in your life? Is it your father? Or is it your mother? Is the king the uncle who paid your school fees? Or is it your very own wife? How will these people punish me for my decision to be in full-time ministry? Will they stop their financial support? Will they strike my name out of their family? To be in full-time ministry, you must overcome the fear of every kind of king!

Full-time ministry involves conquering your raging fears. It is truly a frightening thing to abandon everything and enter into full-time ministry.

Questions abound: Will I survive? Will I have food to eat? Will I ever drive a car? Will I ever be happy? Will my children ever go to school? By how much will my life change? What will people think of me? These are just a few of the fears you may have but the Lord will deliver you from all your fears (Psalm 34:4).

8. Full time ministry is to choose to follow invisible things.

> **...for he endured, as seeing him who is invisible.**
>
> **Hebrews 11:27**

Moses endured full-time ministry. He did this by looking at invisible things. Once again, it is only by focusing on unseen eternal realities that full-time ministry is possible. Today's church can hardly produce missionaries.

It is a materialistic church whose trust is in this world's physical wealth. Both pastors and congregation are earthly-minded with dreams of material success and wealth. How can such people look at invisible things? How can such people send young men to jungles, villages to win the forgotten souls of this world?

What are invisible things? They are Heaven, Hell, angels, devils, eternity, eternal rewards and all the things spoken of in the book of Revelation. God Himself is invisible. Jesus is also invisible.

What are the visible things? They are cities, buildings, banks, money, wealth, clothes, diamonds, gold, cars and the like. You cannot do full-time ministry with your eyes on visible things.

Lift up your eyes and see the invisible, then you will be well able to last in full-time ministry!

Chapter

41

The Privileges of Full-Time Ministers

CHAPTER SUMMARY

41.1 Full-time ministers have the privilege of no longer following after dung

41.2 Full-time ministers have gained the privilege of being found in Him

41.3 Full-time ministers have gained the privilege of knowing Him

41.4 Full-time ministers have the privilege of becoming fellow sufferers with Christ

41.5 Full-time ministers are privileged to fight for a glorious resurrection

41.6 Full-time ministers are delivered from complacency

41.7 Full-time ministers have the privilege of attaining the reason for which they were saved

41.8 Full-time ministers have a chance to forget the past

41.9 Full-time ministers can have a special prize

Full-time ministry affords the minister some of the highest privileges ever given to human beings. There is nothing more precious than these blessings.

1. Full-time ministers have the privilege of no longer following after dung.

> **...and do count them but dung, that I may win Christ,**
>
> **Philippians 3:8**

The call to full-time ministry delivers you from the pursuit of dung. Coprophilia is a disease in which a person loves watching people defecate or loves to be defecated upon. This is a terrible disease - to love faeces.

If someone delivered you from coprophilia would you not be grateful? According to Paul the pursuit of Christ with the attendant loss of all things (full-time ministry) is like being delivered from following faeces.

2. Full-time ministers have gained the privilege of being found in Him.

> **And be found in him...**
>
> **Philippians 3:9**

Instead of being found in the library, the market or the bank you can be found in the presence of the Lord. What a privilege this is - to be found in Him!

3. Full-time ministers have gained the privilege of knowing Him.

> **That I may know him...**
>
> **Philippians 3:10**

By coming to work for God and with God, the great blessing will be that you should know Him better. If you work with someone, you get to know the person.

Whilst others are getting to know the Managing Director better, you are getting to know the Lord better. Whilst others are getting closer to Professors you are getting closer to God and to His servants.

4. Full-time ministers have the privilege of becoming fellow sufferers with Christ.

> **...and the fellowship of his sufferings...**
>
> **Philippians 3:10**

What a privilege it is to share in the sufferings of someone great. It will earn you a crown when it really matters. Anyone who suffers with an honourable man will never be forgotten.

Abiathar Suffers with David

King David appointed Solomon to be heir of his throne. Unfortunately, some people (including Abiathar) tried to displace Solomon and ascend the throne. The evil plot was quelled and Solomon became king and took his rightful place.

Solomon executed all the people who tried to usurp his throne, except one person - Abiathar the priest.

Solomon told Abiathar that he deserved to die. However, instead of executing him, he spared his life for one reason - Abiathar had been through much suffering with his father David.

> **Then to Abiathar the priest the king said, "Go to Anathoth to your own field, for you deserve to die; but I will not put you to death at this time, because you carried the ark of the Lord GOD before my father David, and because you were afflicted in everything with which my father was afflicted."**
>
> **So Solomon dismissed Abiathar from being priest to the LORD, in order to fulfill the word of the LORD, which He had spoken concerning the house of Eli in Shiloh.**
>
> **1 Kings 2:26-27, NASB**

The Disciples Suffer with Christ

Jesus said the same thing to His disciples. They had been through much suffering with Him and he would never forget it. He promised them special rewards just because they had suffered with him.

> **Ye are they which have continued with me in my temptations. And I appoint unto you a kingdom, as my Father hath appointed unto me;**
>
> **Luke 22:28-29**

One of the privileges of full-time ministry is to join Christ in the shame and humiliation of true ministry. Surely, sharing the shame and suffering of Christ will not be in vain.

5. Full-time ministers are privileged to fight for a glorious resurrection.

> **If by any means I might attain unto the resurrection of the dead.**
>
> **Philippians 3:11**

Instead of being presumptuous, full-time ministers fight to ensure they are part of the glorious resurrection.

6. Full-time ministers are delivered from complacency.

> **Not as though I had already attained, either were already perfect: but I follow after...**
>
> **Philippians 3:12**

The lack of labourers and harvesters becomes apparent when you become a full-time minister.

Through full-time ministry, your personal inadequacies are revealed. The daunting task of ministry removes the feeling of being perfect.

The harvest fields of lost souls weigh on the true minister. You will not be able to say you have arrived. You will never feel accomplished no matter how much you work. This reality saves you from the sin of complacency.

What a privilege to be delivered from the deception of thinking we are something that we are not!

7. Full-time ministers have the privilege of attaining the reason for which they were saved.

> **...that I may apprehend that for which also I am apprehended of Christ Jesus.**
>
> **Philippians 3:12**

When I was a student, the aging founder of the Church of Pentecost preached to the university fellowship of his denomination from this text. That is how I always remember this Scripture. I always imagine this seasoned warrior saying, "That I may apprehend that for which I was apprehended!"

Sadly, most Christians never apprehend that for which they were apprehended. Is this not the most important thing in the world? To accomplish the things for which Christ saved you?

Why did He save you? Why did He love you? Why did He call you? Why you and not somebody else?

Thank God for a divine opportunity to attain to your divine destiny!

8. Full-time ministers have a chance to forget the past.

> **...forgetting those things which are behind...**
>
> **Philippians 3:13**

Full-time ministry will swallow up your life. There will be no time or energy to remember the past. Paul's past was wiped away as he pursued the Lord in full-time ministry. He was now able to press towards the things of God that lay ahead.

9. Full-time ministers can have a special prize.

> **I press toward the mark for the prize of the high calling of God in Christ Jesus.**
>
> **Philippians 3:13-14**

All full-time ministers are privileged to target the prize of the high calling. This is not the prize for the best student in French. It is the prize of the high calling. It must be something special and I am blessed to aim for this wonderful prize.

Chapter

42

Why Some People Leave the Work of Ministry

CHAPTER SUMMARY

There are several subtle defections from ministry. Actually, many people depart from ministry in their hearts before they get involved in business, social work and politics.

- **Types of Returnees**

42. 1 **Type 1: The Subtle Type**

42. 2 **Type 2: The Demas Type**

42. 3 **Type 3: The Lot's Wife Type**

42. 4 **Type 4: The Mark Type**

42. 5 **Type 5: The Peter Type**

42. 6 **Type 6: The Bored Type**

> **But we are not of them who draw back...**
>
> **Hebrews 10:39**

Years ago, I sat in a restaurant with a seasoned minister of God. He had built a large church in a city and had several other branch churches. As we chatted, he told me something that stunned me.

He said, "I have decided to leave the ministry and go into business."

He explained, "I find the ministry boring. It does not challenge me anymore."

Then he said, "I can't imagine myself doing this for the rest of my life."

He told me how he had decided to go to university so that he could accomplish many more things.

I was bewildered, as I had never met anyone like that.

To me, coming into ministry was the greatest step of my life. Leaving medicine behind was such a big upward step.

I wondered, "Why would anyone do something like that?" What would make someone who is successful in ministry abandon everything and return to the secular world?

Well, I was to find out that he was not the first, and neither would he be the last to return.

■ Types of Returnees

Type 1: The Subtle Type

Some people partially desert the ministry because of attractions to other vocations.

I have heard of different ministers going into politics, business, medical work, social work, government work and all sorts of other occupations.

In a sense, the ministry becomes a thing of the past. It no longer consumes their whole being as it used to.

Sadly, the work of the ministry is relegated to the position of a stepchild. They maintain the title Reverend and continue to pastor their churches, but they have actually metamorphosed into part-time ministers and part-time something else. Surely, there has been a subtle but significant shift from true ministry.

Is There Nothing to Do?

All these subtle defections from the ministry are done against the background of six billion souls waiting to be won to Jesus. As nations fall to Islam, Christian ministers charged with spreading the Gospel rather find time for a host of other things!

Ironically, as millions continue to die and go to Hell, the urgency of our calling seems to be weaker. Perhaps backslidden pastors who are possessed with the spirit of worldliness and who value wealth more than the anointing lead the church.

It is because we are a backslidden church that the idea of substituting the ministry of the cross and the blood of Jesus with business, politics or humanitarian works can even be suggested in the church community.

Type 2: The Demas Type

> **For Demas has forsaken me, having loved this present world...**
> **2 Timothy 4:10, NKJV**

Demas was in full-time ministry with the Apostle Paul. Yet he forsook Paul and returned to his old life. Paul explained why this had happened: Demas had loved this present world. No one who loves this present world will do well in full-time ministry. You must not love this earthly, physical world. Your heart must be fixed on eternal things.

The worst type of person to mistakenly be in full-time ministry is someone who loves this present world. If you love the glamour and wealth of the cities of this world, how can you be sent to villages where the poor and needy await salvation?

Sadly, many Christians are in love with this world and they are incompatible with full-time ministry. A lover of cars, money, clothes, and houses should not apply to work in full-time ministry. The ministry is not a place for people with earthly goals. Your earthly ambitions will soon be in conflict with the goals of ministry.

Do you desire fame and acknowledgement from the world? Do you desire earthly laurels? Do you want to be seen as one of the young, upwardly progressive people of this era? Well, that is not compatible with full-time ministry. Full-time ministry will lead to rejection by the world.

The medical community from which I emanate did not hail or praise me for entering into full-time ministry. They despised me and called me names. One doctor asked if I had gone mad. I don't blame them. I am not trying to impress them.

Type 3: The Lot's Wife Type

> **Remember Lot's wife.**
> **Luke 17:32**

> **But his wife looked back behind him, and she became a pillar of salt.**
> **Genesis 19:26, NKJV**

Lot's wife turned into a pillar of salt because she looked into the past. Do not look back; otherwise, your ministry will freeze. You cannot have the same friends, the same cars, the same income, the same clothes, the same pastimes that you had when you were in the world. If you look back longingly at these things, you have troubled yourself.

He Looked Back

One day, a brother who was in full-time ministry began complaining about his work. In one of his outbursts, he made a pronouncement, which was revealing.

He blurted out, "If I was still working at King Kong Fishing Company, I would be earning thousands of dollars by now."

You see, this fellow used to be a Manager for King Kong and it was now five years since he had resigned and entered into full-time ministry. He was looking back at his income. He was considering what his income might have been. When you look back, you have all sorts of imaginations about what you could have become. This paralyses you in full-time ministry and makes you want to return.

If we all look back and imagine what we might have been, our ministries may come to a grinding halt. Looking back is not an option once you are in full-time ministry.

Type 4: The Mark Type

Barnabas wanted to take John, called Mark, along with them also.

But Paul kept insisting that they should not take him along who had deserted them in Pamphylia and had not gone with them to the work.

Acts 15:37-38, NASB

Mark is an example of someone who abandoned the ministry midstream. I have seen this several times. These people suddenly resign from full-time ministry without much explanation. They abruptly disengage from the ministry without obvious reason. This type of desertion is distressing as it is never clear why the individual is departing.

Once, I had a pastor I loved dearly and to whom I had assigned a very important job. Everything seemed to be going well until I suddenly got a letter by which he resigned from the ministry. I found out later that this fellow was offended about various things.

Several other ministers who have behaved in this "Mark" fashion had hidden reasons in their hearts.

And then shall many be offended, and shall betray one another, and shall hate one another.

Matthew 24:10

Alas, unhealed wounds are not compatible with the priesthood. No minister will flourish if he keeps bitterness within.

I tell you, unforgiveness will remove you from the ministry faster than you can imagine. Unforgiveness and a lack of communication are the cause of this kind of desertion.

Type 5: The Peter Type

> **Simon Peter said to them, "I am going fishing." They said to him, "We are going with you also." They went out and immediately got into the boat, and that night they caught nothing.**
>
> **John 21:3, NKJV**

After Peter had received training for three years, he decided to go back to fishing. Peter's return to fishing was one of his most unfortunate choices. He carried along with him people that looked up to him.

This is the type of desertion in which people do not appreciate their ministerial training. Such people do not realize the investments that have been made in their lives. They disregard years of Bible school training and simply put it aside.

The Bible School Picture

Years ago, Dr Yonggi Cho told a story of how he found an old picture of his Bible school mates. He noted that most of them were dead. Just a couple of them were still alive and those were the ones still in ministry. You see, instead of preaching, many of them had become welders, carpenters, drivers, etc. Bible school training had not meant much to some of them.

In the "Peter type" of desertion, the person does not know the greatness of his calling! The entire church of Jesus Christ depended on Peter becoming a rock and a foundation. Yet here he was fishing. And he was not alone, but he was fishing with all the other rocks and foundations of the church. Mercy!

How was the church to be built if Peter returned to fishing? Did the three years with Christ mean nothing? Did all the teachings and private discussions found in the book of John mean nothing? What was Peter looking for?

You Will Not Prosper When You Return

Peter caught nothing that night. He was looking for fish but there was no fish to be found for the returning apostle.

Jesus called out and told the struggling defectors what to do. Once again, our Lord proved that we can do nothing without him, including our professions. They ran to the shore and found Jesus grilling the very fish they were looking for.

God knows what we need. There is no need for us to abandon our calling to chase our needs.

It is only when they fished on the instructions of Jesus that it yielded anything. Everything else was useless.

> **Simon Peter said to them, "I am going fishing." They said to him, "We will also come with you." They went out and got into the boat; and that night they caught nothing.**
>
> **But when the day was now breaking, Jesus stood on the beach; yet the disciples did not know that it was Jesus.**

So Jesus said to them, "Children, you do not have any fish, do you?" They answered Him, "No."

And He said to them, "Cast the net on the right-hand side of the boat and you will find a catch." So they cast, and then they were not able to haul it in because of the great number of fish.

Therefore that disciple whom Jesus loved said to Peter, "It is the Lord." So when Simon Peter heard that it was the Lord, he put his outer garment on (for he was stripped for work), and threw himself into the sea.

But the other disciples came in the little boat, for they were not far from the land, but about one hundred yards away, dragging the net full of fish.

So when they got out on the land, they saw a charcoal fire already laid and fish placed on it, and bread.

Jesus said to them, "Bring some of the fish which you have now caught."

Simon Peter went up and drew the net to land, full of large fish, a hundred and fifty-three; and although there were so many, the net was not torn.

Jesus said to them, "Come and have breakfast." None of the disciples ventured to question Him, "Who are You?" knowing that it was the Lord.

Jesus came and took the bread and gave it to them, and the fish likewise.

John 21:3-13, NASB

Sheep or Fish?

It was after this that Jesus asked, "Do you love me?" When Peter said, "I love you", Jesus asked him to go back to ministry work. In other words, "Please don't go back to fishing. Concentrate on the sheep and feed them." How many ministers have left the sheep and gone back to fishing? Perhaps countless have. Could it be that we do not love Jesus anymore? May God have mercy on our souls!

Type 6: The Bored Type

Then shall we know, if we follow on to know the LORD...

Hosea 6:3

There is a type of desertion in ministry, which comes from not continuing to follow the Lord. It is easy to start out in the ministry but it is not that easy to continue. To be steadfast in ministry is important.

Steadfastness is a word borrowed from the navy. It speaks of the ability to stay on course. It also speaks of the ability to come back to course after you have drifted off. Many ministers do not have steadfastness. They cannot fulfil the calling of a pastor. It takes steadfastness to continue preaching divine and mystical truths in spite of the pressure to change the message and make it more "relevant".

Following the Lord is an exciting adventure. It is a quest without parallel. You will find yourself running, fighting, thinking, surviving and strategizing all the time.

Paul described the tension of ministry in the second book of Corinthians. He said,

> **For we do not want you to be unaware, brethren, of our affliction which came to us in Asia, that we were burdened excessively, beyond our strength, so that we despaired even of life; indeed, we had the sentence of death within ourselves so that we would not trust in ourselves, but in God who raises the dead; who delivered us from so great a peril of death, and will deliver us, He on whom we have set our hope. And He will yet deliver us,**
>
> **2 Corinthians 1:8-10, NASB**

How can ministry be boring? It is because you have ceased to follow the Lord that ministry has become boring to you. Many have taken detours because their eyes are set on natural goals rather than God-given tasks.

I feel no rest and I feel no ease after all these years in ministry. There is always a certain kind of tension within me. It is as though I just began. The closer I get to God the more worried I am for my state.

The whole world lies in wickedness! Billions of souls are waiting for us!

The forgotten ones sleep and awake everyday in their villages hoping it will be the day when the good news will be brought to them.

Seeking for the Lord in full-time ministry will never be boring. It will challenge you to the very core.

Do not let any minister deceive you into thinking that there is time and space for earthly pursuits. It is time to spend and be spent!

Paul's last words do not give the impression of someone who was bored. His last words do not give the impression of someone looking for a new job.

He had no time for a political or social role in Rome where he was a citizen. You can sense the exhaustion, the intensity and the dedication to the original purpose.

> **For I am now ready to be offered, and the time of my departure is at hand.**
>
> **I have fought a good fight, I have finished my course, I have kept the faith:**
>
> **2 Timothy 4:6-7**

Full-time ministry is the best thing that could ever happen to you. There is no parallel to this high calling. There is no greater opportunity that a person could have.

I highly recommend that your life be spent in absolute surrender and full-time commitment to the purpose and prize of the Gospel!

Section

3

LAIKOS

The Greek word LAIKOS means "having no skills". History has taught us over and over again that great things have been accomplished through people who "lacked skills". Learn, through this section, what happens where there are no laymen working in the church; how to share the burden with lay people and why we must fight to protect the lay ministry.

Chapter

43

LAIKOS: The Layman

CHAPTER SUMMARY

The word layman comes from the Greek word LAIKOS which means "having no skills". History teaches us that great things can be accomplished through people who "lack skills". A quick glance at the achievements of lay people or common people will inspire you to use them in the ministry. Through laymen, souls will be saved, cells will be established, churches will grow and God's work will flourish.

The following are a few definitions of the word layman:

1. A layman is an ordinary person.
2. A layman is a normal person.
3. A layman is a commonplace person.
4. A layman is a usual person.
5. A layman is a regular person.
6. A layman is a common person.
7. A layman is an everyday person.
8. A layman is an average person.
9. A layman is someone who is not a professional.
10. A layman is someone who is not an expert.
11. A layman is someone who is not specialized.
12. A layman is someone who is not skilled.
13. A layman is someone who is not trained.
14. A layman is someone who is not certified.
15. A layman is someone who is not licensed.

■ Great Achievements in the Church World

1. Lay people were the pillars of the great reformation of the church.

Martin Luther's translation of the Bible into the language of the common people changed the world. Instead of just being in Latin, the Bible was made more accessible to the common people. Once the common/lay people had revelation knowledge in their hands they changed the world. Realising that salvation was available to all men through the grace of God they rose up and championed what we now know as the Reformation.

2. Lay people are the pillars of the great Methodist Church.

By the middle of the 20th century, Methodism was the largest Protestant denomination in the United States. The great Methodist church has ridden on the backs of lay people.

A very early tradition of preaching in the Methodist churches was for a Lay Preacher to be appointed to lead services of worship and preach in a group of churches called a "circuit".

The lay preacher walked or rode on horseback in a prescribed circuit of the preaching places according to an agreed pattern and timing.

After the appointment of ministers and pastors, this lay preaching tradition continued with "Methodist Local Preachers" being appointed by individual churches, and in turn approved and invited by nearby churches, as an adjunct to the minister or during their planned absences.

3. Lay people were the pillars of the largest single church in the world.

One of the foundational principles on which the Yoido Full Gospel Church is built is the principle of working through lay people.

The Yoido Full Gospel Church, founded by David Yonggi Cho and his mother-in-law, Choi Ja-shil, both Assemblies of God pastors, held its maiden worship service on May 15, 1958 with four other ladies in the home of Choi Ja-shil.

Membership of the church had reached fifty thousand by 1977, a figure that doubled in only two years. On 30 November 1981, membership topped two hundred thousand. By this time, it was the largest single congregation in the world and was recognized as such by the Los Angeles Times.

In 2007 its membership stood at 830,000, with seven Sunday services translated into sixteen languages.

4. Lay people are the pillars of huge networks of churches originating from Nigeria and Ghana.

Both the Redeemed Christian Church of God with its home in Nigeria and The Church of Pentecost with its headquarters in Ghana are known to make good use of lay people. Both of these ministries have huge networks of churches and regularly employ the services of lay people for preaching and pastoring.

The Church of Pentecost was founded by James McKeon, an Irish missionary sent by the Apostolic Church, Bradford, UK to the then Gold Coast.

It has grown to have a membership of over 1.7 million members. The Church of Pentecost has over 13,000 churches in 70 countries across all the continents of the world.

In 1952, Pa Josiah Akindayomi founded the Redeemed Christian Church of God in Nigeria.

Under the leadership of its General Overseer, Reverend E.A. Adeboye, it has grown to have churches in more than 140 countries, with millions in attendance.

Truly, these are great achievements and they have been made possible through the inputs of lay people.

■ Great Achievements in the Secular World

1. The great government system of democracy was birthed through lay people.

Democracy is giving common people the opportunity to act and change the government if they wish.

Democracy is the common man's power to refuse to live under unacceptable conditions.

Democracy is the common man's participation and influence in a country.

Democracy is built upon the principle of equal opportunity given to all common people.

2. The great super-power was given birth to through lay people.

The American Revolution is a classic example of the power of the common or lay people in shaping history. The common man gave birth to a superpower. At the turn of the last century, the American Revolution was a successful experiment that marked the transition of a world controlled by a few to a world controlled by the many.

The Revolution was largely shaped by small revolutionary organizations such as the Sons of Liberty. These organizations were not controlled by the rich and powerful landowners but common people of average social status came together to plant the seeds of the Revolution.

3. The historic election victory of Barack Obama came through lay people.

In May 2008, Barack Obama, first black president of the United States of America, clinched the Democratic nomination for the presidency of the United States.

Even though the country's rich and influential Democrats were Clinton supporters and provided the millions of dollars, Obama raised more than any other presidential candidate in history by using the power of the common person.

Obama raised over $80 million in his campaign, most of which came from common people making small individual contributions.

Chapter

44

What Happens When There Are No Laymen and Volunteers

CHAPTER SUMMARY

The symbol of Christianity is the cross. The cross speaks of suffering and dying. God spoke to Abraham and asked him to give up his most treasured possession - his son. Don't listen to anyone who tells you that the day of suffering, sacrificing, losing and dying is over. The day of suffering, sacrificing, losing and dying has come! God is requiring us to give up our treasured possessions so that we can serve Him. The church is being filled with people who are not aware that God is calling them to sacrifice. Christianity is a religion of sacrifice. Christianity is based on the cross. Christianity is based on losing your life so that you gain a new life.

1. If you do not allow volunteers to work in the ministry you will kill the Christian principle of sacrifice in the church.

> **Then said Jesus unto his disciples, If any man will come after me, let him deny himself, and take up his cross, and follow me.**
>
> **Matthew 16:24**

Different Sacrifices for Different People

But some people have the mistaken view that God asks everyone to sacrifice their "Isaac". But God did not ask Joseph to sacrifice his sons. Neither did He ask Jacob or Isaac to sacrifice their sons. King David was a man after God's own heart, but God did not ask David to sacrifice his son.

God deals with everyone differently! What God requires of me may be different from what He requires of you. God has asked me for my profession. Perhaps God will not ask you for your profession. *But He will ask you for something and you will have to give it up.*

Christianity always involves sacrifice. If you do not allow lay people to work in the ministry, they will never learn to give up the smallest things for Christ. If they cannot give up their time, their evenings and their leisure for Christ what will happen if the Lord asks them for their "Isaac"? It is important to expose the lay people in your church to this basic principle of sacrifice.

2. If you do not allow laymen to work in the ministry you will remove the opportunity for people to demonstrate faithfulness.

The Bible teaches clearly that he that is faithful with little will be faithful with much.

> **He that is faithful in that which is least is faithful also in much: and he that is unjust in the least is unjust also in much. If therefore ye have not been faithful in the unrighteous mammon, who will commit to your trust the true riches? And if ye have not been faithful in that which is another man's, who shall give you that which is your own?**
>
> **Luke 16:10-12**

If somebody is not faithful as a layperson, how will he be faithful when he is in full-time ministry? Many people do not do well in full-time ministry because they did not do well as lay people.

Did you work for the Lord as a layperson who did not need supervision? Did you need anybody to tell you to get up to pray? Did you need anybody to tell you to study your Bible? Were you faithful when you were in school?

I was a committed worker in the Scripture Union fellowship in my school. I was heavily involved as an organist in a Christian singing group to which I belonged. I was a drummer and pianist for Victory Church in London. I was involved with the fellowships in the university. Yet it never once crossed my mind that I should be paid for these things.

This lay ministry is an important background for a future full-time ministry. He that is faithful with lay ministry will be faithful with full-time ministry. Many people who have worked as lay people work even better as full-timers.

3. If you do not allow lay people to work in the ministry you will employ people to do jobs that do not occupy them fully.

Not every ministry needs a full-time pastor. Many churches can be pastored by unpaid lay pastors. If there are only twenty-five people in the church, it is obvious that it cannot sustain and does not need a full-time minister. Many of the church members secretly ask, "What does the full-time pastor do all day?"

Many people think that pastors sleep from morning to evening. The fact is that there isn't so much to do with a congregation of thirty. The ministry has to develop to the point where it needs a full-time worker. The other reality is that most of the members are at work during the day and only become available in the evenings.

Pastors are not bankers, accountants or pharmacists. They are shepherds who are supposed to look after sheep. Working hours are different for different professions! I do not work from nine to five every day because I am not an accountant. I am a pastor! When the sheep become available in the evenings I become very active. That is why I work late into the night. Some pastors become idle and lazy as they wait for Sunday when they can deliver their next sermon.

> **For we hear that there are some which walk among you disorderly, WORKING NOT AT ALL…**
>
> **2 Thessalonians 3:11**

Let us be honest! Let us be realistic! Does your church need so many full-time pastors? Does it need even one full-time pastor? Can the income of the church sustain the pastor and his family? Can the pastor not find a secular job to do? Pastors are frustrated and fearful because they are not sure whether they will be able to survive until the next month.

You can overcome that frustration today! Get a job and pastor the church on the side until it grows and demands your full attention!

The Swiss missionaries who were sent to Ghana many years ago were sent as *self-sustaining ministers.* They came equipped with skills that would enable them to work in Africa as they did their ministry work. That is a good example to follow. We need self-sustaining ministers today more than ever before. Most churches cannot bear the burden of maintaining so many full-time pastors.

You must keep your ministry staff as small as possible so that you can pay them properly. You must not have idle and discontented people around you. Idleness leads to laziness and laziness leads to discontentment and discontentment leads to disloyalty.

> **And withal they learn to be idle, wandering about from house to house; and not only idle, but tattlers also and busybodies, speaking things which they ought not.**
>
> **1 Timothy 5:13**

4. If you do not allow volunteers to work in the ministry everything done in the church will be related to money.

> **He that loveth silver shall not be satisfied with silver; nor he that loveth abundance with increase: this is also vanity.**
>
> **Ecclesiastes 5:10**

The ministry is not an alternative source of employment for anyone. It was never intended to be! It is a special job that God gives to those whom He has called. **As the church becomes larger, it often deteriorates into a source of employment for the unemployed.** This attracts many people who have no better options. What happens to the church? It becomes full of seekers of wealth and lovers of silver. The church is filled with pastors who constantly fight for better salaries and conditions of service.

I started ministry as a layperson, so the idea of being paid in full-time ministry came up much later. I started my church as a medical student and found myself pastoring while at the same time practising medicine. Later on, I went into business and combined it with pastoral work.

At the end of 1990, the Lord told me to leave everything I was doing and enter into full-time ministry. It was not an easy decision for me. Since January 1st, 1991 I have been full-time in the ministry for the Lord Jesus.

There are many people who are in full-time ministry who should not really be there. There are many people who I believe should find secular jobs! How can a church with sixty members sustain eight full-time pastors and their families? Yet, this is the case in many ministries. Success in the ministry requires both power and wisdom.

> **But unto them which are called, both Jews and Greeks, Christ the power of God, and the wisdom of God.**
>
> **1 Corinthians 1:24**

Many pastors see the ministry as a way to travel around the world and to drive nice cars. I did not enter the ministry in order to drive a nice car. I do drive a nice car now but I did not come into the ministry because I wanted to have the nice things of this world. In fact, coming into full-time ministry was, for me, the end of all hopes of ever having the nice things of this world.

> **Yea doubtless, and I count all things but loss for the excellency of the knowledge of Christ Jesus my Lord: for whom I HAVE SUFFERED THE LOSS OF ALL THINGS, and do count them but dung, that I may win Christ,**
>
> **Philippians 3:8**

A minister who is going to serve God properly must have died to the love for silver and gold. Why is this? The Bible teaches that those that love silver are never satisfied with silver. The more you give them, the more they want. Why is it that the richest people in this world are often the biggest thieves? Is it because they are poor? Is it because they are in need? Certainly not! It is because of the greed for more and more and more!

You cannot satisfy people who want more and more money. From experience, whenever I have felt under pressure to raise salaries, I have often discovered it does not solve the problem!

Senior pastors, if you feel under pressure to raise salaries and give more and more benefits, you will discover that the problem never goes away. Full-time ministers must be people who just want to serve the Lord at heart. This does not mean that people will be poor but it means that the heart is not craving endlessly after more and more.

Soon the church becomes unionized with the workers against the management, and the management against the workers! The "management" are often the senior pastors who make decisions and the "workers" are the other pastors and workers who are not involved in the decision-making. You should see the bitterness, petty jealousies and bickering amongst the full-time staff of many churches and ministries. This often extends to their families and pastor's wives pick up quarrels with other pastor's wives.

I would rather have one or two workers with peace than to have a hundred unhappy and discontented full-time staff.

5. If you do not allow laymen to work in the ministry people will not learn obedience and submission.

As you enter into full-time ministry you must be open for whatever the future will bring. You may be rich or you may be poor. You may have abundance or you may live in the "want of all things". Are you ready for anything?

> **Verily, verily, I say unto thee, When thou wast young, thou girdedst thyself, and walkedst whither thou wouldest: but when thou shalt be old, thou shalt stretch forth thy hands, and another shall gird thee, and carry thee whither thou wouldest not.**
>
> **This spake he, signifying by what death he should glorify God. And when he had spoken this, he saith unto him, Follow me.**
>
> **John 21:18-19**

Jesus told Peter to be ready for anything. Be ready to be carried anywhere. It will no longer be your will, but God's will. You are not the commander, you are just one of God's workers. One of the reasons why I am in the ministry is because I have no choice.

> **...woe is unto me, if I preach not the gospel!**
>
> **1 Corinthians 9:16**

There are detractors, faultfinders, analysts and commentators who talk about me all the time. I have no time for empty chatter. I prefer to hear my dogs barking in the morning than to listen to their hateful and sarcastic comments. I must continue doing what God has called me to do. Some people love me for what I do and others hate me. I thank God for them all. But I press on for the mark of the prize of the high calling.

I am totally surrendered to fulfilling the call of God upon my life, so help me God!

Chapter

45

Seven Reasons Why God Operates through Lay People

CHAPTER SUMMARY

- **Why God Operates through Lay People**

45. 1 **The gift of ministry is *measured.***

45. 2 **God has decided to give everyone *a different office*.**

45. 3 **God gives some people *only one talent*.**

45. 4 **Some people *do not have the ability* for full-time ministry.**

45. 5 **The *Holy Spirit works* through all ministries no matter how diverse they are.**

45. 6 **God *administers* His power in different ways.**

45. 7 **God *operates* in different ways. God Almighty can operate through a volunteer.**

All through the Scriptures, you see God giving different gifts to different people. To some He gives one talent and to others He gives many talents. I believe that it is the ministry of the one talent. However, it is important to value this ministry even if it is only one talent. Your judgment for despising the one talent will be severe.

Why do I call it the ministry of one talent? Those in full-time ministry give all their days, nights, weeks and months to the Lord's work whilst those who are volunteers may give one day in the week for this ministry. You cannot compare the output and the sacrifice of a one-evening-a-week ministry with that of a hundred per cent full-time dedicated ministry. Does that mean that the lay ministry is not valid? Not at all! Some people have been called by the Holy Spirit to work for God with one talent. "But all these worketh that one and the selfsame Spirit, dividing to every man severally as he will" (1Corinthians 12:11).

It is the will of God that some people have one talent while some have ten. It is the will of God that some people work for God once a week whilst others work for Him every day. Your judgment will be based on your faithfulness to your mission and your call.

■ Why God Operates through Lay People

1. **The gift of ministry is *measured*.** Some people receive a larger measure than others. That is the will of God.

> **For I say, through the grace given unto me, to every man that is among you, not to think of himself more highly than he ought to think; but to think soberly, according as GOD HATH DEALT TO EVERY MAN THE MEASURE OF FAITH.**
>
> **Romans 12:3**

2. **God has decided to give everyone *a different office*.** Some have the office of the all-out minister working full time. Others are given the office of a lay person.

> **For as we have many members in one body, and ALL MEMBERS HAVE NOT THE SAME OFFICE:**
>
> **Romans 12:4**

3. **God gives some people *only one talent*.** You cannot ask God why He gives some people only one talent. That is His decision. Those with only one talent are able to work for the Lord in a much smaller capacity.

> **For the kingdom of heaven is as a man travelling into a far country, who called his own servants, and delivered unto them his goods and UNTO ONE HE GAVE FIVE TALENTS, TO ANOTHER TWO, AND TO ANOTHER ONE; To every man according to his several ability; and straightway took his journey.**
>
> **Matthew 25:14-15**

4. **Some people *do not have the ability* for full-time ministry.** If you force people who do not have the divine ability to be in full-time ministry, you will only create rebels and spiritual tragedies. Accept the reality that everyone has been given different abilities by the Lord.

> **For the kingdom of heaven is as a man travelling into a far country, who called his own servants, and delivered unto them his goods and unto one he gave five talents, to another two, and to another one; to every man ACCORDING TO HIS SEVERAL ABILITY; and straightway took his journey.**
>
> **Matthew 25:14-15**

5. **The *Holy Spirit works* through all ministries no matter how diverse they are.**

This is why the lay ministry can be as anointed as full-time ministry. That is why the contribution of lay ministers and volunteers can be as powerful and meaningful as a full-time minister. The Holy Spirit works through the lay ministry just as much as He does through the full-time ministry. There are many Spirit-anointed laymen who walk in God's wonderful calling.

> **But ALL THESE WORKETH THAT ONE AND THE SELFSAME SPIRIT, dividing to every man severally as he will.**
>
> **1 Corinthians 12:11**

6. **God *administers* His power in different ways.** God Almighty can administer His love for mankind through a layman.

> **And there are DIFFERENCES OF ADMINISTRATIONS, but the same Lord.**
>
> **1 Corinthians 12:5**

7. **God *operates* in different ways. God Almighty can operate through a volunteer.** Who can question God's operations?

> **And there are DIVERSITIES OF OPERATIONS, but it is the same God which worketh all in all.**
>
> **1 Corinthians 12:6**

Chapter

46

Seven Things You Must Know about the Lay Ministry

CHAPTER SUMMARY

46. 1 The Lay ministry will greatly enhance the work of church planting

46. 2 It is possible to combine secular work with the ministry

46. 3 The best New Testament example of a lay pastor is the Apostle Paul. The best Old Testament example is the Prophet Daniel

46. 4 Sometimes it is the will of God for you to be a volunteer and sometimes it is the will of God for you to be in full-time ministry

46. 5 Lay pastors and volunteers will become prominent in the last days

46. 6 Paul practised the lay ministry so that others would follow his good example

46. 7 Lay pastors and volunteers can be just as fruitful as full-time ministers

1. The Lay ministry will greatly enhance the work of church planting.

One of the greatest keys to extensive church planting is the lay ministry. The lay ministry is the sacrifice of pastors and evangelists, who labour without being paid for their services. The enormity of the work is such that, without the strategy of lay ministry, very few churches will be planted. Almost every ministry I know has ground to a halt because of mounting bills, and the high cost of maintaining staff. It is virtually IMPOSSIBLE for the church to employ the people that are needed for the work of God.

The lay ministry is not popular in some circles. In some cultures everybody must be paid for his services. The organist must be paid! The guitarist must be paid! The sound controller must be paid and the pastor constantly seeks a higher salary for his services.

Dear friend, most of the ripened harvest fields are in the poor regions of the world. How will the poor people of the earth be reached in their poverty? Most of these people cannot pay for the services of good pastors and evangelists. The ministry of unpaid pastors and evangelists is the key to continued church planting.

Where the sacrificial nature of Christianity is compromised, church planting comes to an end. The church was born on the sacrifice of Christ. The church grew through the sacrifice of the apostolic church. Once again, the church will only expand through sacrifice.

Paul left Athens and went to Corinth, where he met Aquila, a Jewish man from Pontus. Not long before this, Aquila had come from Italy with his wife Priscilla, because Emperor Claudius had ordered the Jewish people to leave Rome. Paul went to see Aquila and Priscilla and found out that they were tent makers. PAUL WAS A TENT MAKER TOO. So he stayed with them and they worked together.

> **EVERY SABBATH, PAUL WENT TO THE JEWISH MEETING PLACE. He spoke to Jews and Gentiles and TRIED TO WIN THEM OVER.**
>
> **Acts 18:4 (Contemporary English Version)**

2. It is possible to combine secular work with the ministry.

Lay ministry requires the ability to combine secular work with real ministry. The best example of the lay ministry was the Apostle Paul's ministry. It is a ministry in which you support yourself. You may ask, "Is this the way that God planned for ministry to be?" "Does the Bible not teach that they that preach the gospel must live of the gospel?"

> **Even so hath the Lord ordained that they which preach the gospel should live of the gospel.**
>
> **1 Corinthians 9:14**

I combined being a medical student with ministry. I know many people who are effectively ministering the Word of God and continuing in their professions. Paul was the great church planter of the New Testament. He was able to accomplish great things for the Lord whilst he supported himself with the tent making business. The lay ministry is even more vital for church planting today.

3. The best New Testament example of a lay pastor is the Apostle Paul. The best Old Testament example is the Prophet Daniel.

Daniel had three jobs:

i. He was a Member of Parliament for the Babylonian Province.

> **Then the king made Daniel a great man, and gave him many great gifts, and made him ruler over the whole province of Babylon, and chief of the governors over all the wise men of Babylon.**
>
> **Daniel 2:48**

ii. He was the Second Vice President to Belshazzar.

> **Then commanded Belshazzar, and they clothed Daniel with scarlet, and put a chain of gold about his neck, and made a proclamation concerning him, that he should be the third ruler in the kingdom.**
>
> **Daniel 5:29**

iii. He was the Prime Minister during the rule of Darius.

> **It pleased Darius to set over the kingdom an hundred and twenty princes, which should be over the whole kingdom; And over these three presidents; of whom Daniel was first: that the princes might give accounts unto them, and the king should have no damage.**
>
> **Daniel 6:1-2**

4. Sometimes it is the will of God for you to be a volunteer and sometimes it is the will of God for you to be in full-time ministry.

In one breath, the right thing to do is to be fully supported by the ministry, but in another breath the right thing to do is to support yourself. It is important that we follow the leading of the Spirit at all times. Isn't it amazing that the right thing can become the wrong thing ("Anomia"), because God said so? Paul declared that he was instructed by the Lord to be both full and hungry.

> **I know both how to be abased, and I know how to abound: every where and in all things I AM INSTRUCTED BOTH TO BE FULL AND TO BE HUNGRY, both to abound and to suffer need.**
>
> **Philippians 4:12**

5. Lay pastors and volunteers will become prominent in the last days.

Paul's ministry still lives on today. The best way some people can help in the ministry is to be like Paul - secular work during the week and then "reasoning in the synagogue with the Jews on the Sabbath day".

And because he was of the same craft, he abode with them, and wrought: for by their occupation they were tentmakers. AND HE REASONED IN THE SYNAGOGUE every sabbath, and persuaded the Jews and the Greeks.

Acts 18:3-4

6. Paul practised the lay ministry so that others would follow his good example.

I now place you in God's care. Remember the messages about his great kindness! This message can help you and give you what belongs to you as God's people. I have never wanted anyone's money or clothes. You know how I HAVE WORKED WITH MY OWN HANDS TO MAKE A LIVING FOR MYSELF and my friends.

By everything I did, I showed you how you should work to help everyone who is weak. Remember that our Lord Jesus said, "More blessings come from giving than from receiving." After Paul had finished speaking, he knelt down with all of them and prayed.

Acts 20:32-36 (Contemporary English Version)

For yourselves know how ye ought to follow us: for we behaved not ourselves disorderly among you; Neither did we eat any man's bread for nought; but wrought with labour and travail night and day, that we might not be chargeable to any of you: Not because we have not power, but to make ourselves an ensample unto you to follow us.

2 Thessalonians 3:7-9

I am talking about a fruitful and lasting ministry. Paul was a powerful church planter. It is time for many who are called to follow this good example.

7. Lay pastors and volunteers can be just as fruitful as full-time ministers.

I do not know of anyone who will say that the Apostle Paul was inferior to any of the other apostles. He laboured more abundantly and travelled more extensively. He planted more churches than any one else did. He was truly an effective, anointed and fruitful pastor.

Chapter

47

Why You Must Become a Lay Pastor

CHAPTER SUMMARY

47.1 Become a lay pastor so that you can live in certain geographical locations and do the ministry

47. 2 Become a lay pastor so that you are not a burden to anyone

47. 3 Become a lay pastor so that you can survive in ministry without being paid by the church

47. 4 Become a lay pastor so that you are "free" from all men

47. 5 Be a lay pastor so that you can be in the ministry whether finances permit it or not

47. 6 Be a lay pastor to ensure that you have a part in this great ministry

47. 7 Be a lay pastor so that you will be able to relate better with other volunteers

47. 8 Be a lay pastor so that you can sacrifice to the Lord.

47. 9 Be a lay pastor to overcome selfishness in your life

47. 10 Become a wise lay pastor

47. 11 Be a lay pastor so you can be a financial support to the ministry

47. 12 Be a lay pastor to overcome laziness and idleness in the church

1. Become a lay pastor so that you can live in certain geographical locations and do the ministry.

When missionaries were sent from Switzerland to Ghana two hundred years ago, they had to support themselves on the mission field. Many of them became farmers, teachers etc. There was obviously no way of making bank transfers to these missionaries. It is important for ministers to understand that there are times when secular work gives you the legitimate basis for being in particular places. I have pastors in certain countries that do secular work simply because they need to be able to live in that country legally.

Are we ready to do anything for Christ Jesus our Lord? If you have to hold down a secular job so that you can live and minister in a strange land will you do it? Is that asking too much? How do you think the Prophet Daniel was able to flourish in Babylon? He maintained his job as a Member of Parliament.

2. Become a lay pastor so that you are not a burden to anyone.

> **Neither did we eat any man's bread for nought; but wrought with labour and travail night and day, THAT WE MIGHT NOT BE CHARGEABLE TO ANY OF YOU.**
>
> **2 Thessalonians 3:8**

There are times when being a full-time minister is a burden to a small congregation. Sometimes a particular person in the congregation is burdened by the fact that he has to support you all the time. There are times I wouldn't want to stay in certain people's homes. This is because I feel that my presence is burdensome to my host.

Once we went out preaching and we got back home very late. It was past midnight. Our hostess came out of her room looking very sleepy and tired.

She said, "Oh, are you guys back?"

"What time is it?" she mumbled.

We found out that it was about one a.m.

"Would you like to eat?" She asked.

I thought to myself, "Of course I would like to eat. I am starving; I haven't eaten the whole day." But I muttered some non-committal and diplomatic answer.

My hostess continued, "I have some fish in the freezer, I can defrost it and make some stew."

I was quiet but she continued, "I have some rice which I can also prepare."

Then she asked again, "Would you like me to make the food?"

I thought to myself, "Should a Christian ask someone to defrost fish and boil rice at one a.m.?" I decided that I didn't want to be a burden to this dear hostess.

I smiled sheepishly and said, "Oh, it is alright."

I went to bed on an empty stomach. I simply did not want to be a burden to my hostess.

I have learnt to carry secret supplies of food with me when I travel so that I do not become a burden to people. This is what Paul was talking about. He did not want his ministry to become a burden to anyone.

3. Become a lay pastor so that you can survive in ministry without being paid by the church.

> **Neither did we eat any man's bread for nought; but wrought with labour and travail night and day, that WE MIGHT NOT BE CHARGEABLE TO ANY OF YOU:**
>
> **2 Thessalonians 3:8**

■ Four Ways That Paying a Pastor Can Hinder the Ministry

a. Building projects are slowed down or stopped.

b. The church cannot buy the equipment it needs.

c. Missionaries cannot be sent out.

d. Immature church members who do not understand why pastors should be paid certain amounts of money could cause trouble in a new church. Some people simply do not understand why people who work for God should be blessed. I advise pastors to keep their lives as private as possible.

4. Become a lay pastor so that you are "free" from all men.

> **For though I be FREE FROM ALL MEN, yet have I made myself servant unto all, that I might gain the more.**
>
> **1 Corinthians 9:19**

Many times people who give money develop an attitude because of the size of their donations. It is very important for pastors to be free from the negative attitudes of church members. The prophets were warned, "Don't be afraid of their faces." This is because the facial expression on people's faces often intimidates us. There are times when our being lay ministers eliminates the need for people's gifts and donations hereby eliminating these bad attitudes.

> **For though I preach the gospel, I have nothing to glory of: for necessity is laid upon me; yea, woe is unto me, if I preach not the gospel! For if I do this thing willingly, I have a reward: but if against my will, a dispensation of the gospel is committed unto me. What is my reward then? Verily that, when I preach the gospel, I may make the gospel of Christ without charge, that I abuse not my power in the gospel.**
>
> **For though I BE FREE FROM ALL MEN, yet have I made myself servant unto all, that I might gain the more.**
>
> **1 Corinthians 9:16-19**

5. Be a lay pastor so that you can be in the ministry whether finances permit it or not.

> **For though I preach the gospel, I have nothing to glory of: for NECESSITY IS LAID UPON ME; yea, woe is unto me, if I preach not the gospel!**
>
> **For if I do this thing willingly, I have a reward: but if against my will, a dispensation of the gospel is committed unto me. What is my reward then? Verily that, when I preach the gospel, I may make the gospel of Christ without charge, that I abuse not my power in the gospel.**
>
> **1 Corinthians 9:16-18**

Paul said, "Woe is me if I preach not the gospel." Sometimes we do not have a choice! We have to do His will whether there is a salary or not.

That is exactly how I feel. I do not think that I have a choice. I am bound to obey God. I feel that if I do anything apart from preaching His Word, God will destroy me. I have heard other pastors say the same thing.

One pastor said to me, "Before I was in the ministry, I knew that God had called me. At one time I felt that God would kill me if I didn't go into the ministry."

He continued, "That is why I am in full-time ministry today."

6. Be a lay pastor to ensure that you have a part in this great ministry.

> **For he was numbered with us, and HAD OBTAINED PART of this ministry.**
>
> **Acts 1:17**

Many of us may never play a part in building the kingdom unless we do it as lay people. Are all apostles? Are all prophets? Are all evangelists? Are all pastors? Obviously not! But thank God you can support yourself and make a significant contribution to the ministry as a lay pastor.

7. Be a lay pastor so that you will be able to relate better with other volunteers.

Many full-time pastors are unable to relate to lay pastors. The lay ministry is a good foundation for a pastor. Because ministers of the gospel have never practised the lay ministry, they do not encourage laymen in the church to rise up and be volunteers. God is merciful and He makes a way for all kinds of people to help in the ministry.

8. Be a lay pastor so that you can sacrifice to the Lord.

The lay ministry is essentially sacrificial in nature. Unlike what many people think, the ministry is very tiring and stressful. Even paid ministers are often called upon to sacrifice.

Many pastors do not have a normal family life because their family life is constantly interrupted by the incessant demands of the congregation. When it is holiday time, instead of the pastor having time for his family, he has to attend various church and social functions. No one really cares about it until the pastor's children become rebels.

There are many pastors' children who hate the ministry. They feel the ministry steals their parents from them. Besides this, there are many stresses that come to the pastor and his wife by virtue of the position they hold. He is the focus of every spiritual attack; many people do not know this.

One time, when Israel went to war with Syria, the Syrian king gave a very revealing command to his generals and to his captains. He said to them, "Do not fight with anyone. DON'T FIGHT WITH THE GREAT AND DON'T FIGHT WITH THE SMALL, FIGHT ONLY WITH THE KING PERSONALLY."

> **But the king of Syria commanded his thirty and two captains that had rule over his chariots, saying, Fight neither with small nor great, SAVE ONLY WITH THE KING OF ISRAEL.**
>
> **1 Kings 22:31**

You can see from this instruction that no target was significant enough except the King of Israel himself. The king represents the leader or the pastor who becomes the focus of the attack.

When a person takes on the sacrifices of ministry without being paid, he makes a double sacrifice.

> **Am I not an apostle? am I not free? have I not seen Jesus Christ our Lord? are not ye my work in the Lord? If I be not an apostle unto others, yet doubtless I am to you: for the seal of mine apostleship are ye in the Lord. Mine answer to them that do examine me is this, HAVE WE NOT POWER TO EAT AND TO DRINK? HAVE WE NOT POWER TO LEAD ABOUT A SISTER, A WIFE, AS WELL AS OTHER APOSTLES, AND AS THE BRETHREN OF THE LORD, AND CEPHAS? Or I only and Barnabas, have not we power to forbear working?**
>
> **Who goeth a warfare any time at his own charges? who planteth a vineyard, and eateth not of the fruit thereof? OR WHO FEEDETH A FLOCK, AND EATETH NOT OF THE MILK OF THE FLOCK? Say I these things as a man? or saith not the law the same also? For it is written in the law of Moses, Thou shalt not muzzle the mouth of the ox that treadeth out the corn. Doth God take care for oxen? Or saith he it altogether for our sakes? For our sakes, no doubt, this is written: that he that ploweth should plow in hope; and that he that thresheth in hope should be partaker of his hope.**
>
> **If we have sown unto you spiritual things, is it a great thing if we shall reap your carnal things? If others be partakers of this power over you, are not we rather? Nevertheless we have not used this power; but suffer all things, lest we should hinder the gospel of Christ. Do ye not know that they which minister about holy things live of the things of the temple? and they which wait at the altar are partakers with the altar? Even so hath the Lord ordained that they which preach the gospel should live of the gospel. But I have used none of these things: neither have I written these things, that it should be so done unto me: for it were better for me to die, than that any man should make my glorying void.**

> **For though I preach the gospel, I have nothing to glory of: for necessity is laid upon me; yea, woe is unto me, if I preach not the gospel! For if I do this thing willingly, I have a reward: but if against my will, a dispensation of the gospel is committed unto me. What is my reward then? Verily that, when I preach the gospel, I may make the gospel of Christ without charge, that I abuse not my power in the gospel.**
>
> **1 Corinthians 9:1-18**

The lay ministry will test your Christian character. Virtues like self-control and temperance will be tested. When I was a medical student and doctor on the wards of the hospital, I had to sacrifice my resting times for the ministry. When people were watching TV, I could not afford that luxury. I didn't have time for useless socializing and chatting. All my spare time was taken up.

9. Be a lay pastor to overcome selfishness in your life.

Selfishness is the principal reason why many people do not get involved in the lay ministry. Most people are basically self-centred in their outlook of life; they have no concerns for anyone except themselves. They are engrossed in the little world they have built around themselves. Selfishness speaks of self-centredness, self-concern, self-awareness, self-help and self-gratification.

A selfish person can never be a servant of the Lord. Selfishness makes you think about yourself but ministry makes you think about people you don't even know. The Apostle Paul lamented about this phenomenon. He noted that all men seek for their own welfare.

He said, "No one cares for the things of the Lord."

> **For I have no man likeminded, who will naturally care for your state. For all seek their own, not the things which are Jesus Christ's.**
>
> **Philippians 2:20-21**

We are all selfish by nature but the deeper we get in the Lord, the less selfish we become. The barrenness of most Christians is a result of the spirit of selfishness.

Who cares if they go to Hell? At least I am going to Heaven. Who cares if there is a village somewhere that has not heard the gospel? At least my family and I are okay. Who cares if somebody is sick and lying on the hospital ward? At least I am well. Who cares if there is some dirty old prisoner languishing in jail? At least I am free!

That is the spirit of selfishness at work in the church and the Christian.

If Jesus had been selfish, He would not have left His throne in glory and come to this rotten world.

10. Become a wise lay pastor.

> **Behold, I send you forth as sheep in the midst of wolves: be ye therefore wise as serpents, and harmless as doves.**
>
> **Matthew 10:16**

Because of the intrinsic hatred for God and the ministry, many people would like to pick on someone who claims to be a pastor.

> **There was a man of the Pharisees, named Nicodemus, a ruler of the Jews: The same came to Jesus by night, and said unto him, Rabbi, we know that thou art a teacher come from God: for no man can do these miracles that thou doest, except God be with him.**
>
> **John 3:1-2**

People often look out for your faults at work or at school. They say things like, "I am surprised that a pastor would do that. I never knew that pastors also come to work late."

I remember when I worked at the Korle Bu Teaching Hospital, the biggest hospital in my country, as a doctor; I never told them I was a pastor. I knew that at the slightest opportunity they would use it against me. While a student and a pastor, I never indicated that I was even religious. I didn't want them to know anything about me.

It is foolishness to go announcing to the whole world that you are a pastor or a religious leader. Jesus said we should be as wise as serpents. What does it mean to be as wise as a serpent? What wisdom does the serpent have? It has the wisdom to exist quietly in the midst of people who hate it.

The serpent is universally hated and killed on sight, with no questions asked. And yet, snakes flourish all around us. There are millions of snakes all over the world. How has the snake managed to live and multiply in a world that hates it utterly? By discretion, carefulness, judgment, secrecy, prudence and caution!

11. Be a lay pastor so you can be a financial support to the ministry.

> **I have shewed you all things, how that so labouring ye ought to SUPPORT THE WEAK, and to remember the words of the Lord Jesus, how he said, It is more blessed to give than to receive.**
>
> **Acts 20:35**

It is amazing that a large amount of financial support comes from my lay pastors. Many times when there is a special appeal for financial support, it is my lay pastors who often support me most. When you are involved in the ministry; you know the needs of the ministry. Lay ministers are a good support base for every church.

12. Be a lay pastor to overcome laziness and idleness in the church.

> **For we hear that there are some which walk among you disorderly, working not at all, but are busybodies.**
>
> **2 Thessalonians 3:11**

After people have been in the church for some years, they seem to know all your sermons. No matter what tricks you use, they are able to see through the message and identify where it is coming from.

I remember preaching a powerful series in church. People were really blessed. Many commented on how powerful the services had been. Then I had a note. This note was from a long-standing church member.

He wrote, "Dear pastor we were tremendously blessed by your message tonight."

He continued, "This is exactly what you preached five years ago. You only changed the title."

He went further and enumerated the messages from where he claimed I had duplicated my current series.

Then to reassure me he said, "We were mightily blessed anyway so keep on doing the good work."

You see, it is important that Christians get involved with the ministry otherwise they become critical busy bodies, analyzing and commenting on things that they do not even understand.

LORD, my heart is not haughty, nor mine eyes lofty: neither do I exercise myself in great matters, or in things too high for me.

Psalm 131:1

Chapter

48

How I Operated as a Lay Pastor

CHAPTER SUMMARY

I have experienced two worlds of ministry: full-time ministry and lay ministry. Most pastors are only aware of the existence of the full-time dimension of ministry. My intention is to help you to discover the reality of how lay people can cause the church to grow.

If pastors understand that their *lay people can do much more than just give money* to the church, they would help themselves and their churches a great deal. That is what this section is about - showing how lay people can help the church to grow.

A lay person is someone who maintains his secular job and yet is active in the ministry of the Lord Jesus. A full-time minister is someone who has abandoned his secular job to concentrate fully on the ministry.

Many ministers who are in full-time ministry are not comfortable with the idea of lay people participating in the ministry. This is because they want to maintain the ministry as the exclusive preserve of a few "called" men of God. Some full-time ministers do not want to accept the reality that lay people are capable of making a substantial (non-financial) contribution to ministry. Many full-time ministers are happy to maintain their lay people as mere financial supporters.

Pastors want to feel special as they perform their exclusive ministerial duties. "Why should a lay person do what I do?" they say. They think, "After all, if you can do the job I'm doing, what makes me special? What makes me (the pastor) different if lay people can do the things I do?"

Many ministers are not convinced that lay people can do the work of the ministry. I have had pastors ask me, "Will they have time to attend to the needs of the flock?", and "Can they handle emergencies?" "Can they minister powerfully the way we do?" The answer to these is very simple - a resounding YES! I have been in the lay ministry for many years and have found it to be practically possible.

Churches that have experienced phenomenal growth have all employed the principle of using lay people. I believe that it is the key to fulfilling the Great Commission. There is no way we are going to win this world with a few priests and pastors. Everyone must get involved. Many people must get involved at a higher ministerial level. There must be a revival of the lay ministry in the church.

There is such a thing as a lay pastor, i.e., a pastor who combines both his secular job and does the ministry as well. Ninety percent of the pastors in my church are lay pastors.

Full-time pastors must be secure in their positions in order to encourage lay people to get involved. There is nothing mystical about the ministry! There are pastors who want the ministry to be shrouded in mystery so that their members feel dependent on them.

It is something that many can get involved with. What a blessing it is for lay people to discover that they can be useful in the ministry! What a blessing for the pastor when he discovers that the contributions of lay people can make his church grow. I am not saying that there is no need for full-time ministers. I am myself a full-time minister. There is a great need for full-time ministers to be one hundred percent involved in ministry work. There are things that only full-time ministers can do.

I Was a Lay Pastor

At the age of about fifteen, in secondary school, I met the Lord. From the day I gave my life to Christ, I became very active in ministry. I was involved in soul winning and following up converts. I was also involved in singing and playing musical instruments for the Lord.

In the first phase of my Christian life, I was not a traditional Sunday morning church attendee. In fact, I hardly went to church on Sundays. My Christian life was so active from Monday to Saturday that I ended up resting on Sundays! On Mondays and Wednesdays I had a prayer meeting and Bible study. On Tuesdays and Thursdays I had music rehearsals. On Fridays we had fasting and prayer meetings. And then on Saturdays we would have a retreat from ten in the morning until six in the evening.

Whilst I was involved in these activities I did not give up my schooling. I completed my GCE 'O' levels and passed with a distinction - I had seven ones (one is the highest mark of distinction). That was a great accomplishment by any standards. In my GCE 'A' levels I topped my class and was one of only three people from my school admitted into the medical school. Throughout this period, I was fully involved in ministry. I preached! I won souls! I visited people in their homes! I counselled many people! I fasted and prayed! At one point, I fasted so much that I became as thin as a rake. Someone even asked me, "Do you think that you will get to Heaven by being a skeleton?"

Never did it occur to me that I had to be paid for the ministry work that I was involved in. By the time I was nineteen years old, I was fully involved in the ministry. I had many sheep who looked up to me for direction and prayer. By 1980, I was a strong preacher and leader of the Scripture Union fellowship. The point I am making is that ministry is possible alongside other pursuits. I entered the university in October 1982. I was privileged to be studying medicine - one of the most difficult and time-consuming courses. Whilst in the university I began a Christian fellowship that is still in existence today.

During my fourth year, I began to establish the foundations for a church. I then became a pastor and was acknowledged as such whilst I was still a medical student. During this time I was not being paid by anyone to do the work of the ministry. Neither did I slacken in my academic work. On the contrary, I did extremely well and won prizes in the medical school. I applied wisdom and sacrificed my leisure time so that I could be involved in ministry.

■ Sacrifice and Wisdom

These are the two keys to being in the lay ministry - *sacrifice and wisdom.* What is the main task of a pastor? Is it to perform funerals and to officiate weddings? Certainly not! These are certainly duties of a minister but they are not main duties. If your ministry has deteriorated to the point where your main functions are to conduct marriages and bury people, then you need to read your Bible again! The main duty of a minister is to fulfil the Great Commission.

Go ye therefore, and teach all nations, baptizing them in the name of the Father, and of the Son, and of the Holy Ghost: Teaching them to observe all things whatsoever I have commanded you: and, lo, I am with you alway, even unto the end of the world. Amen.

Matthew 28:19, 20

The reason why it is called the Great Commission is because it is the great commandment to all ministers. It is sad to see ministers of the Gospel who have become mere social functionaries. Sometimes pastors are under pressure to be accepted by society. As a result, they want to do nice things that relate to health, education, etc., so that they may gain the approval of society.

Apostle Peter came under the same pressure to leave his principal duties and to perform mainly social tasks.

And in those days, when the number of the disciples was multiplied, there arose a murmuring of the Grecians against the Hebrews, because their widows were neglected in the daily ministration.

> **Then the twelve called the multitude of the disciples unto them, and said, It is not reason that we should leave the word of God, and serve tables.**
>
> **Wherefore, brethren, look ye out among you seven men of honest report, full of the Holy Ghost and wisdom, whom we may appoint over this business.**
>
> **BUT WE WILL GIVE OURSELVES CONTINUALLY TO PRAYER, AND TO THE MINISTRY OF THE WORD.**
>
> **Acts 6:1-4**

You can see from this Scripture that Peter's main duty was to pray and to minister the Word. This is something that can be done by lay people.

Lay people can be taught to visit and counsel younger Christians!

Lay people can be taught how to preach!

Lay people can be taught how to witness!

Lay people can be taught how to minister the Word with power!

Lay people can be taught to make spiritual gains through prayer!

What I have just described is the work of a pastor. Any honest reader will agree that a lay person can become a lay pastor.

What you need is a systematic way of training your lay people to become ministers. Do not limit your lay people because they are professionals in other fields. Do not say that your doctors, lawyers, architects, carpenters, engineers, tailors, masons, nurses and secretaries, cannot be pastors. They can!!

I remember visiting one of our churches that was pastored by a female nurse. There were hundreds of people in the church and I gave glory to God for that. In a large house there are many vessels. God is using all kinds of people. Do not limit God to what you have been used to.

> **But in a great house there are not only vessels of gold and of silver, but also of wood and of earth; and some to honour, and some to dishonour. If a man therefore purge himself from these, he shall be a vessel unto honour, sanctified, and meet for the master's use, and prepared unto every good work.**
>
> **2 Timothy 2:20-21**

When I was in my first year at the university, I was told by the Christian fellowship that *I could not be a leader because I was a medical student.* Medical students were considered too busy to be involved in ministry work. How unfortunate! They had effectively eliminated a whole group of potential leaders from the fellowship.

This is what many pastors do. They look at the doctors in the church and think to themselves, "Sit down quietly, receive your Sunday sermons and pay your tithes. Be a nice principled Christian doctor who does not perform abortions and you will please God!!"

I want you to know that a doctor can also please God by winning souls. It is true that God wants principled doctors. But God also wants doctors who will win souls and do the work of ministry. Today, I have doctors who own clinics and at the same time pastor churches with hundreds of members.

There are many architects who do full-time architectural work and are very fruitful in ministry. There are pastors who work in banks but pastor large churches. I have seen teachers, pharmacists, university lecturers, accountants, students, doctors, nurses, army officers, civil servants, air conditioner repairers, computer scientists, computer technicians, businessmen, and lawyers become great lay pastors. Many people cannot believe that our long lists of pastors are lay people who are not paid by the church.

Please do not misunderstand me; not every lay person must become a pastor. Some of the lay people can function as ordinary shepherds (cell leaders). But there are others who have the call of God upon their lives and who will become pastors.

The Pineapple Patch

One day as I was walking on a hillside I saw something that I want to share with you. I was praying in tongues and walking along a footpath on one of the hills in Ghana. The entire hillside was covered with wild bushes and tall untamed grass. As I walked along, I saw a section within the wild grass measuring about 20 meters by 20 meters. In that particular section there were neatly planted pineapple plants. I could see the baby pineapples sprouting. That section of the hillside was very different from everywhere else.

The Spirit of the Lord spoke to me and said, "That section of the hillside is different because certain seeds have been planted there. That area of the hillside is different because some special investment has been made on that patch of ground." The Lord told me that the rest of the hillside can be likened to the general congregation which receives seeds of normal preaching. The special patch of ground that was yielding pineapples could be likened to the part of the church that received the special seeds of leadership and pastoral training.

If you sow the seeds of pastoral training you will soon have many more pastors and leaders around you.

Many people do not invest the seeds that give rise to leaders, pastors and shepherds. If you sow the seeds that train leaders, you will harvest a crop of well-seasoned leaders. I spend more time with my leaders than I do with the general congregation. The teachings in this book are examples of some of the things I have taught ordinary people over the years.

This investment has turned many people into shepherds and lay pastors! Invest specially in leaders and potential pastors and they will grow up to become great ministers!

I have heard people criticizing me for starting churches with people whom they consider not to be pastors. Do not criticize someone who has been holding Shepherds' Camps to train people. Criticize yourself for not having spent hours training your own lay people to be in the ministry.

You must encourage your lay people to become something more than principled citizens of the country. You must encourage them to become soul winners for Jesus. You must want them to be shepherds of God's flock. You must want them to fulfil the Great Commission.

Dear pastor friend, I wrote this book for you! God told me to write it so that you will understand that lay people can and will help you to build your church.

God has a ministry for you. Please do not go to Heaven and discover that you did not even begin your ministry! Take what you are reading seriously and learn the art of shepherding and pastoring. Discover for yourself the joy of serving God as a layman.

Chapter

49

How to Share the Burden with Lay People

CHAPTER SUMMARY

- **There Is a Real Burden**
- **Don't Exclude Anyone**
- **Share the Burden and Have a Larger Church**

49. 1 Lay people will help you deal with ungrateful and forgetful sheep

49. 2 Lay people will help you overcome disloyalty in the congregation

49. 3 Lay people will help to deal with disrespectful and rebellious church members

49. 4 Good lay people encourage others to respond positively to the Word

49. 5 Lay people will cause the church to expand by becoming part of the workforce

49. 6 Lay people will help you with prayer, visitation, counselling and interaction

49. 7 Lay people will help you to account for the sheep on the Day of Judgment

> **And the Lord said unto Moses, Gather unto me seventy men of the elders of Israel, whom thou knowest to be the elders of the people, and officers over them; and bring them unto the tabernacle of the congregation, that they may stand there with thee. And I will come down and talk with thee there: and I will take of the spirit which is upon thee, and will put it upon them; and they shall BEAR THE BURDEN of the people with thee, that thou bear it not thyself alone.**
>
> **Numbers 11:16, 17**

One of the most difficult tasks in life is to "lead" people. Moses delivered the Israelites from bondage but struggled to lead them to the Promised Land. They were too difficult for him to handle. Moses' job of leading difficult people is the job that all pastors have to do.

God graciously gave Moses spectacular and sensational miracles. These signs and wonders helped to establish his authority over God's flock. In spite of this, the burden of leading the people was more than he could carry. The Bible calls it a burden - and that is what it is! Moses eventually succumbed to the pressures of leading difficult people and lost his chance to enter the Promised Land.

■ There Is a Real Burden

If you have a pastor's heart and love people, you cannot disassociate yourself from their problems. Their problems will become your problems and their burdens will affect you! When God uses you to minister to a large number of people, he expects you to share the burden. Failure to share this burden simply means that you may collapse or come to a standstill in ministry. There are many standstill churches around. They grow to a point but can grow no further. The reason is that they fail to share the burden of ministry.

A balanced church is one that has people of all sorts within it; young, old, educated and uneducated, rich and poor, and male and female. All these people must be drafted in to the share the burden.

■ Don't Exclude Anyone

I notice that most churches exclude the educated and the rich from ministry. Usually, the rich are expected to contribute money whilst the educated enhance the image of the church. However, I have found that both the rich and the educated can be spiritually useful. There are many medical doctors, carpenters, plumbers, specialists, lecturers, architects, and engineers, who serve as lay pastors. These lay pastors share the burden of ministry.

The burden of the ministry cannot be borne by one person. It is simply impossible.

■ Share the Burden and Have a Larger Church

If you want to have a greater ministry than what you currently have, you must share the burden. Sometimes people do not share the burden because they want to take all of the glory for themselves. They want people to feel that they are the only ones with a supernatural gift. They want people to show appreciation to them alone.

Others are afraid of rebellion in the camp. How common is the story of associate pastors rebelling. Many senior pastors fear their assistants will outshine them one day. Fear not, only believe! You cannot expand without trusting people. The work is so great that you will never ever be able to do it all alone.

1. Lay people will help you deal with ungrateful and forgetful sheep.

...in the last days... men shall be... unthankful...

2 Timothy 3:1-2

There will always be lay people who are very grateful for your ministry. They will love you and appreciate your efforts for them. These people will help to neutralize the presumption that is common in the congregation. Their grateful speeches will neutralize rebellion in the camp.

You will notice ungratefulness in people by the way they complain. Moses led the Israelites out of bondage and slavery and yet they murmured and complained bitterly against him. Aaron even had to make a golden calf to calm them down. If something ever goes wrong, you will be surprised at the reactions of people you have ministered to. Many quickly forget what you have done for them. The things a pastor does are not physically tangible, but spiritual. Many therefore think that the pastor has done nothing for them.

Church members can sin against you after you have been a blessing to them. Don't be shocked! The prophet Jeremiah experienced the same thing from his people. He said, "Shall evil be recompensed for good?" (Jeremiah 18:20).

The Sin of Hezekiah

Once, a pastor told a very disturbing story. He said that he was surprised when one of his church members came to his house one night to assault him. He couldn't believe that this young man whom he had led to Christ, trained up in the Lord, whose marriage he had blessed, and helped through various crises would attack him in that manner.

Dear friend, do not be surprised! Do not expect gratitude from man; expect your rewards from God. Hezekiah was blessed. But he did not "render again". That means he did not show gratitude for all the blessings he had received.

But Hezekiah RENDERED NOT AGAIN according to the benefit done unto him...

2 Chronicles 32:25

This is the nature of man. This is the nature of the people God wants you to lead.

2. Lay people will help you overcome disloyalty in the congregation.

With the help of lay people, you will be able to fight disloyalty in the church. The presence of zealously committed lay workers always inspires more loyalty in the ranks. Lay people, who do not earn money from the church, are a great support to every pastor. Lay people who are loyal will report what is going on in the congregation.

Though Judas walked and ministered with Jesus for three years, he eventually betrayed him for a small amount of money. Betrayal is a part of ministry. It is also a part of life. If you have yet to experience betrayal, I can assure you that you will. The disturbing thing about betrayal is that it comes from people who are supposedly close to you.

You are not greater than your master Jesus! The fact that someone may betray you one day makes it very difficult for you to happily interact and flow with the people. Look closely at the ministry of any great man of God. You will discover that they have all had their fair share of traitors. All of this contributes to the burden and difficulty of ministry.

> **Yea, mine own familiar friend, in whom I trusted, which did eat of my bread, hath lifted up his heel against me.**
>
> **Psalm 41:9**

Paul experienced sudden desertions by some of his colleagues, like Demas. I remember one young man whom I trained. He was about to take up an important position in the ministry that we had been preparing for, for over a year. On the day he was to fill the position, he suddenly informed me that he was leaving the country. I couldn't believe my ears! All of our months of preparation meant nothing to him. He just abandoned ship without notice. These experiences are all part of the ministry. Abandonment also occurred under the ministry of Apostle Paul.

> **For Demas hath forsaken me…**
>
> **2 Timothy 4:10**

Because people can abandon you at any time, it is burdensome to lead them. The presence of committed lay people will always help to share the burden of abandonment. God wants us to be involved in His work. God wants us to be shepherds!

3. Lay people will help to deal with disrespectful and rebellious church members.

> **And Miriam and Aaron spake against Moses… Hath the Lord indeed spoken only by Moses? HATH HE NOT SPOKEN ALSO BY US?**
>
> **Numbers 12:1-2**

There are lay people who will sort out disrespectful and rebellious church members for you. You always need people on the ground to deal with church members who make light of pastors. There are people who think their money and status in the secular world gives them a right to say and do anything in the church.

Miriam and Aaron (the closest assistants and closest relatives) spoke against Moses. They most probably said things like, "God also speaks by us" and "Are you the only one God uses?" With time, familiarity creeps in and arrogant people now consider you as an equal. They tend to think, "We can all do it. What's the big deal? You are no different from us!"

This is unfortunate, but real. People easily take you for granted. They murmur and complain against you, forgetting all that you have done for them. When some church members lose their temper, they will speak to you as though you are a little child.

"You Remind Me of My Father"

One church member approached her pastor after Sunday service. The pastor thought she was about to compliment him for the powerful sermon he had just preached.

She started, "Pastor, you know something? I felt I should tell you that you remind me of my father."

"Oh really?" the pastor responded. He thought he reminded her of some good traits in her father.

She continued, "He was so full of himself and so are you!"

The pastor was taken aback but had to smile and continue as though he had received a compliment. This church member was telling the pastor exactly what she thought of him. Moses also experienced rebels who thought he was "too big" for his shoes. Moses also had people who wanted to cut him down to size. That is why Moses had to share the burden with seventy other elders.

> **Now Korah... and Dathan... and Abiram... and On... rose up before Moses... and said... wherefore then lift ye up yourselves [Moses and Aaron] above the congregation of the Lord?**
>
> **Numbers 16:1-3**

4. Good lay people encourage others to respond positively to the Word.

> **When any one heareth the word of the kingdom, and UNDERSTANDETH IT NOT...**
>
> **Matthew 13:19**

The domino effect is when one thing leads to another. When one lay person responds positively to your teaching, others are inspired to do the same. It is always a blessing to have ordinary congregants who are outspoken in their support of you. Sometimes large sections of the congregation do not understand the Word.

Often they do not understand why you have to do fundraising. Consequently, many do not respond in giving. Many times, I have to explain that they are giving to build a nice church where they can have their weddings, their baby dedications and their ceremonies.

Leading people who have all the above characteristics: ungratefulness, disloyalty, etc., is a major task. One person cannot do it alone. The burden must be shared with others. Sharing the burden is hard work.

5. Lay people will cause the church to expand by becoming part of the workforce.

The use of lay people as part of the workforce is the secret to unlimited expansion of the church.

Sometimes people think that lay people cannot do much ministry work. Do not be deceived - try using lay people and you will discover how much work they can do.

Lay people can join the pastors to share the burden of the people. Let your lay people know that they are called to share the burden of ministry with you. They will share the burden on earth and they will share the burden of accounting for the sheep in Heaven.

When we established churches in the universities, we entrusted the preaching and pastoring responsibilities to students. I am very proud of these student ministers because of the great job that they have done on the different campuses. I don't have to rush to the different universities every Sunday morning to minister the Word. Ordinary saints have joined in to help.

These saints must be perfected (prepared, trained) to do the work of the ministry. Ordinary saints can do the work.

> **For the perfecting of the saints, for the work of the ministry, for the edifying of the body of Christ:**
>
> **Ephesians 4:12**

The principal strategy for distributing the burden is to involve lay men and women in ministry. No church is capable of employing an endless number of people. Every church has a limit to its resources.

It is not possible to pay salaries and rent an unlimited number of houses for the staff of the ministry. Full-time staff are limited in the amount of work that they can do.

6. Lay people will help you with prayer, visitation, counselling and interaction.

Lay people can help you with the burden of praying, visiting, counselling and interacting with the sheep.

Moses was breaking down under the burden of having to pray, visit, counsel and interact with so many people. God saw a disaster waiting to happen and decided to take of the "spirit" that was on Moses and put it on the seventy leaders "to bear the burden" with him.

> **And the Lord said unto Moses, Gather unto me SEVENTY MEN of the elders of Israel... THAT THEY MAY STAND [work] THERE WITH THEE.**
>
> **Numbers 11:16**

Involving students, workers, and professionals helps to distribute the burden to all saints in the church. The Lord wants everyone to be fruitful no matter what they do in life.

7. Lay people will help you to account for the sheep on the Day of Judgment.

> **...for they watch for your souls, AS THEY THAT MUST GIVE ACCOUNT, that they may do it with joy...**
>
> **Hebrews 13:17**

The burden of answering for the sheep cannot be borne by one person or a few people who supposedly have a "call". The burden of accounting for hundreds of different people cannot be borne by one person. When I stand before the judgment seat and God asks me about certain souls, I intend to refer to the lay pastors and shepherds I put in charge of these souls.

When the Lord asks me about some souls in the church, I intend to find out who was in charge and tell the Lord to ask that person. I cannot possibly answer for all these different people personally.

Every pastor will have a lot to answer for when he stands before the Lord in Heaven. Your burden is to be able to lead all your sheep to Heaven. Make sure you lose none of them. Every pastor must hope to say, "Of all that you have given me, I have lost none!" Jesus said this phrase in three different places – John 6:39, John 17:12; and John 18:9.

Chapter

50

The Ideal Lay Pastor

CHAPTER SUMMARY

50. 1 The ideal lay pastor is a volunteer for life

50. 2 The ideal lay pastor is a good shepherd and a good pastor

50. 3 The ideal lay pastor is a good businessman or professional

50. 4 The ideal lay pastor is good at combining the pastoral work with secular work

50. 5 The ideal lay pastor has a great respect for full-time ministry, even though he himself does not leave his secular profession for the ministry

50. 6 The ideal lay pastor is sacrificial

50. 7 The ideal lay pastor is loyal and persistent in ministry, even through the mid-life crises of his life

1. The ideal lay pastor is a volunteer for life.

He does not turn aside from his commitment to volunteer himself to the ministry. The best lay pastors are those who give themselves to the lay ministry for life. They do not waver from their initial commitment.

2. The ideal lay pastor is a good shepherd and a good pastor.

He has learnt how to be a good shepherd and how to care for the sheep.

3. The ideal lay pastor is a good businessman or professional.

He has learnt how to flourish in his chosen secular profession or business. Most of the lay pastors who become rebellious have financial problems and are tempted to use the ministry as an additional source of income.

4. The ideal lay pastor is good at combining the pastoral work with secular work.

He has overcome all the difficulties and challenges of combining these two very different activities.

5. The ideal lay pastor has a great respect for full-time ministry, even though he himself does not leave his secular profession for the ministry.

The ability to genuinely respect full-time priests, even though you are not entering it yourself, is a mark of the ideal lay pastor.

6. The ideal lay pastor is sacrificial.

The ideal lay pastor will give up much of his rest and leisure time for the ministry.

7. The ideal lay pastor is loyal and persistent in ministry, even through the mid-life crises of his life.

Non-ideal lay pastors fall away during their mid-life crises and during their financial dry seasons.

Chapter

51

What Is the Proper Attitude of a Lay Pastor?

CHAPTER SUMMARY

To be a successful volunteer or lay pastor, you must have the right heart and the right attitude towards real ministry. If you do not respect full-time ministry you will not walk in the full anointing of your calling.

Render therefore to all their dues: tribute to whom tribute is due; custom to whom custom; fear to whom fear; honour to whom honour.

Romans 13:7

The right attitude for a lay pastor is to respect the full-time ministry!

Great honour is due men who have given up everything to be in the ministry. The secular world may not respect the office of a priest. Non-believers may have no regard for the work of a full-time minister. But a lay pastor must definitely have the greatest respect and understanding for the work of a full-time pastor.

How a Lay Pastor Can Prove His Respect for Full-Time Ministry

1. A lay pastor proves his respect for full-time ministry when he is not non-committal on the subject of full-time ministry.

Some lay people and volunteers say little or nothing when it comes to the subject of full-time ministry. Their silence on this subject reveals hidden misgivings about the need for people to be in full-time ministry. Indeed, a lay pastor must have a clear and positive attitude towards full-time ministry.

2. A lay pastor proves his respect for full-time ministry when he honestly admits that he does not have the courage or boldness to be in full-time ministry.

The reality is that many lay pastors were afraid to take the bold step of entering into full-time ministry and that is why they are still lay pastors. An honest admission of this weakness will deliver them from dishonesty, untruths and continuing self-deception.

When you admit that you were afraid to enter into full-time ministry, you honestly admit that full-time ministry is a great thing and only great people are able to enter it.

3. A lay pastor proves his respect for full-time ministry when he speaks highly of full-time ministry.

Words of honour and words of respect for the priesthood and those who have entered it reveal your utmost respect for full-time ministry.

4. A lay pastor proves his respect for full-time ministry when he is able to encourage others to be in full-time ministry even though he is not.

A healthy respect for full-time ministry is revealed when you are able to encour-age others to do something that you were unable to do. When outsiders support people who are in ministry, it reveals a deep-seated love and respect for the ministry. Hannah showed her support for her son's ministry by making a coat for him every year.

But Samuel ministered before the Lord, being a child, girded with a linen ephod.

> **Moreover his mother made him A LITTLE COAT, and brought it to him FROM YEAR TO YEAR, when she came up with her husband to offer the yearly sacrifice.**
>
> **1 Samuel 2:18-19**

5. A lay pastor proves his respect for full-time ministry when he is able to defer to and receive counsel from a full-time pastor.

A lay pastor can show his respect and esteem for full-time ministry by deferring to full-time ministers. The ability to receive counsel from a person fully dedicated to ministry is a sign of respect for the ministry. Unfortunately, some lay people despise full-time ministers, thinking that they have no knowledge or input to make in secular life and work. Because they obviously despise the ministry, they are kept away from committing themselves to the profession.

Chapter

52

Double-Minded Lay Pastors

CHAPTER SUMMARY

52.1 Double-mindedness about lay and full-time ministries introduces instability into your life

52.2 Double-mindedness about lay and full-time ministry reveals a lack of honesty and truth

52.3 Double-mindedness about lay and full-time ministries exposes you to a love-hate relationship with the ministry

52.4 Double-mindedness about lay and full-time ministries introduces a long period of confusion into your life and ministry

52.5 Double-mindedness about lay and full-time ministries is a demonstration of immaturity

52.6 Double-mindedness about lay and full-time ministries will cause you to have a faulty ministry

You must make up your mind about whether to be a layperson or to go all out into ministry. A double-minded man is unstable in all his ways. The last thing you must be double-minded about is your career! You cannot be double-minded about your ministry! Are you in full-time ministry or in lay ministry? Which is your calling? Choose you this day whom you will serve!

■ Evil Effects of Double-Mindedness on the Ministry

1. Double-mindedness about lay and full-time ministries introduces instability into your life.

When a layperson is undecided about what he is doing, he is uncertain as to whether he should go all out in his secular ambitions or he should give himself to ministry.

> **A double minded man is UNSTABLE in all his ways.**
>
> **James 1:8**

2. Double-mindedness about lay and full-time ministry reveals a lack of honesty and truth.

You must be truthful to yourself. You must not deceive yourself about what your calling is. If God has called you to the ministry, then give yourself to that cause. Do not wait until you see financial opportunities before you switch from lay ministry to full-time ministry. Which side do you belong to? What is your calling? Be truthful to yourself about who you are and about what God wants you to do. When the belt of truth is loose, you open yourself up to corrupt thoughts of wickedness.

> **Draw nigh to God, and he will draw nigh to you. Cleanse your hands, ye sinners; and PURIFY YOUR HEARTS, YE DOUBLE MINDED.**
>
> **James 4:8**

3. Double-mindedness about lay and full-time ministries exposes you to a love-hate relationship with the ministry.

You cannot serve mammon and God. In a sense, full-time ministry represents serving God whilst lay ministry represents serving mammon.

In lay ministry, your principal job is to do with secular work, whereas in full-time ministry your principal job is to do with the church. Many lay men and volunteers are double-minded and end up either loving the ministry and hating their secular jobs or hating the ministry and loving their secular jobs. Make up your mind today! Be a lay preacher for life or be a full-time preacher for life! You cannot serve two masters. You must choose who will be your master.

> **No servant can serve two masters: for either he will hate the one, and love the other; or else he will hold to the one, and despise the other. Ye cannot serve God and mammon.**
>
> **Luke 16:13**

4. Double-mindedness about lay and full-time ministries introduces a long period of confusion into your life and ministry.

Confusion is the fruit of double-mindedness. God is not the author of confusion. You must decide where you belong. How long will you waver between two opinions? People who have wavered between two opinions have ended up neither prospering in the secular world nor flourishing in the ministry.

> **And Elijah came unto all the people, and said, HOW LONG halt ye between two opinions? If the Lord be God, follow him: but if Baal, then follow him. And the people answered him not a word.**
>
> **1 Kings 18:21**

> **And if it seem evil unto you to serve the Lord, CHOOSE YOU THIS DAY whom ye will serve; whether the gods which your fathers served that were on the other side of the flood, or the gods of the Amorites, in whose land ye dwell: but as for me and my house, we will serve the Lord.**
>
> **Joshua 24:15**

5. Double-mindedness about lay and full-time ministries is a demonstration of immaturity.

Your ability to choose something and to stick to your choice reveals maturity. This is why certain jobs are only given to people who are married. Marriage reveals a person's ability to choose one of many options that are available to him.

Immature flighty young men cannot make up their minds! But the mature person will decide on one person and stay with his choice. Indeed, it is maturity that enables a person to choose either the lay ministry or full-time ministry for the rest of his life.

> **That we henceforth be no more CHILDREN, TOSSED TO AND FRO, and carried about with every wind of doctrine, by the sleight of men, and cunning craftiness, whereby they lie in wait to deceive;**
>
> **Ephesians 4:14**

6. Double-mindedness about lay and full-time ministries will cause you to have a faulty ministry.

I have observed many faulty ministers who have wavered between lay ministry and full-time ministry for many years. God is calling you to make up your mind and do what is right. If God has given you one talent, make the most of it and be a good lay minister. If God has given you ten talents, make the most of it and be a good full-time minister.

> **THEIR HEART IS DIVIDED; NOW SHALL THEY BE FOUND FAULTY: he shall break down their altars, he shall spoil their images.**
>
> **Hosea 10:2**

Chapter

53

Understanding How Lay Ministry Is a Measure of Ministry

CHAPTER SUMMARY

53. 1 Lay ministry is a measure of ministry

53. 2 Lay people have the grace of God for their measure of ministry

53. 3 Lay people must not think of themselves more highly than they ought to

53. 4 Lay people must not exalt themselves above full-time ministry

53. 5 Lay people should assess their ministry by the things they have suffered

1. Lay ministry is a measure of ministry.

Indeed, every one of us has only a measure of ministry. Jesus is the only one who was given the ministry without a measure. "For he whom God hath sent speaketh the words of God: for God giveth not the Spirit by measure unto him" (John 3:34). Jesus Christ is the only one whose ministry was not limited. He did not receive a portion. Everybody has been given a measure of a gift. A lay pastor is a measure of the pastoral gift.

2. Lay people have the grace of God for their measure of ministry.

Everyone has grace for what he is called to do. Some people wonder how a medical doctor can also pastor a church. Some people are surprised that an accountant can run a church. Where do they find the time to do the work? How can they study and prepare? Will the church ever be able to grow? Indeed, laymen can help the church to grow. God uses laymen to do great things. They are able to accomplish great things because of the grace that is upon their lives. A full-time pastor may not have that grace and may have to prepare much more to be able to run his church.

> **But unto every one of us is given GRACE ACCORDING TO THE MEASURE of the gift of Christ.**
>
> **Ephesians 4:7**

3. Lay people must not think of themselves more highly than they ought to.

The lay ministry is a small measure of ministry. No matter how long you have been a lay pastor, you are still only a lay pastor. You are not a professional priest who is dedicated to the things of God. You have been granted grace to operate as a lay minister. It is the grace of God that allows lay people to be part of this wonderful ministry.

> **For I say, through the grace given unto me, to every man that is among you, NOT TO THINK OF HIMSELF MORE HIGHLY THAN HE OUGHT to think; but to think soberly, according as God hath dealt to every man the measure of faith.**
>
> **Romans 12:3**

4. Lay people must not exalt themselves above full-time ministry.

You must not boast of things that are outside your measure. You must accept the measure you have been given. A lay pastor must not exalt himself above a full-time minister. A lay pastor must be humble in the presence of someone who is fully dedicated to the ministry. In the same way, when a full-time pastor visits the workplace of the lay pastor, he will accord the lay pastor the necessary respect in his chosen profession.

When lay pastors begin to think they are what they are not, the church suffers loss. I have seen churches that are hijacked by laymen who feel they are as good as full-time dedicated pastors. As a result, the church suffers decline and full-time ministry is despised. Can you imagine a bank that is run by laymen who work elsewhere and visit the bank at weekends and on some evenings? What would be the hope of that bank?

> **NOT BOASTING OF THINGS WITHOUT OUR MEASURE, that is, of other men's labours; but having hope, when your faith is increased, that we shall be enlarged by you according to our rule abundantly,**
>
> **2 Corinthians 10:15**

5. Lay people should assess their ministry by the things they have suffered.

Lay people protect themselves from suffering, sacrifice and loss by maintaining their jobs in the secular world. How did Paul assess his ministry? How did he know that he was a minister of Christ? Was it by the size of his church? Was it by how old he was? Or was it by how much money he had? Indeed, it was by the things he had suffered and endured in the ministry. When a person gives himself into full-time ministry, he risks having a lifetime of poverty and suffering. He will go through many difficulties which a lay person shields himself from through his secular career.

Lay people achieve great things for themselves in the secular world. Lay people protect themselves from suffering, sacrifice and loss by maintaining their jobs in the secular world. This is the principal difference between a lay pastor and a full-time minister of Christ. This is why Paul revealed his true rank by the things that he suffered and not by the things he had achieved.

> **Are they ministers of Christ? (I speak as a fool) I am more; in labours more abundant, in stripes above measure, in prisons more frequent, in deaths oft.**
>
> **Of the Jews five times received I forty stripes save one.**
>
> **Thrice was I beaten with rods, once was I stoned, thrice I suffered shipwreck, a night and a day I have been in the deep;**
>
> **In journeyings often, in perils of waters, in perils of robbers, in perils by mine own countrymen, in perils by the heathen, in perils in the city, in perils in the wilderness, in perils in the sea, in perils among false brethren;**
>
> **In weariness and painfulness, in watchings often, in hunger and thirst, in fastings often, in cold and nakedness. . . .**
>
> **The God and Father of our Lord Jesus Christ, which is blessed for evermore, knoweth that I lie not.**
>
> **In Damascus the governor under Aretas the king kept the city of the Damascenes with a garrison, desirous to apprehend me: And through a window in a basket was I let down by the wall, and escaped his hands.**
>
> **2 Corinthians 11:23-27, 31-33**

Chapter

54

Understanding How Lay Ministry Is a Type of Helps Ministry

CHAPTER SUMMARY

Lay ministry is simply another form of the helps ministry. The main line of work in the church is the ministry of apostles, pastors, teachers, evangelists and prophets. There are, however, people who are called to help these principal ministers of the body of Christ.

> **And God hath set some in the church, first apostles, secondarily prophets, thirdly teachers, after that miracles, then gifts of healings, HELPS, governments, diversities of tongues.**
>
> **1 Corinthians 12:28**

The word, helps comes from a Greek word antilepsis which means "*to aid, to participate, to support, to relieve* and *to assist*". In a sense, the helps ministry is a vague, limitless and undefined ministry. Help is not easy to define and it can take almost any form. There are many things that are helpful and so anything that is helpful can be considered as the helps ministry.

The Bible has several examples of helps ministers and these examples help to reveal what a true helps minister is. Indeed, lay ministry is one of the largest sections of helps ministry. An unpaid lay person can assist an apostle, prophet, teacher or apostle in many different ways. A lay person can assist by preaching the Word of God. A lay person can assist by doing administrative work. A lay person can assist by caring for and supporting a minister of God.

When someone does any of these things without charge he is a layman in the helps ministry.

■ Examples of Helps Ministers

1. Onesiphorus the helps minister of Paul

> **But God bless Onesiphorus and his family! Many's the time I've been refreshed in that house. And he wasn't embarrassed a bit that I was in jail. The first thing he did when he got to Rome was look me up.**
>
> **May God on the last day treat him as well as he treated me. And then there was all the help he provided in Ephesus – but you know that better than I.**
>
> **2 Timothy 1:16-18 (The Message)**

2. The seventy lay elders, the helps ministers of Moses

These seventy elders were to help him in his pastoral care of the people of Israel. Laymen also help in the pastoral care of the flock of God. The seventy elders were lay people who were not part of the priesthood.

> **And the LORD said unto Moses, Gather unto me seventy men of the elders of Israel, whom thou knowest to be the elders of the people, and officers over them; and bring them unto the tabernacle of the congregation, that they may stand there with thee.**
>
> **And I will come down and talk with thee there: and I will take of the spirit which is upon thee, and will put it upon them; and they shall bear the burden of the people with thee, that thou bear it not thyself alone.**
>
> **Numbers 11:16-17**

3. The seventy, helps ministers of Jesus' evangelistic ministry

Jesus was assisted by the seventy elders whom He sent out to prepare the way for His evangelistic campaign. Every evangelist needs forerunners who will prepare the way for the big campaign that is coming up.

> **After these things the Lord appointed other seventy also, and sent them two and two before his face into every city and place, whither he himself would come.**
>
> **Therefore said he unto them, The harvest truly is great, but the labourers are few: pray ye therefore the Lord of the harvest, that he would send forth labourers into his harvest.**
>
> **Luke 10:1-2**

4. Priscilla and Aquila, helps ministers of Paul

> **Greet Priscilla and Aquila my helpers in Christ Jesus:**
>
> **Romans 16:3**

5. Urbane

> **Salute Urbane, our helper in Christ, and Stachys my beloved.**
>
> **Romans 16:9**

Chapter

55

Understanding the Deficiencies of Lay Ministry

CHAPTER SUMMARY

55. 1 The lay ministry is deficient because it lacks the full consecration of a Levite.

55. 2 The lay ministry is deficient because lay pastors do not wholly belong to the Lord

55. 3 The lay ministry is deficient because lay pastors cannot and do not take care of the tabernacle in the way Levites do

55. 4 The lay ministry is deficient because lay pastors do have an inheritance in the world

55. 5 The lay ministry is deficient because lay pastors do not have the time to assist the high priest in many of his duties

55. 6 The lay ministry is deficient because only real Levites are fit to do the work of the priesthood

55. 7 The lay ministry is deficient because lay pastors cannot give the hours necessary for quality work

55. 8 The lay ministry is deficient because it is not God's ordained purpose and plan

55. 9 The lay ministry is deficient because in the lay ministry, God does not have the first honoured position that He deserves

55. 10 The lay ministry is deficient because lay people are unable to make full proof of their ministry

> **So you shall appoint Aaron and his sons that they may keep their priesthood, but THE LAYMAN WHO COMES NEAR SHALL BE PUT TO DEATH.**
>
> **Numbers 3:10 (NASB)**

1. The lay ministry is deficient because it lacks the full consecration of a Levite.

The full consecration that was required of Levites can never be given by a lay pastor. A study of the Bible reveals the extent to which priests had to be consecrated to God and to the ministry.

2. The lay ministry is deficient because lay pastors do not wholly belong to the Lord.

The Levites are the Lord's. When you work at the bank, there is a sense in which the bank owns you. The bank tells you when to come to work and when to go home. These are simply realities of life.

> **And I, behold, I have taken the Levites from among the children of Israel instead of all the firstborn that openeth the matrix among the children of Israel: therefore THE LEVITES SHALL BE MINE;**
>
> **Numbers 3:12**

3. The lay ministry is deficient because lay pastors cannot and do not take care of the tabernacle in the way Levites do.

Lay pastors are busy taking care of the business of the bank and other secular institutions that they work for.

> **But the Levites shall pitch round about the tabernacle of testimony, that there be no wrath upon the congregation of the children of Israel: and the LEVITES SHALL KEEP THE CHARGE OF THE TABERNACLE of testimony.**
>
> **Numbers 1:53**

4. The lay ministry is deficient because lay pastors do have an inheritance in the world.

The inheritance of lay pastors is their jobs. Real pastors do not have an inheritance in the world. They are wholly dedicated to the Lord and all their hope is in the Lord.

> **But the tithes of the children of Israel, which they offer as an heave offering unto the Lord, I have given to the Levites to inherit: therefore I have said unto them, AMONG THE CHILDREN OF ISRAEL THEY SHALL HAVE NO INHERITANCE.**
>
> **Numbers 18:24**

5. The lay ministry is deficient because lay pastors do not have the time to assist the high priest in many of his duties.

Lay pastors will be at their secular jobs when needed by the high priest. A real Levite is wholly given to the work of ministry.

> **You shall thus give the Levites to Aaron and to his sons; THEY ARE WHOLLY GIVEN TO HIM from among the sons of Israel.**
>
> **Numbers 3:9 (NASB)**

6. The lay ministry is deficient because only real Levites are fit to do the work of the priesthood.

Lay men were not allowed to approach these holy tasks.

> **So you shall appoint Aaron and his sons that they may keep their priesthood, but THE LAYMAN WHO COMES NEAR SHALL BE PUT TO DEATH.**
>
> **Numbers 3:10 (NASB)**

7. The lay ministry is deficient because lay pastors cannot give the hours necessary for quality work.

The hours spent on your profession logically define who you are.

The amount of time necessary for quality fruits and results can never be provided by a part-time input. The curse of Adam requires several hours of input and sweat for any good results. Quality time must be spent on quality work. It is only in sorrow and hard work that our work on earth will yield fruits.

> **And unto Adam he said, Because thou hast hearkened unto the voice of thy wife, and hast eaten of the tree, of which I commanded thee, saying, Thou shalt not eat of it: cursed is the ground for thy sake; in sorrow shalt thou eat of it all the days of thy life;**
>
> **Thorns also and thistles shall it bring forth to thee; and thou shalt eat the herb of the field;**
>
> **In the sweat of thy face shalt thou eat bread, till thou return unto the ground; for out of it wast thou taken: for dust thou art, and unto dust shalt thou return.**
>
> **Genesis 3:17-19**

8. The lay ministry is deficient because it is not God's ordained purpose and plan.

God's purpose is the plan that must be pursued and not our ideas. His ordained method is for His priests to work and to live off their work and be sustained by it. Lay people are not paid or sustained by the ministry. They earn money from the secular jobs they do. God's ordained plan is full-time ministry. Read the Scriptures for yourself!

> **Do ye not know that they which minister about holy things live of the things of the temple? and they which wait at the altar are partakers with the altar?**
>
> **Even so HATH THE LORD ORDAINED that they which preach the gospel should live of the gospel.**
>
> **1 Corinthians 9:13-14**

9. The lay ministry is deficient because in the lay ministry, God does not have the first honoured position that He deserves.

God will never accept to be secondary to anything or to anyone. The honoured position which God deserves is the first position; that which comes before everything else.

His work comes before the work of the bank, the work of the university, the work of private companies or even the work of the government. Everyone who works for God after working for mammon has placed God in second position. God is aware of this reality. Yet out of grace and mercy, He receives those who still want to do something for His sake.

> **But seek ye first the kingdom of God, and his righteousness; and all these things shall be added unto you.**
>
> **Matthew 6:33**

10. The lay ministry is deficient because lay people are unable to make full proof of their ministry.

Because a lay person cannot fully perform certain duties, he cannot make full proof of his ministry. His ministry can never develop to its ultimate level of fruitfulness.

> **But watch thou in all things, endure afflictions, do the work of an evangelist, MAKE FULL PROOF OF THY MINISTRY.**
>
> **2 Timothy 4:5**

> **... fully perform all the duties of your ministry.**
>
> **2 Timothy 4:5 (AMP)**

> **... do a thorough job ...**
>
> **2 Timothy 4:5 (Message)**

Chapter

56

Understanding Why God Allows Lay Ministry to Exist

CHAPTER SUMMARY

56. 1 Lay ministry comes about because of a deceptive response from those called to the work

56. 2 The lay ministry came about because of a lack of labourers

56. 3 The lay ministry came about because of the great need

56. 4 The lay ministry came about because of people's inability to pay for true ministry

1. Lay ministry comes about because of a deceptive response from those called to the work.

We all know that lay ministry is not the God-ordained kind of ministry. So why does God allow the lay ministry to carry on? When those who promised to go do not go, God is forced to fall back on lay people and even on women. Read it for yourself!

> **But what think ye? A certain man had two sons; and he came to the first, and said, Son, go work to day in my vineyard. He answered and said, I will not: but afterward he repented, and went. And he came to the second, and said likewise. And he answered and said, I go, sir: AND WENT NOT.**
>
> **Matthew 21:28-30**

2. The lay ministry came about because of a lack of labourers.

There is a genuine lack of labourers for the work of God. If you were Almighty God and you needed to save seven billion dying souls from going to Hell, would you not raise up lay men to help in this unbelievable, gargantuan harvest?

> **But when he saw the multitudes, he was moved with compassion on them, because they fainted, and were scattered abroad, as sheep having no shepherd.**
>
> **Then saith he unto his disciples, the harvest truly is plenteous, but the LABOURERS ARE FEW;**
>
> **Pray ye therefore the Lord of the harvest, that he will send forth labourers into his harvest.**
>
> **Matthew 9:36-38**

3. The lay ministry came about because of the great need.

There is a great need in the church for labourers, pastors and evangelists. Paul said, "Necessity is laid on me!" I have to do it! I need to go! Perhaps the great needs that exist in the church have forced the lay ministry to become an important arm of ministry today.

> **For though I preach the gospel, I have nothing to glory of: for NECESSITY IS LAID UPON ME; yea, woe is unto me, if I preach not the gospel!**
>
> **1 Corinthians 9:16**

4. The lay ministry came about because of people's inability to pay for true ministry.

Many times the church is unable to pay a good pastor to look after the people. Many small congregations do not have the money or resources to look after their shepherd. This results in pastors preaching and teaching the Word of God without being paid. The apostle Paul was a good example of someone who kept preaching the Word without charging for it.

> **For ye remember, brethren, our labour and travail: for labouring night and day, because we would not be chargeable unto any of you, we preached unto you the gospel of God.**
>
> **1 Thessalonians 2:9**

Chapter

57

Develop the Four Essential Skills of a Lay Pastor

CHAPTER SUMMARY

A lay pastor must develop four essential skills. Just as there are four engines that power a jumbo jet, there are four engines that power up a lay pastor's life and ministry. In this chapter, I want you to think about these four essential skills that make a lay pastor complete.

1. Pastoral skills

A lay pastor must develop himself as a good pastor. He must be a good shepherd and lead the flock of God as though he were in full-time ministry. People under his care must experience the love of God and enjoy the richness of the Word of God that he preaches.

2. Business and professional skills

If the lay pastor is a businessman, he must develop very good business skills. These business skills will cause him to prosper and be successful in his business. It is dangerous to have a lay pastor who is a failure in his business. It will make him desperate and begin to have an evil eye towards the ministry.

Such people blame the ministry for their failures in business. If you are a professional such as a lawyer or a doctor, you must excel in your chosen profession. You must get to the highest possible rank that you can and become an example to other laymen. Once again, when you do not prosper in your profession, you begin to have an evil eye towards the ministry. Lay pastors who became corrupt were often failures in their chosen professions or business. In their poverty and desperation they turned on the church for financial relief.

3. Flourishing skills

A lay pastor must also develop himself in the art of flourishing. This is the art of becoming rich and prosperous. There are many people who develop themselves in their businesses or professions but are unable to convert it into real prosperity. It is important to use the art of leadership and the art of strategic thinking to help yourself to flourish. We all know many doctors and lawyers who don't have much money. They are professionals alright, but they have not flourished and do not have much money to spend. We all know many lecturers who live from hand to mouth. They are professors alright and they did earn their PhD's from famous universities. But many of these highly educated men have simply not learnt the art of flourishing.

A lay pastor must flourish; otherwise, in his midlife he will turn against the ministry he has loved and blame the church for his difficulties. Midlife crisis that begins from around the age of forty, causes men to re-evaluate all they have been involved in. Unfortunately, many laymen begin to blame the ministry for their poor performance at work and their poor flourishing skills.

A flourishing lay pastor must have an income that is far more than his expenses. A flourishing lay pastor must be able to give larger and larger amounts to the ministry.

4. Early retirement skills

A lay pastor must have early retirement skills. Perhaps the most important of these four is the early retirement skills. These skills are important to a lay pastor because as he goes forward, he is likely to want to give himself more to the work of the Lord. However, if he has not developed early retirement skills, he will be unable to retire from his secular work. He will need to go to the clinic every day and earn his living.

If a lay pastor cannot take long periods off from work, to give himself to God's work he will not be able to retire soon from his secular work. If, however, he has been successful in investing in real estate or other income-generating projects, he will be able to retire early from secular work and give himself to ministry. A lay pastor with early retirement skills will have ensured that he is genuinely free from debts and lives in his own house. Indeed, a lay pastor with early retirement skills is able to stay away from work longer and longer until one day he never has to return!

Chapter

58

The Struggles of Lay Pastors

CHAPTER SUMMARY

58.1 Lay pastors struggle with the concept of full-time ministry

58.2 Lay pastors struggle with independence

58.3 Lay pastors struggle with keeping rank

58.4 Lay pastors struggle with offences from transfers

58.5 Lay pastors struggle with corrections and rebukes

58.6 Lay pastors struggle with delegated authorities

58.7 Lay pastors struggle with combining their secular life with ministry

58.8 Lay pastors struggle with the transition into full-time ministry

58.9 Lay pastors struggle with closeness

58.10 Lay pastors struggle with pride

58.11 Lay pastors struggle with hypocrisy

58.12 Lay pastors struggle with deceptions and delusions

58.13 Lay pastors struggle with endurance

1. Lay pastors struggle with the concept of full-time ministry.

> **Lest there be any fornicator, or PROFANE PERSON, as Esau, who for one morsel of meat sold his birthright.**
>
> **Hebrews 12:16**

A lot of lay pastors struggle with the concept of full-time ministry. However, a good lay pastor should be able to preach about full-time ministry. To despise the concept of full dedication to the house of the Lord is a mistake of grandiose proportions. Esau profaned and despised sacred things and was rejected by God. Lay pastors must not despise the concept of full-time ministry. Indeed, there must be no struggle to acknowledge the importance and validity of full-time ministry.

2. Lay pastors struggle with independence.

Many lay pastors struggle with obedience and conformity. Obedience becomes difficult as pride increases in your heart. Through disobedience and non-conformity, the spirit of independence develops. But God did not design us to be independent beings. It is obvious that we have not recognised what being independent really is. When Satan tempted Adam and Eve, an offer for independence was made to them (which is the same offer made to each of us today). Satan offered independence when he said, "You will be like God; you will not need God."

All men have this inherent struggle with independence. The seed of Satan leads the drive to independence, even when it is self-destructive. Men have more of a drive for independence than women. Research has shown that women remain faithfully in their jobs once they are treated well. Women are not as likely to change jobs as men are. On the average, men change their jobs about seven times in their lifetime.

A great difference between human beings and the rest of creation is our desire to be independent from God. Unlike the rest of the creation, human beings are always struggling to be independent of God who created them. Similarly, people who were birthed into a ministry struggle to be independent of the person who birthed them. The stars are not independent! God numbers the stars and calls them by name.

> **He telleth the number of the stars; he calleth them all by their names.**
>
> **Psalm 147:4**

The lions look to God for their food. The lions have never desired independence from God.

> **The young lions roar after their prey, and seek their meat from God.**
>
> **Psalm 104:21**

The birds and beasts look to God for their food. They have never gone away from their creator. Human beings have forsaken God and put Him out of our minds.

> **He giveth to the beast his food, and to the young ravens which cry.**
>
> **Psalm 147:9**

Jesus told us how the Father feeds the birds of the air:

> **Behold the fowls of the air: for they sow not, neither do they reap, nor gather into barns; yet YOUR HEAVENLY FATHER FEEDETH THEM.**
>
> **Matthew 6:26**

Whilst all of creation looks to God for their food, we (human beings) rather become more independent of God. Human beings are alone in their desire and pursuit of independence.

> **O Lord, how manifold are thy works! in wisdom hast thou made them all: the earth is full of thy riches. So is this great and wide sea, wherein are things creeping innumerable, both small and great beasts.**
>
> **There go the ships: there is that leviathan, whom thou hast made to play therein.These wait ALL UPON THEE; that THOU MAYEST GIVE THEM THEIR MEAT in due season.**
>
> **Psalm 104:24-27**

Our struggle to be independent from God has always resulted in confusion. When you struggle to be independent from the ministry that gave birth to you, you may be motivated by Satan. Satan is the salesman of independence.

Beware! The desire for independence is not a new thing. Adam was offered this independence and he took it, landing the whole universe in utter confusion. A lay pastor must not become independent of the source of his authority.

Some lay pastors quickly become independent when they are appointed to the ministry. They feel they know everything and disconnect spiritually from the source of their spiritual existence. They no longer listen to messages or advice from their spiritual father. What a tragedy! The appointment to the pastoral office often destroys people.

3. Lay pastors struggle with keeping rank.

Lay pastors must stay in line and try not to move out of their position. The lay ministry is a layman's ministry. It is not "real" ministry and people who are practising the lay ministry must acknowledge who they are and who they are not. That is what it means to keep rank! When I drive to any court of law, I am not acknowledged as a professional lawyer even though I have written a few contracts in my lifetime. I am a lay person as far as the law profession is concerned and I have to accept that. I must stay within my rank and not think of myself more highly than I ought to.

> **Of Zebulun, such as went forth to battle, expert in war, with all instruments of war, FIFTY THOUSAND, WHICH COULD KEEP RANK: they were not of double heart.**
>
> **1 Chronicles 12:33**

4. Lay pastors struggle with offences from transfers.

> **Then Joab arose, and came to Absalom unto his house, and said unto him, Wherefore have thy servants set my field on fire?**
>
> **And Absalom answered Joab, Behold, I sent unto thee, saying, Come hither, that I may send thee to the king, to say, Wherefore am I come from Geshur? IT HAD BEEN GOOD FOR ME TO HAVE BEEN THERE STILL: now therefore let me see the king's face; and if there be any iniquity in me, let him kill me.**
>
> **2 Samuel 14:31-32**

Absalom was transferred to Geshur. On his return he wanted to live in the same house as the king. He reacted angrily when the king would not see him.

People who struggle with being transferred from place to place are often agitated by spirits of rebellion. Just like Absalom, they do not want to be where they are placed.

Lay pastors are support staff in ministry and ought not to struggle with any kind of transfers. Pride makes a lay pastor offended with a transfer. It is pride that makes a pastor resign because he has been transferred. A lay person must accept that he is a helper to those who are in full-time ministry. He cannot dictate what must be done and how the church must be run. I know several lay pastors who were greatly offended when they were asked to move and serve in another capacity.

5. Lay pastors struggle with corrections and rebukes.

> **Reprove not a scorner, lest he hate thee: rebuke a wise man, and he will love thee.**
>
> **Proverbs 9:8**

A pastor must not be angry when he is rebuked. He must receive correction like a child who is humble and open. Unfortunately, some lay pastors are puffed up because of their long service. After some years in lay ministry, they consider themselves too big to be corrected or rebuked. Such "big" pastors must be shown the exit sign and made to leave. Their continued presence in the ministry will pollute younger ones and the leaven of pride and rebellion will spread. There is no place for these "big" men in the work of the Lord.

6. Lay pastors struggle with delegated authorities.

> **... He that believeth on me, believeth not on me, but on him that sent me.**
>
> **John 12:44**

Lay pastors must receive delegated authorities with joy. As the church grows larger, people you do not know will be appointed and may have authority over you. The air hostess on a plane may not know who the pilot is but she has to respect his rank as the commander of the aircraft. It is the rank and the appointment that she must respect. In the same way, lay pastors must receive and accept people who are appointed over them. Failure to accept delegated authority is a recipe for anarchy and confusion in the ministry. How is it that a lay pastor can accept authority in his secular job but reject authority in the church world? Away with these rebels! Let them leave the house of the Lord for those who are humble enough to accept delegated authorities.

7. Lay pastors struggle with combining their secular life with ministry.

Lay pastors struggle to combine secular work with ministry. This is a struggle that will always be there. Indeed, it is not easy to handle two completely different jobs and be successful at both. It takes the grace of God. But that is what lay ministry is all about. There are many people who have successfully combined secular work with their spiritual work. God will bless them for the sacrifices they have made.

Beside those things that are without, that which cometh upon me daily, the care of all the churches.

2 Corinthians 11:28

8. Lay pastors struggle with the transition into full-time ministry.

Verily, verily, I say unto you, He that entereth not by the door into the fold of the sheep, but climbeth up some other way, the same is a thief and a robber.

John 10:1

There is a proper way to enter full-time ministry. Without humility, lay pastors are unable to bow down and go through the entrance door to priesthood. To come into full-time ministry involves giving up everything and sacrificing yourself for the ministry. Transitioning into full-time ministry is not the same as getting an alternative job. The ministry is not an alternative to secular work. It is a calling that must be entered into soberly, advisedly and with lowliness of mind.

The transition to full-time ministry is not the grasping at an alternative source of income. Sadly, some lay pastors begin to see the church as a source of income. When these lay pastors were offered the opportunity to work for the Lord, they rejected it because they thought they would lose everything by working for God. When they began to see the possibility of earning money from the ministry, they suddenly changed their minds about lay ministry and grasped at full-time ministry with their greedy hands.

Why did they not give themselves to the ministry when they were young, fresh, energetic and intelligent? Why did they wait until they were having a midlife crisis and in need of additional income to pay their children's university fees? Do they now look upon the church as a source of money which can cater for their needs? No, no, no! The ministry is not a business and the ministry must not be entered because of your need for money. That is not the legitimate door to ministry. You must enter into ministry in obedience to the call of God. You must enter into ministry because it is the will of God. You must enter into ministry because you love God and because you desire to please Him. Above all, you must enter full-time ministry because God has called you to do so.

9. Lay pastors struggle with closeness.

> **Draw nigh to God, and he will draw nigh to you. Cleanse your hands, ye sinners; and purify your hearts, ye double minded.**
>
> **James 4:8**

Lay pastors struggle to stay close to the anointing which they need. It is important to draw near and stay near. Being close is both an art and an act of humility. Pride creates a gap and brings the aloofness that is so common in some lay pastors and volunteers. They stand at a distance and stare as though they are not welcome. Guilt keeps them away when indeed they should be close by, helping in the ministry.

Don't stand far away! You are loved! You are wanted! You are needed! Come closer and be as involved as you can.

10. Lay pastors struggle with pride.

> **Be of the same mind one toward another. Mind not high things, but condescend to men of low estate. Be not wise in your own conceits.**
>
> **Romans 12:16**

Pride comes from being around for a long time. Sometimes, pride grows in lay pastors when they pastor a successful church. Pride is also seen in pastors who have churches in rich cities. Pride also filters into the lives of lay pastors when they are successful at their secular work.

You must overcome the temptation of the pride that comes by being an opinion leader and a prominent person. Korah is a perfect example of a lay pastor who went berserk because of his position in society. Success in the secular world must not destroy a lay pastor! Korah's outrageous demands to Moses are recorded in the Bible. Korah was a layman who challenged the holiness of Moses, telling him off and informing him that he was not the only holy person who could pray to God. Watch out Mr. Layman!

> **Now Korah, the son of Izhar, the son of Kohath, the son of Levi, and Dathan and Abiram, the sons of Eliab, and On, the son of Peleth, sons of Reuben, took men:**
>
> **And they rose up before Moses, with certain of the children of Israel, two hundred and fifty princes of the assembly, famous in the congregation, men of renown:**
>
> **And they gathered themselves together against Moses and against Aaron, and said unto them, Ye take too much upon you, seeing all the congregation are holy, every one of them, and the Lord is among them: wherefore then lift ye up yourselves above the congregation of the Lord?**
>
> **...**
>
> **And Moses said unto Korah, Hear now, ye sons of Levi: Seemeth it but a small thing unto you, that the God of Israel hath separated you from the congregation of Israel, to bring you near to himself, to do the service of the tabernacle of Jehovah, and to stand before the congregation to minister unto them;**

And that he hath brought thee near, and all thy brethren the sons of Levi with thee? And seek ye the priesthood also?

Numbers 16: 1-3, 8-10

11. Lay pastors struggle with hypocrisy.

Hypocrisy involves appearing to be more committed and righteous than you really are. Ananias and Sapphira suffered from this. They pretended that they were giving more than they actually did. But there is no need to pretend to be more committed, more sacrificial and more spiritual that you really are.

Some lay pastors constantly pretend that they want to be in full-time ministry. All through their lives, they pledge, they promise and they affirm that full-time ministry is all that they want to do with their lives. Like Ananias and Sapphira, they make commitments they cannot keep.

They present themselves as being more zealous and more committed than they really are. Relax my brother and be yourself! Not everyone has been called to full-time ministry! It is not a sin to be a lay pastor! It is a privilege! It is an honour and it is a great thing that you are a lay pastor.

Do not live your life pledging to be somebody you cannot be. Be happy with what God has made you and rejoice in your portion of the lay ministry. **Do not live a life of unnecessary guilt!** God is happy with your contribution to the ministry.

But a certain man named Ananias, with Sapphira his wife, sold a possession, And kept back part of the price, his wife also being privy to it, and brought a certain part, and laid it at the apostles 'feet.

But Peter said, Ananias, why hath Satan filled thine heart to lie to the Holy Ghost, and to keep back part of the price of the land? Whiles it remained, was it not thine own? and after it was sold, was it not in thine own power? why hast thou conceived this thing in thine heart? thou hast not lied unto men, but unto God.

Acts 5:1-4

12. Lay pastors struggle with deceptions and delusions.

And with all deceivableness of unrighteousness in them that perish; because they received not the love of the truth, that they might be saved.

2 Thessalonians 2:10

■ Why Lay Pastors Struggle with Delusions

a. **Lay pastors struggle with delusions because they use the same titles and uniforms as full-time ministers**.

Lay pastors struggle with deception. It is easy to believe you are something that you are not. The roots of the deception of lay pastors lies in their using the same titles and sometimes wearing the same uniforms as full-time ministers. There are lay pastors of small churches who use the title "General Overseer" whilst some founders of huge denominations are also called General

Overseers. Such use of similar titles leads to deceptions about who a lay pastor really is. Many laymen wear a collar whilst full-time priests also wear a similar collar. Of course, they are deceived into thinking that they are priests of the same rank. But this is not the case!

A lay person wearing a collar has been given the privilege to share in the ministry that the few full-time pastors can never fulfil on their own.

b. **Lay pastors struggle with delusions because they engage in the same activities as full-time ministers.**

Delusions also come to lay pastors because they engage in the same activities as full-time ministers. Lay pastors often preach as much as full-time ministers. The ability of laymen to officiate weddings and funerals leaves them with the delusion that they are equal to full-time priests and pastors. What they do not realise is that they are simply helping the full-time pastors to carry out some of their many tasks.

c. **Lay pastors struggle with delusions because they receive appreciation and offerings from church members**.

Delusions abound even more when lay pastors receive offerings from church members. When lay pastors receive letters of love and appreciation from their church members, they feel appreciated for their ministry efforts. At their secular work place, no one writes letters of love to the lay pastor and no one gives him love offerings. All these offerings can establish delusions in a lay pastor until he thinks he is as good as a full-time priest. It is important that a lay pastor continually affirms that he is simply a helper of a full-time priest.

d. **Lay pastors struggle with delusions because they minister under the covering, good name and calling of a large ministry**.

Deceptions and delusions come when people minister under the momentum and good name of a large ministry. Usually, the covering of an apostle's call provides the momentum for lay pastors to function. It is unfortunate that these lay pastors would begin to think that they themselves are apostles.

Lay pastors, guard yourselves from delusions! I have seen many lay pastors fall flat on their faces as they dived out of their God-given covering.

13. Lay pastors struggle with endurance.

> **Therefore, my beloved brethren, be ye stedfast, unmoveable, always abounding in the work of the Lord, forasmuch as ye know that your labour is not in vain in the Lord.**
>
> **1 Corinthians 15:58**

Lay pastors struggle with endurance. A lay pastor must be steadfast, unmoveable, always abounding in the work of the Lord. Many lay pastors give up ministry in their midlife. But you must survive the tests of a lay pastor and persist in the lay ministry. A lay pastor must continue ministering through his middle age, through the midlife crisis zone and into retirement.

Midlife crisis is a syndrome which many people go through. In their midlife beginning from the age of forty, people begin to experience certain well-known symptoms. These are:

1) A search for an undefined dream or goal.

2) A deep sense of regret for goals not accomplished.

3) A fear of humiliation among more successful colleagues.

Indeed, this problem peaks at about the age of forty-six. Many people in this age group experience these symptoms and struggle with the desire to do something new and different. But what new and different thing can you do apart from serving the Lord faithfully? A spiritual person cannot be led by midlife crises. You must overcome the midlife crisis. You must endure to the end. Endurance is a key characteristic of a true spiritual pilgrim.

Chapter

59

The Example-Setting Ministry of Volunteers

CHAPTER SUMMARY

59. 1 Volunteers are an example of zeal

59. 2 Volunteers are an example of hard work

59. 3 Volunteers are an example of Christ-likeness that others can follow

59. 4 Volunteers are an example of a pattern of good works

59. 5 Volunteers are an example to be remembered in a good way, even if dead

1. Volunteers are an example of zeal.

A volunteer is an example of someone zealous for the Lord. Without the zeal of the Lord you will not be able to combine secular work and ministry. When I was a medical student, I needed extra zeal to add any non-medical activities to my life. Indeed, it took the zeal of the Lord to start a church through witnessing and door-to-door evangelism. Every step of the lay ministry was a step of great zeal and faith in the Lord.

> **For I know the forwardness of your mind, for which I boast of you to them of Macedonia, that Achaia was ready a year ago; and YOUR ZEAL HATH PROVOKED VERY MANY.**
>
> **2 Corinthians 9:2**

2. Volunteers are an example of hard work.

A volunteer sets the example of hard work. It is hard work to preach and teach the Word of God and at the same time do your secular duties. A lazy person can never be a successful lay pastor. Many lay pastors are exhausted and weary after a day of this combined effort.

> **And I have been a constant example of how you can help those in need by working hard. You should remember the words of the Lord Jesus: 'It is more blessed to give than to receive.'**
>
> **Acts 20:35 (NLT)**

3. Volunteers are an example of Christ-likeness that others can follow.

Volunteers are an example of Christ. Jesus Christ gave up His life and had no thought for His own well-being. He gave His everything to fulfil the will of His father. Today, every step you take in lay ministry is a step towards being like Jesus Christ the Saviour. I honour lay pastors because they are a good example of Jesus Christ. May God increase the number of lay pastors and volunteers in our churches so that the sacrificial character of Jesus Christ will be evident to all!

> **Be ye followers of me, even as I also am of Christ.**
>
> **1 Corinthians 11:1**

4. Volunteers are an example of a pattern of good works.

Lay pastors reveal a pattern of good works. Without being paid they give off everything they have, expecting their reward from Heaven. This pattern of sacrifice reveals real Christian virtues that can be emulated by the rest of the church. I pity any minister who does not have lay pastors and volunteers eagerly working around in the church.

> **In all things SHEWING THYSELF A PATTERN OF GOOD WORKS: in doctrine shewing uncorruptness, gravity, sincerity,**
>
> **Titus 2:7**

5. Volunteers are an example to be remembered in a good way, even if dead.

I have officiated a number of funerals of lay pastors. Indeed, in their death, their works speak and testify of how fruitful and sacrificial they were in their lifetime. Today, on our Wall of Remembrance are the names of lay pastors who laid down their lives to build the church. Without the contribution of lay pastors and volunteers, a church will never experience a certain level of fruitfulness.

> **By faith Abel offered unto God a more excellent sacrifice than Cain, by which he obtained witness that he was righteous, God testifying of his gifts: and by it he being dead yet speaketh.**
>
> **Hebrews 11:4**

Chapter

60

Why We Must Fight to Protect the Lay Ministry

CHAPTER SUMMARY

Every church that has embraced the lay ministry must fight to preserve it. There will always be people who start out as volunteers but metamorphose into hawks who want to be paid for everything they do. When people realise that the church is not as poor as they thought, they see their lay ministry as an alternative job and want to get as much as they can out of it.

- **Fight the Enemies of Lay Ministry**

60. 1 **Do not allow people to corrupt the good news that lay people can also work for the Lord**

60. 2 **Openly oppose those who corrupt the purity of the ministry**

60. 3 **Do not build the lay ministry and destroy it afterwards**

60. 4 **Do not frustrate the grace of God that works through lay people**

60. 5 **Do not allow witchcraft in the church to manipulate and corrupt the truth about lay ministry**

60. 6 Fight for the birth of the lay ministry

60. 7 Cut off the little leaven that will leaven the whole lump

60. 8 Do not be weary of lay ministry.

There is good news for laymen! I have good news for all volunteers who perform their services willingly and without pay. The message that laymen can have a part in this great work is truly good news for those who love God but are unable to give themselves wholly to this calling. This good news is that in a large house, there are many vessels. God is able to use different kinds of vessels to do His work. He can use volunteer vessels and He can use dedicated full-time priests.

You must not allow anyone to destroy this wonderful provision that the Lord has made. It is important that you do not pervert the concept of lay people being in the ministry. The lay ministry must remain pure and must continue as unpaid volunteer work. When the lay ministry is corrupted, volunteers want to be paid and begin to ask for money. Corrupted lay pastors want to be paid for their volunteer services and begin to grasp after benefits.

The leader of a large denomination once lamented about the lay preachers in his denomination who were demanding cross-country vehicles to be given to them on their retirement from the lay ministry. They demanded money and benefits that are reserved for people who do the ministry on a full-time basis. Obviously, the concept of lay ministry was corrupted and changing into something totally different from what it started as.

Fight the Enemies of Lay Ministry

1. Do not allow people to corrupt the good news that lay people can also work for the Lord.

> **As we said before, so say I now again, if any man preach any other gospel unto you than that ye have received, let him be accursed.**
>
> **Galatians 1:9**

Paul was sure of what he was teaching. He believed in the gospel being sent to the ends of the world free of charge. Freely have you received, freely give. That is the gospel that we preach. Do not give place to people who turn the ministry into a business. No not even for an hour! "To whom we gave place by subjection, no, not for an hour; that the truth of the gospel might continue with you" (Galatians 2:5). The absence of lay people working for God is a tragedy. The absence of volunteers in a church is a mistake. Everybody can do something for God. If everyone has to be paid for every little thing he does, what hope is there for the church? We are standing in the midst of seven billion souls who need to find Jesus Christ before it is too late. To remove lay people and volunteers is to remove a large section of God's working force. Let us resist all those who corrupt the lay ministry and destroy the army of the Lord from within.

2. Openly oppose those who corrupt the purity of the ministry.

> **But when I saw that they walked not uprightly according to the truth of the gospel, I SAID UNTO PETER BEFORE THEM ALL, If thou, being a Jew, livest after the manner of Gentiles, and not as do the Jews, why compellest thou the Gentiles to live as do the Jews?**
>
> **Galatians 2:14**

Paul opposed Peter when he walked in hypocrisy. He rejected the very scent of corruption as it tried to enter the ministry. We must also reject those who corrupt the ministry! The ministry can be corrupted from many angles, including from the laymen. The lay ministry can be destroyed by those who no longer want to sacrifice themselves for the ministry. If we allow this, there will be no more volunteers in the ministry. Without lay people, most of the world will not be reached and the gospel will be hindered.

3. Do not build the lay ministry and destroy it afterwards.

> **For if I BUILD AGAIN THE THINGS WHICH I DESTROYED, I make myself a transgressor.**
>
> **Galatians 2:18**

It is madness to build up an army of volunteers and then destroy it by killing the culture of self-sacrifice. Churches that have worked with lay people must always value them, even when full-time workers become prominent. It is madness to promote lay ministry and later destroy it because you have some new ideas.

4. Do not frustrate the grace of God that works through lay people.

> **I DO NOT FRUSTRATE THE GRACE OF GOD: for if righteousness come by the law, then Christ is dead in vain.**
>
> **Galatians 2:21**

When lay people are able to grow a church as though they were full-time priests, it is because of the grace of God. The grace of God helps the layman to do things as though he is in full-time ministry. Through the grace of God, a lay person may minister as though he was a prophet, an apostle, an evangelist, a teacher or a pastor. When the grace of God is at work, a person is supernaturally lifted up.

Unfortunately, some lay people take the grace of God for granted and begin to think that being in full-time ministry is not necessary. They feel that they, as laymen, have been able to accomplish just as much as full-time ministers. They do not realise that it is God who has worked supernaturally to enable them do certain things.

Some lay people who are helped so much by the grace of God begin to think they are even better than full-time priests because they are not paid by the church.

5. Do not allow witchcraft in the church to manipulate and corrupt the truth about lay ministry.

> **O foolish Galatians, WHO HATH BEWITCHED YOU, that ye should NOT OBEY THE TRUTH, before whose eyes Jesus Christ hath been evidently set forth, crucified among you?**
>
> **Galatians 3:1**

People who operate in witchcraft try to manipulate the truth and cast a slur on lay ministry. They attack full-time ministers and say that full-time ministers enjoy benefits while they work for nothing. Such words corrupt the sacrifice of ministry and stir up people to think that they are being cheated.

People who once sacrificed their lives happily in the service of the Lord, begin to have an evil eye towards the ministry and no longer want to sacrifice or pay the price. Watch out for witchcraft that prevents people from obeying the truth of God's Word. As Paul said, "I am afraid of you, lest I have bestowed upon you labour in vain." Indeed, such people must be feared because they can wipe out the entire volunteer force that is needed to work in the ministry. I remember a lay pastor who wrote a letter to me with a calculation of how many miles his car had driven as he did pastoral work. He wanted the church to pay for his car because of the mileage it had accrued. How sad it is when laymen begin to calculate their sacrifices and present a bill to the Lord.

6. Fight for the birth of the lay ministry.

My little children, of whom I TRAVAIL in birth again until Christ be formed in you.

Galatians 4:19

Paul was fighting for Christ to be formed in the church of Galatia. What did Paul mean by that?

Paul wanted the character of Christ to be formed in the people who had been born again. What is the character of Christ? It is the character of humility, obedience and self-sacrifice. Such traits do not come to people easily. Such traits do not enter a church easily! A church can easily have a vampire culture in which everyone wants to drink the finances of the church of Jesus Christ. In the vampire culture, no one does anything for free. To change such a culture, you must fight with all your might.

You must travail in birth until the sacrificial and humble character of Christ is formed in your church. You must fight to have an army of volunteers in the church. It is not easy to introduce the culture of sacrifice and volunteer service to a church. In today's world, everybody wants to be paid. If you fight for this culture, it will successfully be birthed into the church.

7. Cut off the little leaven that will leaven the whole lump.

A little leaven leaveneth the whole lump.

Galatians 5:9

You must remove people who do not understand what it means to be a lay pastor. You must urgently eliminate those who are not prepared to sacrifice. If you have instrumentalists who are not prepared to play instruments without being paid, get rid of them.

If you have even one musician or talented singer who charges a fee for his services, you must get rid of that person urgently. He will pollute the rest of them and no one will be happy to work for the Lord free of charge.

If you have a lay pastor who begins to eye the offering, you must get rid of him. Volunteers must not think about the money that the church receives. A volunteer is there to work for the Lord without charge. If a volunteer wishes to give himself wholly to the ministry, he is welcome to the ministry. But he must not come to the ministry because he sees it as an opportunity to earn some money.

8. Do not be weary of lay ministry.

> **And let us not be weary in well doing: for in due season we shall reap, if we faint not. As we have therefore opportunity, let us do good unto all men, especially unto them who are of the household of faith.**
>
> **Galatians 6:9-10**

Unfortunately, many volunteers say to themselves, "I've had enough of the church. I cannot continue to spend my time and money serving for nothing." But lay pastors and volunteers must not become tired of the sacrifices they make. The rewards of ministry are great. God has huge harvests waiting for those who have sown the seeds of personal sacrifice and humility. It must be a joy to take up every opportunity that presents itself to lay people. If you are a lawyer, you must be overjoyed that there is a case you can do for the church without charging. If you are an accountant, you must be overjoyed that there are some accounts you can do for the church without charging a fee. What a blessing it is to do something for the Lord!

I noticed how people who became lay pastors in their twenties became weary of the ministry in their forties. Weariness and discouragement had set in! But we must not be weary of well doing. We must continue to work for the King of kings to the very end.

Bibliography

Adams, Jay E. Leaders after God's Heart. Grand Rapids, Michigan: Zondervan Publishers, 1975.

------. Shepherding God's Flock. Grand Rapids, Michigan: Zondervan Publishers, 1974.

Alexander, David et al. Zondervan Handbook to the Bible. Grand Rapids, Michigan: Zondervan Publishing House, 1999.

Anderson, Leith. A Church for the 21st Century. Minneapolis, Minnesota: Bethany House Publishers, 1992.

Armstrong, Michael. A Handbook of Human Resource Management Practice. London: The Bath Press, 1999.

Arn, Win and Charles. The Master's Plan for Making Disciples. Grand Rapids, Michigan: Baker Books, 2004.

Arrington, French L. and Roger Stronstad. Full Life Bible Commentary to the New Testament. Grand Rapids, Michigan: Zondervan, 1999.

-----. Life in the Spirit: New Testament Commentary. Grand Rapids, Michigan: Zondervan, 1999.

Atkinson, David J, and David Field H. ed. New Dictionary of Christian Ethics and Pastoral Theology. Downers Grove, Illinois: InterVarsity Press, 1995.

Bailey, LeRoy. A Solid Foundation. New Kensington: Whitaker House, 2003.

Barker, Alan. How to Be Better at Managing People. London, England: Kogan Page, 2000.

Buckland, Collin. Liberated To Lead. Eastbourne, Sussex: Kingsway Publication, 2001.

Cape, David and Tommy Tenny. God's Secret to Greatness. Ventura, California: Regal Books, 2000.

Charnes, Cy. The Instant Manager. London, U.K.: Kogan Page, 2001.

Cho, David Yonggi and Harold Hostetler. Successful Home Cell Groups . Gainsville, Florida: Bridge Logos Publishers, 2001.

Cho, Paul Yonggi. Solving Life's Problems. South Plainford, New Jersey: Bridge Publishing Inc., 1980.

Cordeiro, Wayne. Doing Church as a Team. Ventura, California: Regal Books, 1997.

Cornwall, Judson. Profiles of a Leader. Gainsville, Florida: Bridge-Logos Publishers, 1980.

Crawfford, Dan. Discipleshape: 12 Weeks to Spiritual Fitness. Peabody, Massachusettes: Hendricks Publication Inc., 1998.

Crowder, Micheal. West Africa: An Introduction to its History. London: Longman Group Ltd., 1977

Daft, Richard L. Leadership: Theory and Practice. Orlando, Florida: Harcourt College Publishers, 1999.

Heward-Mills Dag, Rules of Church Work. Lux Verbi BM, South Africa (2008)

Heward-Mills Dag, Rules of Full-time Ministry. Lux Verbi BM, South Africa (2008)

James D. ed. Leadership Handbook of Management and Administration. Grand Rapids, Berkley, Michigan: Baker Book House Co., 2003.

Kast , Fremont E. and James E. Rosenzweig. Organization and Management. Singapore: McGraw-Hill Book Company, 1985.

Maidment, Fred H. ed. Organizational Behaviour, 1st Edition. Guildford, Connecticut: Dushkin/McGraw Hill Publishing Company, 2000.

Miranda, Jesse. The Christian Church in Ministry. Brussels: International Correspondence Institute, 1980.

Mullins, Laurie J. Management and Organizational Behaviour. Great Britain: Pitman Publishing, 1990.

Munroe Myles. Maximising Your Potential. Slippenburg, Pennsylvania: Destiny Image Publishers Inc., 2003.

Murdock, Mike. The Law of Recognition. Denton, Texas: Wasdom International, 1999.

Orsburn, Jack et al. Self-Directed Work Teams. Homewood, Illinois: Business One Irwin, 1990.

Radcliffe, Robert. Effective Ministry as an Associate. Grand Rapids, Michigan: Kregel Publications, 1973.

Salter, Brian and Naomi Longford-Wood. Successfully Dealing With Difficult People. London: Hodder & Stoughton, 1998.